QUEER MARXISM
IN TWO CHINAS

QUEER MARXISM
IN TWO CHINAS

PETRUS LIU

DUKE UNIVERSITY PRESS

Durham and London 2015

Typeset in Quadraat Pro
by Westchester Publishing Services

Liu, Petrus, author.
Queer Marxism in two Chinas / Petrus Liu.
pages cm
Includes bibliographical references and index.
ISBN 978-0-8223-5972-2 (hardcover : alk. paper)
ISBN 978-0-8223-6004-9 (pbk. : alk. paper)
ISBN 978-0-8223-7508-1 (e-book)
1. Queer theory—China. 2. Philosophy, Marxist—China.
3. Homosexuality—Political aspects—China. 4. Chinese
fiction—20th century—History and criticism. I. Title.
HQ76.3.C6L58 2015
306.7601—dc23
2015020929

Cover Art:
Zhang Huan, 1/2, 1998, Beijing, China.
Courtesy of Zhang Huan Studio.

Duke University Press gratefully acknowledges the
support of Yale-NUS College, which provided funds
toward the publication of this book.

FOR BRIAN

CONTENTS

ACKNOWLEDGMENTS

The germination of this book began with conversations I had with Judith Butler many years ago, and I am indebted to her for her steadfast support and critical intelligence over these years. I also want to thank Claudine Ang, Barney Bate, Kuan-Hsing Chen, Howard Chiang, Tamara Chin, Cui Zi'en, Jonathan Culler, Brett de Bary, Naifei Ding, David Eng, Dustin Friedman, Xiaopei He, Josephine Ho, Hans Tao-Ming Huang, Andrew Hui, Andrew Jones, Wenqing Kang, Bill Kennedy, Dominick LaCapra, Ruhong Lin, Lydia H. Liu, Jen-peng Liu, Colleen Lye, Natalie Melas, Timothy Murray, Chris Newfield, Teng Kuan Ng, Jiazhen Ni, Amie Parry, Rajeev S. Patke, Lisa Rofel, Neil Saccamano, Naoki Sakai, Rebecca Gould, Shi Tou, Shu-mei Shih, Andy Chih-ming Wang, Wang Fangping, Wang Ping, C. J. Wan-ling Wee, and Kenneth Wu for their friendship and guidance.

Portions of this book were given as talks at National Taiwan University, Cornell University, Stanford University, Shanghai University, UC Berkeley, Penn State University, Brandeis University, University of Sydney, University of Miami, Hong Kong University, San Francisco State University, National Central University, National Tsinghua University, CUNY Graduate Center, Brown University, and Yale University. I thank the following colleagues for their warmth, feedback, and encouragement: Andrea Bachner, Tani Barlow, Esther Cheung, Charles Egan, Matthew Fraleigh, Eric Hayot, Gail Hershatter, Andrew Lynch, Tina Lu, Kam Louie, Gina Marchetti, Annie McClanahan, Robin Miller, Gema Pérez-Sánchez, Jeffrey Riegel, Carlos Rojas, Teemu Ruskola, Tze-lan Sang, Shuang Sheng, Matt Sommer, Mirana Szeto, and Jing Tsu. Many thanks to Chris Berry, Marshall Brown, Joe Cleary, Walter Cohen, Sean Connolly, Jed Esty, Fran Martin, and Fredric Jameson for their incisive comments on earlier versions of materials in the book. I also thank several of my Cornell University graduate students whose dissertations deepened my own thinking on topics in this book: Eno Pei Jean Chen, Carl Gelderloos, Zach Howlett, Walter Hsu, Wah Guan Lim, Matthew Omelsky, Jennie Row, Chunyen Wang, Steven Wyatt, and We Jung Yi. In making the final revisions, I am extremely fortunate to have Pei Yun Chia's, Regina Hong's, and Brant Torres's editorial wisdom and invaluable comments. I also thank the National University of Singapore (NUS) and Yale-NUS librarians, Vivien Tan, Rebecca Maniates, and Amy Yung Mei Lin, for their assistance.

The writing of this text was made possible by research support provided by Cornell University and Yale-NUS College. Yale-NUS College has also provided a generous subvention toward the production of this book. Some of the material in chapter 2 appeared in an earlier version in a different form as "Queer Marxism in Taiwan" in *Inter-Asia Cultural Studies* 8, no. 4 (December 2007): 517–39. An earlier version of chapter 3 in a different form appeared as "Why Does Queer Theory Need China?" in "Beyond the Strai(gh)ts," a special issue of *positions: east asia cultures critique* 18, no. 2 (Fall 2010): 291–320. An earlier version of chapter 4 in a different form appeared as "The Peripheral Realism of Two Chinas" in *Modern Language Quarterly* 73, no. 3 (September 2012): 395–414. An earlier version of chapter 5 in a different form appeared as "Queer Human Rights in and against China: Liberalism, Marxism, and the Figuration of the Human" in *Social Text* 30, no. 1 (Spring 2011): 71–90. My revisions greatly benefited from the comments provided by the anonymous reviewers for these journals, and by the four anonymous readers Duke University Press engaged for this book. Indexing was done by Clive Pyne, Book Indexing Services. I am grateful to Ken Wissoker, Jade Brooks, Sara Leone, and Jodi Devine for their editorial guidance in preparing this manuscript.

CHAPTER I

MARXISM, QUEER LIBERALISM, AND

THE QUANDARY OF TWO CHINAS

When hearing about contemporary China, we do not often find the words *queer* and *Marxism* in the same sentence. If anything, it seems that these two categories work against each other: Scholars often attribute the emergence of queer cultures in China to the *end* of Marxism and socialism. If a previous generation of Chinese cultural studies scholars seemed uniformly concerned about the specters of Marxism, today's queer critics are more likely to worry about neoliberalism and gay normalization. The scholarly consensus is that, after Deng's 1978 market reforms, the phenomenon many critics have described as the "new homonormativity" in US culture is taking place in postsocialist China as well. The turn to neoliberalism in queer Chinese studies responds to a global conversation of the highest importance. Lisa Duggan defines homonormativity as "a politics that does not contest dominant heteronormative assumptions and institutions but upholds and sustains them, while promising the possibility of a demobilized gay constituency and a privatized, depoliticized gay culture anchored in domesticity and consumption."[1] Michael Warner argues that homonormativity in the gay liberation movement requires a "more consolidated gay identity" and signals a "retreat from its history of radicalism into a new form of postliberationist privatization."[2] The phenomenon Duggan and Warner describe is well known and seemingly ubiquitous. A popular T-shirt at a Pride March in San Francisco a few years ago illustrates the point particularly well: "My gay lifestyle? Eat, sleep, go to work, pay taxes." With the homonormative turn, many gay men and women now believe that the best strategy for mainstream inclusion and equal rights (such as same-sex marriage) is to show society that they, too, are morally upstanding citizens who are no different from anyone else. Worried about homonormativity, new queer theorists now focus on critiquing "queer liberalism," the economic and social structure underlying this depoliticized consumer space of metrosexual glamor and bourgeois rights. Queer critics point out that liberalism has spawned a homonormative desire to dissociate homosexuality from culturally undesirable practices and experiences such as AIDS, promiscuity, drag, prostitution, and drug use. While it is certainly understandable why gay men and women may wish to combat the conflation of homosexuality with other cultural definitions, the desire for mainstream inclusion has also alienated, disempowered, and further stigmatized gay men and women who *are* prostitutes, drug users, transvestites, promiscuous, or living with AIDS.[3] As Nicole Ferry points out, the homonormative movement is not an equality-based movement, but an inclusion-based assimilation politics with exclusionary results.[4] The situation is clearly worrisome once we recognize that the culture of homonormativity provides a poor political model by suggesting that assimilating to heterosexual norms is the only path to equal rights.

Many instances suggest that a culture of homonormativity has emerged in the People's Republic of China (PRC) after the state officially entered a postsocialist era by adopting experiments in neoliberalism and privatization.[5] Although LGBT political movements have made important advances in mainland China—significantly, the decriminalization of homosexuality in 1997 and its removal from categories of mental disorder by the Chinese Psychiatric Association in 2001—other inequalities have deepened. As Lisa Rofel shows, the advent of neoliberalism produced hierarchically differentiated qualities of desire.[6] China's neoliberal integration into global infrastructures intensifies the process of gay normalization through the discourse of "quality" (suzhi). With the homonormative turn, certain "improperly gay" subjects, such as China's "money boys," are routinely abused from within the gay community. Seeing money boys as a blight on the image of the homosexual community, Chinese gay men are eager to dissociate themselves from money boys in their quest for respectability and global cultural citizenship as China becomes increasingly liberalized, affluent, and cosmopolitan.[7] Rofel describes how the rise of neoliberalism reconfigures the dreams, aspirations, and longings of gay men and women in China, producing novel forms of cosmopolitan aspirations, public culture, identities, and modes of memorializing their pasts. In this way, the differentiation of good and bad forms of gay desire also cements boundaries between rural and urban, elite and common, commercial and privatized.

Queer critics who work on the intersections of Chinese sexualities and neoliberalism provide numerous historical examples that explain why queerness and Marxism are understood in antithetical ways. Rofel's two studies, *Desiring China* and *Other Modernities*, analyze the dominant perception among a broad public in China that Maoist socialism was a distortion of people's natural genders and sexualities. Rofel argues that this view, which has become common sense among many, relies on a revisionist history, a distortion of the past that encourages people to reject their socialist past. Once the past has been constructed this way, postsocialist allegories emerge to represent a desire to free one's gendered and sexual self from the dictates of the socialist state. Accordingly, the queerness of human desire comes to be viewed as what sets limits to any and all utopian efforts to control human productivity and to explain the motions of history through economic categories. The arrival of neoliberalism—which, as Rofel crucially argues, is not a fait accompli but an ongoing series of experiments that are centrally about desire—produces yearnings that propel people to reinvent "the strictures and sacrifices" for their socialist past by way of cosmopolitan consumption.[8] Compared to Rofel's work, Travis Kong's *Chinese Male Homosexualities* paints a bleaker picture of China's newly emergent queer communities, but similarly emphasizes the complicity between a consolidated homosexual identity and the consumer culture of neoliberal capitalism. Kong shows that the emergence of gay and lesbian identities in China was predicated on the relaxation of state control of the private sphere following the replacement of communism by neoliberalism. Song Hwee Lim similarly attributes the rising representations of homosexuality in Chinese screen cultures to neoliberal globalization, arguing that an internationalized, deterritorialized economy of film production "introduced homosexuality as a legitimate discourse in Chinese cinemas in ways that may not have been previously possible."[9] These accounts of China's neoliberal queer culture complement the global narrative developed by David Eng's critiques of the increasingly mass-mediated consumer lifestyle in *The Feeling of Kinship:*

Queer Liberalism and the Racialization of Intimacy (2010). In these studies, queer critics either emphasize the agency of queer desire and bodies *against* state prescriptions, or expose the complicity *between* new sexual politics and advanced liberalism. But in either scenario, the focus is on China's postsocialist character after the neoliberal turn, which implies that Marxism, whether good or bad for queers, has ceased to be a relevant consideration.

The critique of queer liberalism therefore unwittingly naturalizes the assumption that China has unequivocally entered a postsocialist phase. However, we might pause to ask, is neoliberalism truly the dominant cultural logic of contemporary queer Chinese cultures? Are queer cultural expressions always complicit with neoliberal globalization and the politics of gay normalization? Is there a critical, dissident, and, indeed, *queer* Chinese culture anymore? Treating contemporary Chinese queer cultures as a symptomatic expression of a globalizing neoliberalism creates an impression that they are belated copies of the liberal West, evolving along the same path with no local history and no agency. According to this narrative, China's socialist past and dialogues with international Marxism appear to be a detour at best, with no lasting effects on the development of its queer cultures. Ultimately, China has arrived at the same conundrum we see in North America today: queer liberalism and homonormativity.

The story I tell in this book is different. *Queer Marxism in Two Chinas* reconstructs a rich and complex tradition of postwar queer Chinese works that retool and revitalize Marxist social analysis. In assembling this queer Marxist archive, I also propose two intertwined arguments that depart from the scholarly consensus in Chinese queer studies. First, instead of reading contemporary Chinese queer cultures as responses to neoliberal globalization, I argue that a unique local event has centrally shaped the development of Chinese queer thought: the 1949 division of China into the People's Republic of China (PRC) and the Republic of China on Taiwan (ROC). In referring to the PRC and the ROC as two Chinas, I am less interested in making a political provocation than in historicizing the implications of their coexistence for queer practice. My second argument is that postwar queer Chinese writers, many of whom are based in the ROC rather than the PRC, developed a unique theory and literature by fusing Marxism with inquiries into gender and sexuality. The fact that Marxism flourished in anticommunist

ROC may come as a surprise. While the queer Marxist tradition embodies a living dialogue between the ROC and the PRC that attests to the permeability of their boundaries, it also highlights a need to disarticulate Marxism from the communist bureaucracy of the PRC. This little known cultural history of queer Marxism in the two Chinas indicates the vitality and dynamism of Marxism in divergent vectors of queer thought. The geopolitical rivalry between the PRC and the ROC becomes an unexpected kind of productive tension for Chinese queer discourse, which, in turn, is also compelled to revise and reintegrate Marxist thought into the analysis of gender and sexuality in distinctive ways.

Although the book title pluralizes Chinas, and most of my examples come from the ROC, my project is not a Sinophone studies book. My intention is not to bring together materials from the peripheries of the Sinophone world—Singapore, Hong Kong, and the Chinese diaspora in Malaysia, Indonesia, and North America—to develop a non–PRC-centered story of queer lives in Chinese-speaking communities.[10] Rather, I am interested in historicizing the ways in which Chinese writers, in any location, came to view the historical creation of the PRC and the ROC as a foundational event for queer life. Because the aim of my project is not to displace Chineseness with Sinophone, Sinoglossia, or other critical concepts, I am not treating works by Taiwan-based writers as an expression of Taiwaneseness. In choosing my examples, I have also privileged transnational and transcultural texts—for example, Chen Ruoxi's *Paper Marriage*, a novel about an American man and a mainland Chinese woman who cross boundaries of nationality and sexual orientation, which the author wrote based on her experiences in the PRC, the ROC, and the United States. Similarly, because my use of the concept of "two Chinas" is historical rather than ideological, my study also excludes Hong Kong as a primary site of consideration. Certainly, Hong Kong-based authors have also developed important queer reflections on liberalism, socialism, and Marxism.[11] Far from being comprehensive, my archive of queer Marxist practice invites comparisons with not only Hong Kong's neoliberalism but also Singapore's "illiberal pragmatism" as a technique of queer social management.[12] It is my hope that *Queer Marxism in Two Chinas* will initiate critical interest in such transregional studies.

My study of the continuous dialogues and cross-pollination between Marxist and queer thought stems from a desire to understand

Chinese queer cultures' engagement with the geopolitics of the Cold War that produced the two Chinas and their corresponding ideological significations. After all, the ideological legacy of the Cold War cements our habitual readings of the economic fortunes of the PRC and the ROC as the historical vindication of Marxism and liberalism. I argue that any discussion of liberalism in the Chinese context must begin with the Cold War divide, because the rise of liberalism in the PRC's political history is critically informed by Taiwan's historical claim as Free China and by its identity as China's "economic miracle"—namely, what would happen in mainland China if the PRC government had adopted liberalism and capitalism instead of socialism. As an ethnically Chinese state without a colonial administration, Taiwan provided the most relevant and compelling economic model for PRC leaders when they first considered liberalizing the market. While the ideologically retrograde elements of Free China discourses are obvious, the legacy of the Cold War has also given rise to positive and productive queer appropriations. In chapter four, for example, I offer a reading of the 1980s' queer narrative of self-invention, entrepreneurship, and miraculous development, to dissect the historical subjectivity underpinning the two Chinas' transitions to postsocialism and postmartial law market economy. For the queer Marxist cultural producers considered in this book, the geopolitical conflicts between the two Chinas are both a historical burden and an intellectual opportunity. Indeed, I would suggest that a persistent engagement with the geopolitics of two Chinas forms the basis of a Chinese materialist queer theory that sets it apart from its Euro-American counterparts.

One of the aims of this book is to develop a useful account of the insights and distinctive features of Chinese queer theory, since we are used to thinking of queer theory as an exclusively Euro-American enterprise. In writing this way about the connections between Chinese queer theory and geopolitics, I also present theory as a product of historically determinate circumstances rather than as a set of timeless principles we can apply to a variety of cultural situations. At the same time, characterizing theory, queer or nonqueer, as a product of the conditions of its own genesis also risks reifying cultural differences. Without raising the enormously complex questions of cultural essentialism and universalism, I would like to propose at this point some of the distinctive achievements and concerns of queer Marxism in the Chinas in contrast to more familiar intellectual paradigms in the United States. One of the hallmark achievements of US queer theory is the exploration of the intersectionality of identity categories. For example, the "queer of color critique" in recent years provides a powerful framework for exposing the mutual dependency of racialization and sexual abjection.[13] But while US-based queer theory enables a rethinking of the relations between the diacritical markers of personhood—race, gender, class, sexuality, and religion—this queer theory's conception of social differences remains restricted by a liberal pluralist culture of identity politics that is distinctively American.[14] By contrast, Chinese theory of the geopolitical meditations of queer lives does not begin with the concept of social identity; instead, it emphasizes the impersonal, structural, and systemic workings of power. Whereas US queer theory responds to the failures of neoliberal social management by postulating an incomplete, foreclosed, or irreducibly heterogeneous subject of identity, Chinese queer Marxists develop an arsenal of conceptual tools for reading the complex and overdetermined relations between human sexual freedom and the ideological cartography of the Cold War. For these thinkers, to raise the question of queer desire in this context is also to examine the incomplete project of decolonization in Asia, the achievements and failures of socialist democracy, the contradictory process of capitalist modernization, and the uneven exchange of capital and goods.

The intellectual tradition of queer Marxism offers a nonliberal alternative to the Euro-American model of queer emancipation grounded in liberal values of privacy, tolerance, individual rights, and diversity. In my view, contemporary queer critics of homonormativity, queer liberalism, and homonationalism have much to gain from a consideration of this nonliberal queer theory. The existence of Chinese queer Marxism also indicates that LGBTQ communities in the world do not evolve along the same, inevitable path prescribed by a globalizing neoliberalism. Indeed, it would be a mistake to interpret the emergence of queer identities and communities in the two Chinas as belated versions of post-Stonewall social formations in the United States under a singular logic of neoliberal globalization. The archive of queer cultural artifacts and intellectual discourses I assemble in this book disrupts that developmentalist narrative by demonstrating the importance of Marxist reflections on the 1949 division for contemporary queer thought. The confrontation between queer and Marxist discourses in Chinese intellectual scenes reveals a hidden chapter of the global history of cultural materialism that parts company with both metropolitan understandings of capitalism as corporate greed and the standard signification of global Maoism as Third-World revolutionary struggles.

In literary and cultural studies in North America, Marxism has come to be understood as a somewhat specialized academic sub-discipline associated with figures such as Fredric Jameson and Gayatri Spivak, whose monumental works renewed critical interest in Georg Lukács's concepts of totality and reification, Antonio Gramsci's theories of hegemony and mediation, and Louis Althusser's structuralist interpretation of the economic base as an "absent cause." While the American reception of Marxism made critical contributions to both dialectical philosophy and historical materialism, it has also become increasingly divorced from the "economistic" debates in European and Asian Marxisms concerning such technical questions as "the transformation problem," the withering away of law, the value form, the law of the tendency of the rate of profit to fall, and theories of accumulation and crisis. Nonetheless, the culturalist reinterpretations of Marxism have not rescued it from accusations of economic reductionism and foundationalism, against which queer theory and other "postfoundationalist" projects consciously rebel.[15] While the critique of foundationalism is both timely and necessary, the framing of Marxism as a monolithic intellectual orthodoxy plagued by problems of determinism, teleology, utopianism, and economism also misses the opportunity to deploy the insights developed by Marxist authors for queer use.

In schematic terms, the queer writers examined in this book explore four areas of social thought that are historically associated with Marxism: first, the indivisible organicity of the social body (totality); second, the distinction between formal and substantive equality (fetishism); third, theories of community, species-being, and primitive accumulation (alienation); and, finally, the question of social transformation (ideology). The rich tradition of queer Marxism thus differs from orthodox Marxism's emphasis on the primacy of economics. For the queer cultural producers discussed in this book, Marxism is not so much the content of queer reflections, but a methodology. The analysis I offer significantly differs from projects that seek to "queer" Marxism through delightfully perverse (mis-)readings of letters between Marx and Engels, rehistoricizations of deskilled labor as the conditions of possibility for the performance of masculinity and reified desire, or interpretations of capitalism as the production of desiring machines and bodies without organs. These queer Marxist projects share two assumptions: that capitalism is the exclusive property of Euro-American modernity, and that Marxism is a closed system incapable of dealing with the complexities of modern life (such as sexuality) and therefore needs to be "queered." By contrast, the type of Marxism I invoke in this study does not take capitalism's historical development in Europe as its privileged object of analysis. Neither do I regard queerness or biopolitical production as the conceptual tools needed to rescue Marxism from its ideological blind spots. Instead of queering Marxism, the authors I consider in this book bring the methodology of Marxism to bear on queer lives. In their works, Marxism is not a state policy such as the planned economy or collectivized labor, but a living philosophy. As a methodology rather than an ideology, Marxism inspires queer authors who occupy a variety of political positions that may be at odds with the "actually existing Marxism" of the People's Republic of China. While some of the most ingenious and hybrid uses of Marxist theories of social structuration, alienation, and totality come from PRC political dissidents who are openly critical of the Communist Party, ROC-based intellectuals have also developed textured narratives of the failures of liberal pluralism through recourse to Marxist theories of substantive equality. As represented by these texts, queerness exceeds the sexual meaning of homosexuality. Instead, queerness indicates a constitutive sociality of the self that counters the neoliberal imagination of formal rights, electoral competition, and economic growth.

Beyond Neoliberal Homonationalism

In both English and Chinese scholarship, this turn toward a critique of neoliberal homonormativity is informed by two of the most galvanizing developments in queer theory.[16] The first development is the theory of queer temporality, a dynamic body of scholarship that accomplishes many things: it theorizes the conflict between reproductive futurism and queer negativity;[17] excavates a different political historical consciousness from the pleasures of the past;[18] critiques the normative model of temporality that organizes bourgeois reproduction, inheritance, risk/safety, work/play;[19] analyzes movements of sex before the homo/heterosexual definition as figurations of the "untimely";[20] and even writes, proleptically, queer theory's own obituary.[21] The second important development is the much discussed "affective turn" in queer theory, which has also produced an explosive growth of exciting scholarship on gay and lesbian emotion, charting a passage from negative feelings (shame, loss, melancholia, grief, trauma) to positive feelings (outrage, sociability, happiness, public feelings, touching feelings, optimism) in queer history.[22] As generative as these forms of scholarship have been, theories of queer temporality and works in affect studies have a dematerializing tendency. Certainly, the affective turn in queer studies has significantly expanded a Marxist cultural materialism that includes Raymond Williams's analysis of structures of feelings and Herbert Marcuse's syncretic writings on Eros and civilization, attuning us to the mutually constitutive and mutually embedded relations between emergent social forms and queer affect.[23] In their emphasis on the subjective meanings of pleasure, play, and desire, however, new queer studies sometimes give insufficient attention to the impersonal structures and conditions of social change.[24]

There is no question that postsocialist China and postmartial law Taiwan have entered a new era marked by the biopolitical production of the neoliberal subject. Yet this bioproduction has also given rise to a reinvigorated Marxist analysis from within Chinese intellectual circles, which suggests that it is difficult to theorize queer subjectivities as a question of affect and shifting temporalities alone. The phenomenon of China's "pink economy" presents a complex cultural semiotic that the production of the neoliberal subject only partially explains. The metropolitan dreams of China's new queer bourgeoisie, like any dream-text, have manifest contents as well as deep structures. On the surface, many of these developments do suggest that a new era of liberal rights has dawned to bring about the hypervisibility of queer issues in the public domain. At the time of my writing in 2014, Taiwan is in the midst of massive protests against a proposed bill to legalize same-sex marriage, which would make Taiwan the first Asian country to do so. In the PRC, a visible and self-affirmative gay culture has appeared as well. A recent mainstream blockbuster, *Tiny Times* (2013), adapted from the director Guo Jingming's own best-selling trilogy *Xiao shidai* (2008, 2010, 2011), comfortably and confidently presents homoeroticism, male nudity, and sexual experimentations as metropolitan glamor. In Beijing and

Shanghai, gay bars, saunas, cruising spots in parks, and other establishments are surrounded by restaurants that cater to middle-class gay consumers. Gay-themed television shows, lesbian pulp fiction, pop songs, youth culture, film festivals, and money boys abound.[25] Many of these structural transformations have impacted not only popular culture but also high art: as Fran Martin's study shows, contemporary Chinese lesbian cinema has entered a distinctively new phase marked by a "critical presentism" that defines a self-consciously minoritizing lesbian identity, here and now, over and against an earlier, "memorial mode" of narrating same-sex love in the schoolgirl romance genre, where the dominant tendency is to bracket off same-sex experiences as an interlude in an otherwise unilinear and indicatively heterosexual life history.[26] New developments in literature, as well, contribute to this sense of the present as a groundbreaking moment marked by new identities, politics, communities, markets, and bodies in China.[27] As several recent sociological and ethnographic studies have observed, self-identified "tongzhi," "tongren," and "lala," have established their own social vocabulary,[28] new community formations on the internet,[29] affective ties, recreational culture,[30] support networks,[31] relationship strategies, and even marriage rituals.[32] Indeed, since the 1990s, mainland China has seen numerous milestones of gay visibility and social rights: the 1997 repeal of the criminal code of "hooliganism" (under which homosexuals could be prosecuted),[33] Li Yinhe's campaign to legalize same-sex marriage in China in 2001, the 2001 Chinese Gay and Lesbian Film Festival at Beijing University,[34] the removal of homosexuality from the medical category of perversions by the Chinese Psychiatry Association in 2001, the inaugural Shanghai Pride in June 2009, and the appearances of mainstream lesbian, gay, and transgendered television celebrities (such as Jin Xing).[35] As Lisa Rofel describes, while "from one perspective it might seem as if the Chinese state creates strict constraints on political activism, from another perspective the difficulty of doing politics on the terrain of 'rights' opens up a space that enables a different kind of political creativity"—an example being Pink Space (Fense kongjian), founded by He Xiaopei.[36]

Queer culture in the PRC is so developed today that the topic of homosexuality per se, once taboo and subsequently greeted by many people with fascination, can no longer command the attention of the public. Instead, today's China has seen a proliferation of sexual discourses and identities. *Tongqi* is a new item of China's popular vocabulary that refers to gay men's wives. These "beards" or "living widows" are a new social minority and the constituency of a new social movement in China. A hotly debated topic on Chinese internet forums today, the *tongqi* social movement of "living widows" demonstrates the hypervisibility of contemporary queer issues in China. The intensity of the conversation bears witness to the lightning speed at which Chinese reception and culture of sexuality have evolved. In 2011 a former living widow, Yao Lifen, founded *Tongqi jiayuan*, an organization designed to mobilize and empower other living widows.[37] The organization offers resources and counseling for women who unknowingly married homosexual men, but it also emphatically portrays homosexuality as a threat to women's happiness. Its website characterizes women married to homosexual men as victims of domestic abuse and psychological trauma, and homosexual men as selfish liars who abuse women to protect their own secrets. In fact, the organization urges the Chinese government to penalize deceitful homosexual men by criminalizing such marriages as fraud, and claims that such marriages pose a threat to public health by exposing unsuspecting Chinese women to AIDS. While *Tongqi jiayuan* pathologizes homosexuality and homosexual men, other voices have emerged. Pink Space provides a support group for wives of gay men as well, but the goal of the latter group is to promote understanding and dialogue between these women and the gay male community. A recent television show, "What Are We Doing to Rescue Wives of Homosexuals?" described those women as a "new minority in China more disempowered and alienated than homosexuals" and estimated their number to be around 16 million based on a study by Zhang Beichuan, a professor at Qingdao University.[38] According to the study of Liu Dalin at Shanghai University, China has 25 million *tongqi* at the moment.[39] In the realm of arts and literature, *tongqi* is a well-known topic in China. As early as 2003, Andrew Yusu Cheng's feature film, *Welcome to Destination Shanghai*, already presents a kaleidoscopic view of the entangled lives of *tongqi* and other disenfranchised characters on the margins of society. Two recent popular novels, Qing Zizhu's *Tongqi* and Jin Erchuang's *Tongfu Tongqi*, depict the social life and dilemmas of *tongqi*, while a new feature film made in Taiwan, *Will You Still Love Me Tomorrow?* (Arvin Chen, 2013), bears witness to the cultural interest in the topic across the straits. *Tongqi* is therefore a transregional and a transcultural formation. The attention the topic has gained not only indicates that sexuality issues have entered a new phase in the PRC, but also demonstrates that the boundaries between the PRC and the ROC are often more porous than we acknowledge.

While these developments unambiguously suggest a neoliberal transformation of queer identities and discourses, many crucial questions are left unanswered without a materialist analysis. Above all, it is unclear whether the queer community's newfound visibility indicates collective social progress, or the cooptation of the gay movement by neoliberal capitalism. For example, Fang Gang's 1995 book, *Homosexuality in China*, brought about the first legal case against the libel of homosexuality and is for that reason frequently cited as a milestone of gay cultural history in China.[40] For queer Marxist Cui Zi'en, however, Fang Gang's work exemplifies an opportunistic voyeurism that transforms the social plight of homosexuals into a commodity.[41] A similar and earlier example is the publication of Li Yinhe and Wang Xiaobo's coauthored book, *Their World: A Penetrating Look into China's Male Homosexual Community*. No scholar can deny that Li and Wang's book brought about a paradigm shift in gay and lesbian research in China, and that Li, a prominent sociologist, sexologist, and advocate of gay rights, has made numerous contributions to China's LGBT community. In particular, Li is well known for her campaign to legalize same-sex marriage in China. However, Li and Wang's book, as its title shows, has also been criticized for objectifying and exoticizing the gay community. Critics point out that Li and Wang emphatically separate the researchers from the object of their inquiry ("their world"), while establishing the researchers as the authoritative and scientific fact-finders who "penetrate" China's male homosexual communities.[42] A catalogue of queer films, novels, visual arts, conferences, and social movements alone will not provide a meaningful account of how and how much PRC's sexual communities have evolved. These changes need to be recontextualized by an analysis of the political economy of two Chinas.

Excavating the Marxist intellectual roots of contemporary queer thought in the Chinas is one way of answering some of today's most urgent questions: How does being queer matter? If China's popular culture and social science research indicate that homosexuals are not just visible, but already firmly established in their roles as society's latest neoliberal subjects fighting for mainstream inclusion—what's queer about queer studies now, in the two Chinas or elsewhere? My formulation of this question comes from the 2005 special issue of *Social Text* (edited by David Eng, Judith Halberstam, and José Muñoz), but it has, in some form or another, been at the heart of conversations around "being critically queer," the question of social transformation,[43] "queer occupy,"[44] queer antiwar movements,[45] and a host of other concepts. As queer people transform from victims to consumers, queer theory is no longer centered on loss, melancholia, or other feelings associated with the era of the AIDS epidemic. Instead, contemporary queer theory mourns the loss of radicality in queer movements, which have been taken over by the assimilationist logic of commodified desire. Against the backdrop of a perceived universal loss of queer radicality, North American critics have even more reason to consider the historical development of a nonliberal alternative as it has occurred in the Chinas. The insights of Chinese queer Marxist writers are particularly relevant to our times. In this book, I offer an analysis of their thinking on the alliances between labor and queer movements, the material conditions that govern permissible language and democratic participation, and the future of substantive equality. In turning to these ideas, I also hope to show that Marxist methodology has flourished in the two Chinas, both of which are locations that international commentators expect to have been eroded by capitalist penetrations. The vitality of Marxist thought in postsocialist China and anticommunist Taiwan also indicates the limits of a static conception of Marxism and queer struggles as historically successive social movements.

I do not intend to suggest that China alone has a queer Marxist tradition. Certainly, sophisticated meditations on the convergence of Marxism and queer studies are available in North American intellectual circles. A vibrant tradition that encompasses, among others, Kevin Floyd's important *The Reification of Desire: Towards a Queer Marxism* has already standardized the vocabulary for analyzing the relation between biopolitical reproduction and crisis of capitalist accumulation, a topic that received reinvigorated treatment in a 2012 special issue of GLQ.[46] However, as I mentioned already, scholars working in this vein tend to be more interested in queering Marxism than bringing historical materialism to bear on queer studies. But Marxism is not just a critique of capitalism, corporations, and consumption. It is also a philosophy of the totality of the social world, a critique of the bourgeois conception of rights, an analysis of the mechanism that regulates differential access to resources, a social theory of alienation, and a dialectical method of reading historical tendencies and countertendencies. All of these strands of Marxist thought have influenced Chinese queer writings, which in turn provide some of the most powerful, yet underconsidered, resources for contemporary theory and politics.

The dynamic tradition of queer Marxism in the Chinas has produced a nonliberal queer theory, but reaping its insights requires the labor of two kinds of cultural translation. The first is disciplinary: we must take Chinese materials seriously as intellectual resources rather than local illustrations of theoretical paradigms already developed by the canon of queer theory. Doing so also means that we must adamantly reject the common division of intellectual labor in area studies programs between the production of paradigms (queer theory) and the gathering of raw materials (Chinese examples). Hence, we should not assume that queer theory automatically refers to the distinct body of theoretical works produced in 1990s' United States and later translated into Chinese. In my study, queer theory refers to a global discourse that was simultaneously developed by English, Chinese, and other academic traditions. Queer theory is a transnational and transcultural practice of which its US instantiation is only part. Moreover, this global dialogue is necessarily impure in its methodology, entangled in historical trajectory, and varied in modes of dissemination.

The second kind of translation performed in this book is methodological: I read fiction as theory and society as text. Literature is a node of densely woven information and ideas provided by a culture, though its insights are often obscured by its self-declared status as fiction in our habitual search for stable meanings, historical truths, and readily digestible propositions. Similarly, the social text of contemporary Chinese queer cultures often resists our desire to transcode it into political allegories and narratives of emergence. Despite the formidable work of the historians of sexuality, queer Chinese cultures remain recalcitrant, thwarting every effort to produce neatly organized histories from taboo to identity. Instead, those interested in reading, interpreting, or writing about Chinese queer cultures are more likely to be confronted with enigmatic political signifiers and overlapping temporalities. While these aberrant Chinese queer narratives fail to delineate the heroic journey of the self-making of a subculture, they also defy attempts to align their signification to the economic policies of the socialist and non-socialist parts and phases of Chinese cultures. The cultural narratives produced by the two Chinas are too complex to be reduced to expressions of Marxism and liberalism. In turn, queer writings provide precisely the conceptual tools we need to overcome these static Cold War bifurcations.

The Quandary of Two Chinas

Today two nations in the world refer to themselves as China: the People's Republic of China and the Republic of China on Taiwan. The coexistence of two Chinas (and two Koreas) indicates that the Cold War is not yet over in Asia. This reality is significantly absent in the American perspective, which tends to consider the disintegration of the Soviet Union as the beginning of a post-Cold War world order marked by "the end of ideology." The coexistence of two Chinas also limits the usefulness of nation-centered history. From the beginning, the creation of two Chinas signals a sedimentation of multinational interests and conflicts. At the end of the Chinese Civil War in 1949, the Chiang Kai-shek government relocated to Taiwan and, under the protection of the Seventh Fleet, became America's island fortress for the crusade against communism in the Pacific. As part of the United States' strategy of containment, the Sino-American Mutual Defense Treaty prevented both the PRC and the ROC from initiating direct military action against each other, effectively ensuring the division of China. While the two Germanys were unified after the disintegration of the Soviet Union, East Asia remains divided according to the original cartography drawn at the height of the Cold War, and ideologically governed by popular responses to the economic outcomes of socialism and liberal capitalism. In Taiwan, while the rhetoric of "taking back the mainland" has dissipated with the liberalization of political culture and commerce, the stigma of communism (understood as poverty, cultural backwardness, and one-party dictatorship) translates into sinophobia and remains the primary emotional material fueling the Taiwanese independence movement. As Chen Kuan-Hsing argues, decolonization in East Asia is an incomplete project that was hijacked by the US installment of a Cold

War structure of feeling.[47] The Cold War created the spatial fracturing and "worlding" of Chinas (first, second, and third worlds) as well as their temporal desynchronization (pre-, anti-, and postcapitalist). This fracturing is most symptomatically seen in the contradictory senses of center and periphery in the two Chinas: while the PRC is militarily and politically dominant, it is also economically and culturally colonized by the ROC.[48] Although the ROC no longer claims to be the seat of the legitimate government of the whole of China, it continues to see itself as the center of authentic Chinese culture, where standard Chinese writing remains in use and traditional culture remains protected from the disastrous events of the Cultural Revolution. Such claims no doubt carry an imperialistic undertone, although it is far from clear whether it is colonialist to consider Taiwan Chinese or *not* to do so. The interpenetrations of American neocolonial interests, Han Chinese chauvinism, Taiwanese ethno-nationalism, and Sinocentrism often render the operations of power illegible, greatly limiting the application of a dichotomous model of domination and resistance from postcolonial studies to the quandary of two Chinas.[49]

How, then, is the problem of queer liberalism entwined with the quandary of two Chinas? For many international observers, Taiwan has been a poster child of East Asian democratization. Taiwan's highly touted economic "miracle" is causally linked to its political liberalism, although it is hard to say which is the cause and which is the effect. The tentative links between Taiwan's economic and political liberalism aside, one of the most important indices of Taiwan's political liberalism is indeed its queer movement: queer literature has blossomed in Taiwan since the 1990s, producing mainstream and internationally acclaimed titles such as Chu T'ien-wen's *Notes of a Desolate Man*. In addition, the popular gay TV series, *Crystal Boys*, aired in 2003 to wide attention. Taiwan was also the first Chinese community to hold a Gay Pride parade in 2003. Since then, Taiwan has been rumored to be on its way to becoming the first East Asian country to legalize same-sex marriage.[50] Since these significant changes in queer visibility occurred after the lifting of the martial law in 1987 and the multiparty election in 2000, it is natural to assume that queer emancipation is a byproduct of the advent of the liberal-democratic state. This view reinforces the link between political liberalism (queer visibility) and economic liberalism (free trade), which, consequently, implies that any observable degree of queer progress in the PRC must be attributed to the supersession of socialism by international capitalism.

The assumption of free and repressed queer subjects depends on the dichotomy of two Chinas. Since the Cold War period, Taiwan is almost never studied in the West as an object of interest itself. Instead, as Yvonne Chang points out, Taiwan has served either as a surrogate for China as a whole (during the years when scholars could not access mainland China for fieldwork or language training), or as a thought experiment of the "road not taken" in communist studies: "What would have happened to China without the Communist Revolution?"[51] The celebration of Taiwan's liberalism, then, works in tandem with the reduction of China to communist studies, whereby Marxism is caricatured as the planned economy and rigid power structures, and democracy conflated with the ballot box.

Commentators who consider Taiwan to be a formerly Leninist state that has successfully undergone democratization commonly attribute a revolutionary character to the lifting of martial law in 1987. The event ended near four decades of Kuomintang (KMT) autocracy and granted oppositional parties formal political representation. But as Marx once said, "the political revolution dissolves civil society into its elements without revolutionizing these elements themselves or subjecting them to criticism."[52] The creation of a multiparty electoral system does not signal substantive equality and social change; nor can we comfortably equate democratization to the formal competition between parties. Despite the rhetoric of radical break, this common reading of 1987 as the beginning of democratization in Taiwan actually derives in part from a perception that Taiwan was always and already liberal before the lifting of martial law.

It is worth noting that such readings are possible only because liberalism itself is a contradictory ideology whose political and economic meanings are conflated in the cultural imaginary. In the pre–1987 authoritarian phase, Taiwan was the "Free China" that was not yet lost to the revolution against the property system. During this phase, Taiwan was free in the sense of the free market. Like many other capitalist, but not necessarily democratic, regimes supported by the United States, Taiwan played a key role in the global translation of liberty as laissez-faire capitalism. Long before the popularization of the term

East Asian Economic Miracle, triumphant accounts of the Four Asian Tigers already identified Taiwan's high growth rates since the 1960s as the vindication of liberalism over the socialist model. In the period after the lifting of martial law in 1987, Taiwan is again a paradigmatic manifestation of a universal liberalism, whose meaning has suddenly shifted from free trade to the ballot box. Discussed in the Western media mainly as a counterpart of the People's Republic of China, Taiwan stands as a comforting example of how Western liberal principles, such as freedom of expression and free elections, can take root in non-Western cultures. Together with Japan, India, and Namibia, Taiwan is the living proof that "traditional societies," despite their recalcitrant cultural customs and economic backwardness, can also become just like the West. By the twenty-first century, the old world order was turned upside down by a post-martial-law, democratic Taiwan and a post-Maoist, capitalist China. Because formerly stable ideological metaphors are reversed, the revamped Cold War bipolar lens of the differences between the ROC and the PRC has come to depend heavily on the political rivalry between the Democratic Progress Party (DPP) and the KMT for a sense of Taiwan's liberalism. Although the principal justification for the grouping of Taiwan with the liberal West has now shifted from its capitalism to its democracy, the theoretical inconsistencies of global anticommunism have only reinforced the impression that Taiwan is a steadily liberalizing society on the verge of becoming a belated version of multicultural America.

One crucial consequence of this queer emancipatory narrative is the analytical reduction of human emancipation to democratization, to a revolution in the *form of the state* from the one-party rule of the KMT to the present multi-party system in Taiwan. However, since Taiwan's "democratization"—its first multifactional presidential election in 2000—ethnic identity has replaced anticommunism as the dominant political issue in Taiwan. Currently, the Taiwanese polity is divided into two color-coded camps: the Pan-Green Coalition led by the DPP and devoted to the promotion of Taiwan's de jure independence, and the "One China" Pan-Blue Coalition centered on the nationalist party's (KMT) platform of unitary Chinese national identity and close economic cooperation with the People's Republic of China. The Green Camp made the creation of a distinctive Taiwanese identity and "de-Sinicization" (qu Zhongguo hua) major campaign issues, emphasizing the KMT's long record of oppression and martial law, its massacre of Taiwanese protestors in the 228 Incident, and its regime of White Terror that imprisoned and executed 45,000–90,000 intellectuals in the 1950s. The electoral competition between Green and Blue has blocked queer issues from entering the domain of politics. In 2004, a group of concerned intellectuals, writers, artists, and activists in Taiwan formed the Alliance of Ethnic Equality in response to DPP's electoral campaign, which created "a divisive identity politics playing on ethnic friction rather than resolving them."[53] The Alliance recognized that Taiwan did not have a true democracy because elections were monopolized by ethnic identity issues, while other concerns—environmentalism, migrant workers, queer rights—were effectively purged from the domain of electoral politics. More specifically, elections in Taiwan are determined by the ethnic identities of the running candidates—whether the politician in question is Taiwan-born (*bensheng*) or an émigré from the mainland (*waisheng*)—and both camps have been unresponsive to and uninterested in queer and feminist issues.

This analysis suggests that a simple dichotomy between liberal and illiberal regimes, democracies and authoritarian bureaucracies, is insufficient for comprehending the conditions of queer lives. Indeed, sexual dissidents, migrant workers, and other disempowered social groups often bear the brunt of globalization-induced crisis. Threatened by the prospect of reunification with mainland China, Taiwan has focused its diplomatic strategy on integrating into the global economy and on securing popular support from the West by promoting itself as a democratic regime with values similar to those in the United States. As Josephine Ho demonstrated, the realignment of local cultures with the demands of globalization has also created a repressive regime for queer people through the establishment of NGOs, religious groups, psychiatric and health experts, and even human rights watch groups.[54] The queer Marxism project runs counter to the perception that liberalism has advanced queer rights. Giving up the notion of a liberal Taiwan, in turn, frees us of these debilitating habits of thought inherited from the Cold War that are blocking more useful analyses of the complex relations between queer struggles and power. Moreover, disabusing ourselves of the knee-jerk equation of Marxism and liberalism with the correlated Chinas also allows us to recognize these struggles as intellectually hybrid, impure, and even promiscuous formations.

Viewing Marxism as an intellectual resource rather than an economic policy necessarily raises the question of theory in Chinese studies. It should be clear by now that "China" in this study is not an empirical location that refers to the PRC alone. Instead, I focus on how queer cultural producers engage with the problematic of China(s). Treating China as an object of theoretical reflection disrupts a strong tendency in the current field of gender and sexuality studies to separate theory, in particular queer theory, from empirical and historical perspectives on same-sex relations in China. Scholars who separate theoretical and historical perspectives in Chinese gender studies often insist that queer theory is a Euro-American formation of sexual knowledge, and that applying queer theory to the study of China perpetuates a colonialist epistemology. The critique is not unfounded, since Sinophone queer cultures indeed have important and distinctive features that cannot be assimilated into a global history of sexuality.[55] In addition, this critique of queer theory's Eurocentrism is both urgent and necessary, given that it is increasingly common for critics, such as Dennis Altman, to interpret new sexual formations in Asia as the spread of Western models of homosexuality without local history and agency.[56] A stronger version of this view categorically rejects the applicability of the terms queer and homosexuality, insisting that *tongxinglian* and *tongxing'ai* in China are entirely different from these concepts.[57] My study questions the assumption that renders China as antithetical and exterior to queer theory; in turn, I characterize queer theory as an incomplete project that is constantly transformed by China. In my view, limiting the provenance of queer theory to North America misses not only the opportunity for a transcultural dialogue, but also the point of queer theory altogether: that sexual difference necessitates a rethinking of cultural comparison and comparability.

In what follows, I offer some reflections on the historical entanglement between queer theory and cultural comparison as the discipline was practiced in North America. I assert that queer theory, for all its emphasis on sexual difference, was actually founded by a theory of the non-West that was captured by the sign of China. In this context, the proper question to ask in the postcolonial debate is no longer, "Why does China need queer theory?" but rather, "Why does queer theory need the Chinas?" By demonstrating that queer theory has always needed and presupposed the Chinas, and that queer theory is also a theory of the cultural difference between China and the West, I strive to show that queer theory requires a theory of geopolitics. In turn, Chinese queer Marxists' theorization of the intimacy between geopolitics and sexuality, which I reconstruct more systematically in chapter two, serves as a model for queer writings in English. Recognizing Chinese queer theory as a geopolitically mediated discourse, then, helps to correct the perception of it as a derivative discourse. Instead, we can place Chinese queer theory in the proper intellectual context as a globally capacious tradition that prefigures and encompasses its Euro-American variant.

In the United States in the late 1980s and the 1990s, a major question in queer theory was the postulation of a universal patriarchy. In retrospect, it is surprising how many of the founding texts of queer theory were derived from a theoretical argument for a nonidentity between Eastern and Western cultures. Take, for example, Judith Butler's 1990 *Gender Trouble*, a text primarily known today for its theory of performativity and for its critique of the category of women as the universal basis of feminism. In *Gender Trouble* and later elaborations, Butler argues that gender is not an immutable essence of a person but, rather, a reiterative series of acts and a citational practice of norms that are, significantly, culturally variable.[58] The theory of cultural variability underlies the book's central claim, which is that a representational politics based on an idealized and dualistic conception of gender forecloses transgressive possibilities and agency. But Butler means several things by the phrase "culturally variable." The immediate context for Butler's intervention is a structuralist legacy in French feminist theory that she understands to be a dyadic heterosexism. In *The Elementary Structures of Kinship*, Claude Lévi-Strauss maintains that the prohibition against incest is not only a law present in every culture but also what founds culture as such. Lévi-Strauss's understanding of the prohibition against incest as a culturally invariable "elementary structure" of human civilization provides the basis of the Symbolic in Lacanian psychoanalysis, which elevates the incest taboo into a heterosexist theory of the Oedipus complex.[59] Later, Butler wonders what would happen if Western philosophy (and gender theory) began with Antigone instead of Oedipus, and formulates an alternative to the Oedipus complex in *Antigone's Claim*. In *Gender Trouble*, Butler identifies the important links (and discontinuities) between the structuralist legacy of Lévi-Strauss, Ferdinand de Saussure, and Jacques Lacan, and the French feminist theory of Julia Kristeva, Hélène Cixous, and Luce Irigaray. The contributions of French feminist theory are many, but most significant is the view that the fundamental difference between masculine and feminine is a precondition of human signification and communicability. Butler argues that Lévi-Straussian theories of universal structures and fundamentals were indispensable in elevating feminist theory to the center of social analysis: "The speaking subject was, accordingly, one who emerged in relation to the duality of the sexes, and that culture, as outlined by Lévi-Strauss, was defined through the exchange of women, and that the difference between men and women was instituted at the level of elementary exchange, an exchange which forms the possibility of communication itself. . . . Suddenly, [women] were fundamental. Suddenly, no human science could proceed without us."[60]

Why was *Gender Trouble*, the foundational text of US queer theory, so preoccupied with the question of cultural variability in structuralist anthropology? In the 1966 preface to the second edition of *The Elementary Structures of Kinship*, Lévi-Strauss openly acknowledges that his theory of kinship was based on insufficient and secondary sources about China and India.[61] Butler returns to Lévi-Strauss's writings on China in *Undoing Gender*, citing the 2001 anthropological findings of Cai Hua to dismiss the structuralist myth of universal kinship.[62] Here, China occupies a strategic place in Butler's quarrels with the structuralists, many of whom (such as Kristeva and Žižek) have also produced famous statements of their own on China.[63] Butler's goal is not only to reveal the heteronormative and cisnormative assumptions in structuralist and psychoanalytic understandings of kinship, but to demonstrate that these laws, norms, and structures are products of human culture and hence subject to social change and democratic contestations.[64] The thesis of social transformability then requires Butler to demonstrate that such laws must vary from culture to culture. If cultures like China can be discovered to operate outside or, better yet, against the systematic descriptions of universally valid laws and conventions of the human world in Western philosophy, the structuralist project can be finally overcome.[65] In these queer battles against the heterosexism of the Symbolic, observations about the culturally constructed nature of social categories become an argument about cultural differences in the anthropological sense, and the critique of gender norms becomes entangled with theories of Oriental exceptionalism.

In *Gender Trouble*, Butler argues that the category of women is an oppressively restrictive notion that is dependent on an equally restrictive imagination of a singular patriarchy.[66] To make this argument, Butler points out that there must be other cultures that do not share Western ideas about what a woman is or what constitutes oppression and patriarchy. In order to deconstruct the fixity of women as a category, Butler has to first caution her reader against the search for a universal patriarchy in non-Western cultures:

> The effort to include "Other" cultures as variegated amplifications of a global phallogocentrism constitutes an appropriative act that risks a repetition of the self-aggrandizing gesture of phallogocentrism, colonizing under the sign of the same those differences that might otherwise call that totalizing concept into question. . . . The political assumption that there must be a universal basis for feminism, one which must be found in an identity assumed to exist cross-culturally, often accompanies the notion that the oppression of women has some singular form discernible in the universal or hegemonic structure of patriarchy or masculine domination. . . . That form of feminism has come under criticism for its efforts to colonize and appropriate non-Western cultures to support highly Western notions of oppression.[67]

What exactly are these "highly Western notions of oppression" and how do non-Western cultures serve as their conceptual limits, as the *l'impensé de la raison*? More specifically, how does an argument that designates non-Western cultures as the unrepresentable and the unspeakable counter the history of colonial violence and the hegemony of Western thought? In this critique of the foundational ethnocentrism of the West, paradoxically, the non-West becomes excluded from thought, standing in for the epistemological limits of Western reason. This particular postcolonial critique certainly has its political promises and uses, but the more pressing question is why the ethical call to realign what is possible in human gender and sexual relations in queer theory has to rely on an anthropological hypothesis of the incongruity of Western and non-Western cultures, which in turn posits China as the exteriority and lacunae of "Western notions of oppression."

Gender Trouble is not the only text from the 1990s whose theory of gender relies on this particular conception of the non-West. Another pioneering text of early US queer theory, Eve Sedgwick's *Epistemology of the Closet*, makes a different argument about sexuality via the distinction between the totalizability of the West and the nontotalizable nature of the non-West. Sedgwick's work is generally acknowledged as a paradigm shift that establishes the study of sexuality as the foundation of all social analysis, rather than as its footnote. She makes this argument by showing that the definitional crisis of homosexuality/heterosexuality is "epidemic" and central to all organizations of knowledge, even non-sex-specific kinds. In many scenarios that do not appear to be primarily concerned with homosexuality—for example, romantic English poetry—the text's structure of address belies a preoccupation with what Sedgwick calls the triangulation of desire that involves the deflection and disavowal of homosocial desires. In order to show that sexuality is central to *every* node of knowledge, however, Sedgwick has to qualify her argument with the phrase "in Western culture." The West then becomes a totalizable entity, while the non-West is definitionally excluded from this theory of sexuality.

Sedgwick begins *Epistemology of the Closet* with the proposal that the (crisis of the) homo/heterosexual definition is constitutive of "twentieth-century Western culture as a whole."[68] This argument builds on her analysis in *Between Men* (1985) that the disavowal or deflection of same-sex desire, often found in English poetry whose manifest theme is the celebration of heterosexual union, constitutes a culturally policed boundary between homosociality and homosexuality that structures the entire social terrain "in the modern West."[69] Sedgwick argues that although the figure of the closet may appear to be a merely sexual or even trivial question, it is actually the paradigm of knowledge/ignorance that organizes the entire domain of modern social thought. Later, Sedgwick elaborates this argument in the discussion of the "privilege of unknowing" in *Tendencies* (1993). Sedgwick shows that social domination depends on a strategic separation of mutually implied forms of knowledge of which the closet is a paradigmatic case.[70] This point is the basis of Sedgwick's claim that the interpretation of sexuality should be taken as the starting point of social analysis rather than as its afterthought. The future of queer studies depends on the promise that rethinking the sexual can lead to the rethinking of the social as well.[71]

The power of Sedgwick's work comes from her ability to show that sexuality is revelatory of the ways in which an entire culture organizes itself and therefore central to any type of social analysis. Sedgwick, however, cautions that sexuality studies can become the foundation of social analysis only if we do not apply such generalizations, "however sweeping," outside the West: "It is very difficult for [this book's choice of the Euro-American male as its subject matter] to be interpreted in any other light than that of the categorical imperative: the fact that they are made in a certain way here seems a priori to assert that they would be best made *in the same way everywhere*. I would ask that, *however sweeping* the claims made by this book may seem to be, it not be read as making that particular claim [of applying the analysis to non–Euro-American cultures]."[72] In this formula, the mutually constitutive and dialectical relationship between homosexuality and heterosexuality within Western culture "as a whole" is analytically predicated on the categorical rejection of the commensurability between Western and non-Western cultures.

Sedgwick suggests that sexuality can maintain its illustrative power as a paradigmatic instance of the ways discourse organizes the entire social field *only* if we accept that it makes sense to speak of "twentieth-century Western culture as a whole" in the first place, but what are the implications of the insistence on the links between these two arguments? What are the historical and theoretical contexts in which Sedgwick's argument for the centrality of sexuality studies comes to be analytically dependent on the totalizability of the West, on our ability to view "twentieth-century West as a whole" as a coherent unit of analysis? It is unclear whether Sedgwick would consider Spain, Greece, or Serbia part of a West whose definitional axis extends from Marcel Proust to Henry James, Jane Austen, and Herman Melville. But it is clear that the hypothesis of the totality of the West requires the incommensurability between East and West, since it is only in relation to the non-West that the phrase "Western culture as a whole" acquires any meaning and coherence.

While 1990s' US queer theory needed and reified the incongruity between cultures—and for the founding critics, it is not the differences between French and American cultures that matter—the historical tendency to situate China as the paradigmatic Other served a number of important functions in the development of queer theory. The argument that homosexuality was a modern invention (in contrast to, for example, Greek pederasty) is among the most important claims of queer theory.[73] Some queer theorists have argued that the modern period is defined by a newly available conception of homosexuality as the identity of a small and relatively fixed group of people, in distinction from an earlier view of same-sex desire as a continuum of acts, experiences, identities, and pleasures spanning the entire human spectrum. This claim, sometimes known as the "before sexuality thesis," is commonly associated with the work of Michel Foucault, who is quite specific in his dating: Foucault writes that homosexuality as such was invented in 1870 in the West.[74] But in making that claim about the constructedness of homosexuality, Foucault also argues that two different histories, one Western and one Eastern, must be carefully distinguished from each other. Foucault maintains that sexuality is not a timeless, immutable given because sexuality as we know it is absent in the East. The first history, which began somewhere in Greece and migrated to France to produce "the homosexual" as a species in 1870, is called *scientia sexualis*. Foucault's definition of scientia sexualis does not include modern Greece, but draws a line of continuity between modern French culture and ancient Greek culture. The second history, of which Foucault cites China as a primary example, encompasses all non-Western societies without distinguishing their ancient and modern forms. The name Foucault proposes for this second history is *ars erotica* (a term that emphasizes its lack of scientific and logical basis in comparison to scientia sexualis).

Whereas Western civilization (from Greece to France) enjoyed a science of sexuality that discursively produced "the homosexual" as a species in 1870 (in a manner similar to the production of the criminal, the vagabond, the prostitute, the blasphemer, and the insane Foucault analyzes in *Madness and Civilization*), China remains mired in the stage of ars erotica that has blocked the invention of homosexuality: "On the one hand, the societies—and they are numerous: China, Japan, India, Rome, the Arabo-Moslem societies—which endowed themselves with an *ars erotica* [sic] . . . Our civilization possesses no *ars erotica*. In return, it is undoubtedly the only civilization to practice a *scientia sexualis*."[75] Foucault further insists that China's ars erotica is precisely what "we" have shed in order to achieve modernity: "Breaking with the traditions of the *ars erotica,* our society has equipped itself with a *scientia sexualis.*"[76] Here China functions as the constitutive outside of the modern European homosexual's self-definition, as the negative space against which it becomes possible for individuals who are, presumably, genetically unrelated to the Greeks to speak of a "we" and "our society." While the cultural differences between ancient Greece and France of the 1870s are construed as a historical advance, the distinction between ancient China and modern China does not bother Foucault much. In fact, the grouping of ancient Rome and unspecified periods of Chinese history as interchangeable examples of ars erotica is justified precisely by the claim that non-Western societies, due to the lack of scientia sexualis, display a developmental stasis through the millennia. China's ars erotica signifies an ossified cultural essence bearing a collective resemblance to the ancient Mediterranean world. In fact, what Foucault means by the ars erotica of "China, Japan, India, Rome, [and] the Arabo-Moslem societies" is a code name for *non-Christian* societies, whereas Europe is defined by "the development of confessional techniques" and "pastoral care"—namely Christianity.

Noting the glaring absence of race in Foucault's considerations of the bourgeois self in the *History of Sexuality,* Anne Stoler argues that Foucault's Collège de France lectures present a more nuanced treatment of racism and a "shift in analytic weight," where "a discourse of races . . . antedates nineteenth-century social taxonomies, appearing not as a result of bourgeois orderings, but as constitutive of them."[77] If the history of sexuality has always been a history of race as well, Foucault's own insight indicates that European preoccupations with race do not reflect a negotiation of the boundaries between self and other; rather, the concepts of race and sexuality are parts of the metropole's technology of managing social differences within a domestic setting, forming part of the bourgeois state's indispensable defense against itself.[78] The conflation between the global hierarchization of cultures and a liberal pluralist understanding of race in domestic politics is indeed the major problem confronting queer critics writing in the Foucauldian idiom. The influential scholarship of David Halperin is a case in point. In his 2002 *How to Do the History of Sexuality,* Halperin restates the famous thesis of his 1990 *One Hundred Years of Homosexuality* that " 'homosexuality' was a modern cultural production and that there was no homosexuality, properly speaking, in classical Greece, the ancient Mediterranean world, or indeed in most premodern or non-Western societies."[79] Like Foucault, Halperin does not find the distinction between ancient and modern relevant to non-Western societies, and uses "most premodern" and all "non-Western societies" as interchangeable examples. For both Halperin and Foucault, modern China and other non-Western (that is, non-Christian) societies, precisely due to their lack of something that can be called "sexuality," experience an evolutionary stasis that makes them similar to "classical Greece" and the "ancient Mediterranean world."

Writing one full decade after *One Hundred Years of Homosexuality*, however, Halperin acknowledges "the force of [the] postcolonial critique":

> Constructionist discourse about the modernity of sexuality and the historicity of premodern sexual formations often has the effect of aligning marginal or nonstandard sexual practices in postindustrial liberal societies with dominant sexual practices in developing nations, thereby perpetuating the hoary colonialist notion that non-European cultures represent the cultural childhood of a modern Europe. . . . [However, this] irreducible epistemic and social privilege" [of the Western historian] does not mean it's wrong. There are positive uses to be made of inequality and asymmetry, in history as in love.[80]

Halperin is conscientious in his "positive" uses of this "inequality." One detects in his writing no pejorative descriptions of those erotic experiences and expressions that supposedly characterize modern non-Western and premodern Western societies. But one notices how quickly an opportunity to learn from understudied cultures is read as an injunction to suspend moral judgment. Surreptitiously, an engagement with the "postcolonial critique" is replaced by a call to defend and de-stigmatize "nonstandard practices" within modern Western (here defined as "postindustrial" and "liberal") societies themselves. In other words, the *intellectual* critique of Eurocentrism in queer research becomes a commitment to "diversity" as an American social value, and the invitation to think sexuality "transnationally" is understood as an argument for multiculturalism and tolerance for US subjects' alternative sexual practices. In this liberal version of the story, the problem of Orientalism becomes a "hoary colonialist notion" that must be corrected by the enlightened Western historian. Translating the "inequality and asymmetry" between global cultures into the domestic signification of race misses the opportunity to ask how the supposedly "irreducible" "epistemic and social privilege" itself should and can be transformed. In the final analysis, Halperin's approach is a liberal pluralist one whose primary concern lies with diversity in a domestic context instead of transnational dialogues. By contrast, I would insist that transnational dialogues are both possible and necessary, and that we have much to gain from a consideration of the intellectual history of queer China, which provides an important alternative to the liberal pluralist emphasis on tolerance, respect, and diversity as the ethics in dealing with "nonstandard practices."

Queer Marxism: An Alternative to Liberal Pluralist Analysis

In retrospect, we can conclude that the political success of US queer theory—the fact that it was able to make sexuality a legitimate field of social and cultural theory—is rhetorically derived from imagining a binary opposition between East and West. Ironically, the incongruity between East and West, despite its importance to queer theory, does not appear on the famous list of "axiomatic binarisms" Sedgwick enumerates in *Epistemology of the Closet* as the fabric of modern culture, because it is exterior to it.[81] While we are indebted to the works of Foucault, Sedgwick, and Halperin, we cannot afford to keep assuming that queerness or homosexuality has a single origin in Greece or France. Nor can we assume that queer theory should begin with a description of how a certain "we" evolved from a Greek cultural organization of gender and sexuality to the making of the modern French homosexual as a species and then to the twentieth-century homo-/heterosexual definitional crisis. Conversely, it would be erroneous to argue that China disrupts the colonial epistemology of Western universalism by presenting a different history of same-sex relations. However, the problem is not an inherent racism or Orientalism in queer theory. My argument is that postwar theories of sexuality often unwittingly reproduce the logic of liberal pluralism and fail to develop stronger political responses to the dilemmas of the Cold War, which the case of a divided China helps us understand. In other words, queer theory needs the Chinas not because it is ethically imperative to include the Other, but because US theory is itself born in the shadows of the failures of liberal pluralism.

Queer Marxism in the Chinas provides precisely the conceptual tools to illuminate the historical connections between queer theory and liberal pluralism for the global scholarly community.

The queer Marxist approach does not ask society to tolerate or accept "alternative" sexualities. Rather, queer Marxists ask, what kinds of historical processes empower individuals of certain sexualities to decide who should be tolerated and accepted in the first place? Queer Marxists analyze the field of socioeconomic conditions in which desire, pleasure, intimacy, human connectedness, and permissible speech become possible, asking how such social relations are reproduced along unequal axes of power for differently positioned human beings. Similarly, instead of arguing for more "inclusion" of China in queer studies in the hope of undoing the epistemological imperialism of the West, queer Marxists reject inclusion as a mode of social redress, opting instead for an analysis of geopolitically reproduced relations of power. Queer Marxism engages questions of location and situatedness without reifying alterity. The point is neither to return to the primacy of economic determinants by reinstating an intellectual foundationalism for queer theory, nor to reiterate a moralistic critique of bourgeois consumption brought about by transnational capitalism. Rather, queer Marxism emphasizes the possibilities of *systemic analysis* in investigating those configurations of gender, sexuality, and social power that liberal critics characterize as mere contingencies.

Queer Marxism in Two Chinas traces the dynamic traditions of queer art, film, literature, social movements, and popular culture in the Chinas that produce a Marxist philosophy of human sociality. Chapter 2, "Chinese Queer Theory," explores the "theoretical status of theory" in contemporary Chinese queer critical discourses centered on Cui Zi'en, Josephine Ho, Ding Naifei, and the Gender/Sexuality Rights Association, Taiwan. Rather than assuming that anyone producing queer theory in Chinese must be working with a translated concept and hence conflating Euro-American sexual politics and Chinese "tongzhi" in the service of the cultural imperialism of the West, I argue that queer theory itself is an incomplete project with global origins, and that the particular variant of queer theory we have become accustomed to in North American academia is constantly expanded, revised, and displaced by competing sources of knowledge in the Chinas and elsewhere. While the highly transnational, mobile conversations across the straits (between PRC- and

ROC-based scholars) do not represent a univocal queer theory, this body of scholarship is distinct from its North American counterpart in that it has successfully produced an analysis of the relation between geopolitics and sexuality.

Chapter 3, "The Rise of the Queer Chinese Novel," demonstrates that the emergence of queer fiction in Chinese is not merely the result of a consolidated and self-affirmative social identity, as is often assumed, but, rather, a development critically shaped by the geopolitics of the Cold War and the vicissitudes of Chinese Marxism. Tracing the emergence of queer literature and subjectivity back to an earlier generation of writers before the more commonly discussed examples of "tongzhi wenxue" (Chinese queer fiction) writers such as Chu T'ien-wen, Chen Ran, Lin Bai, and Qiu Miaojin, my analysis treats Chen Ruoxi's transnational novel *Paper Marriage* as an exemplary case of the productive tensions between queer feelings and Marxism.

Chapter 4, "Genealogies of the Self," examines the political problem of queer liberalism through a reading of a feminist novel, Xiao Sa's *Song of Dreams*. While the novel makes a feminist claim by representing a self-invented woman who attains both financial and sexual independence in the era of Taiwan's economic miracle, I argue that the novel's feminism is critically predicated on a queer arrangement of desires and commodities, which implies that the gendered "self" is a palimpsest of internally contradictory pasts, rather than the immutable essence of a person. Against the neoliberal fable of middle-class self-transformation and virtuous striving, the novel insists on the need to conduct a genealogical review of the irreducibly queer pasts of a self that appears to be willed into being through sheer determination and hard work. Through a queer critique of economic liberalization and unbridled capitalism, *Song of Dreams* shows a creative way to mobilize queerness for anticapitalist thinking.

The final chapter, "Queer Human Rights in and against the Two Chinas," examines the mutual entanglements between queer human rights discourse and the quandary of two Chinas. Whereas "human rights" remain a sensitive issue in the PRC because of the incomplete character of its independence resulting from US neocolonialism, human rights—including queer human rights—have also become a key tool by which Taiwan disciplines China in order to secure its own independence. While one aim of this chapter is to document the numerous cases of queer human rights violations in Taiwan despite its claims to political liberalism, I also examine the creative guerrilla tactics that queer Marxists have developed that strategically invoke the concept of human rights in the service of progressive ends.

As represented by the queer films, texts, and social movements reconstructed in this book, queerness is not grounded in the subjective meanings of affect, desire, shame, and loss; rather, queerness indicates the constitutive sociality of the self, which shifts the focus of Chinese queer discourse away from questions of cultural diversity and formal electoral competition to the substantive socioeconomic conditions of effective participation in public culture. Inspired by Marxism, these queer movements in the Chinas emphasize the importance of systemic understandings of the material reproduction of power and society, while deploying multilayered, impure, and promiscuous circuits of social exchange to undo habits of thought that congeal around the quandary of two Chinas. Since the underlying structures and causal mechanisms that regulate the conditions of queer democratic participation are necessarily bound up with the dynamics of international capitalism, the specificity of geographical location, and the incomplete project of decolonization, queer Marxism in the Chinas also stands as a historical response to neoliberalism. In this uncanny convergence of queerness, Marxism, and Chinas, we find an alternative imagination of human creativity, fulfillment, and freedom.

CHAPTER 2

CHINESE QUEER THEORY

The Dilemmas of Queer Theory in China

Aibai (short for *aiqing baipi shu*, "White Paper on Love") is one of the earliest internet forums for LGBTQ information-sharing, discussion, and community-organizing in China. The website has hosted debates on topics ranging from Obama's stance on same-sex marriage in the United States to recreational drug use in the LGBTQ community. Recently, an *Aibai* columnist Damien Lu, writing under the penname of Xing Xing (star), published a series of blogs that reignited debates over queer theory's relevance to China's gay liberation movements. Lu is an American-born Chinese (ABC) who writes in fluent Chinese. In his columns, he repeatedly reminds his reader that he holds a Ph.D. from the United States and describes himself as a Western-educated sexologist. Whereas China's famous sexologists from Pan Guangdan to Pan Suiming are devoted to unveiling the mysteries of human sexuality, Lu is invested in a different kind of demystification: he wants to educate the Chinese public about the dangers of queer theory, which he regards as a threat to China's gay liberation movements. Lu argues that queer theory, propagated by Western and Western-educated critics, misleads people into thinking that sexual orientation is fluid, socially constructed, and subject to personal choices. Consequently, the popularization of queer theory in China discourages policymakers from recognizing the legitimacy of homosexuals and their rights.[1] The only way for gay people to free themselves from discrimination, Lu suggests, is to convince the authorities that they are born homosexual rather than choosing to be so.

Without questioning the usefulness of a politics that represents homosexuality as an undesirable but inevitable reality, we can observe that Lu's language conflates the nature/nurture debate (whether homosexuality is genetic or acquired) with the essentialism/constructivism divide (whether the social meanings of homosexuality and heterosexuality are fixed or culturally constructed). Intellectually weak and politically reactionary, Lu's columns are also aggressively nationalist. In "What Is Queer Theory and How Does It Relate to the Gay Movement," Lu defines queer theory as the writings of four culprits: Eve Sedgwick, Judith Butler, Adrienne Rich, and Diana Fuss.[2] Pointing out that "none of these four writers has any training in sociology, psychology, or biology," Lu concludes that "queer theory is the product of the imagination of those living in an ivory tower, rather than the result of scientific research." Such "ivory-tower thinking" has no use for China, Lu maintains, and the Chinese should just stop importing it.

Lu's writing symptomatizes the confluence of two trends that have haunted gender and sexuality studies in China. First, Lu, like many, adopts a narrow definition of queer theory as an American discourse—for Lu, it is specifically the collective oeuvres of Sedgwick, Butler, Rich, and Fuss. As a result, anyone writing in Chinese on queer topics—Li Yinhe, Chang Hsiao-hung, or Pan Suiming, to name just a few—is assumed to be working with a translated Western concept rather than articulating an original thought.[3] Second, Lu's empiricist approach to the gay rights movement is a reaction against theory itself: instead of theory and theorists, Lu argues that China needs more medical, psychological, and public health experts who can produce transparent, easily digestible information to convince the general public and lawmakers that homosexuality is an immutable orientation. In his view, China needs science, not queer theory. How is this dichotomy constructed, and how does it persuade and motivate contemporary Chinese queer publics?

Between 2007 and 2014, I conducted four interviews with Cui Zi'en, China's preeminent queer filmmaker, cultural theorist, and novelist, about these questions. In the 2012 interview, Cui stated:

Compared to the American "ghetto" of academic subspecialization, paradoxically, queer theory in China enjoys a much broader media presence. My queer criticisms and essays have a large readership outside academic circles, not to mention that many works by progressive queer theorists in Taiwan and Hong Kong are avidly consumed in the People's Republic. At the same time, the general climate in China is quite conservative. I am the only openly gay academic in China. With my writings being the only exception, works published in China under the rubric of ku'er lilun (queer theory) or xing yanjiu (sexuality studies) are all produced by heterosexual-identified experts outside the literary fields: Sociologists such as Pan Suiming and Li Yinhe, or medical authorities such as Zhang Beichuan. In China, being openly identified as gay or lesbian detracts from your credibility as an expert on alternative sexuality, which is supposed to be described objectively and studied scientifically, preferably with a quantitative methodology.[4]

Cui's analysis explains the connection between the resistance to theory (which is not limited to sexual knowledge) and Chinese understandings of homosexuality. As Cui points out, homosexuality is recognized in China, but only as an object of medical and psychiatric management, and above all as a threat to public health. Hence, the question of visibility (when does China begin seeing representations of gay people in films and television?) misses the point entirely. Cui's analysis further explains why an enormous amount of funding for gender and sexuality research in China is funneled annually through AIDS-prevention organizations such as Wan Yanhai's Aizhixing Institute of Health Education,[5] while organizations in China devoted to causes unrelated to public health (such as sexual diversity) remain underfunded despite queer cultures' overall increase in visibility in China.[6] The pathologization of sexuality in medical research and social surveillance is matched, on the academic side, by influential studies that present homosexuality as a sociological problem in need of expert dissection. In order to qualify as an expert in this context in China, the researcher must be perceived as a heterosexual. Cui describes the interesting dilemma: in China, being identified or self-identifying as gay undermines one's credibility in producing knowledge about gender and sexuality, whereas in the United States, being an insider or an "authentic native informant" is typically expected to buttress one's authority. The reason is that once sexuality studies in China became a medico-scientific concept tethered to AIDS research and prevention funding, sexuality studies also spawned a group of bureaucrats and medical professionals who are answerable to the interests of the state. As Cui explains, because the state's goal is to contain AIDS rather than combat social stigma and discrimination, homosexuality, even after its removal from the categories of mental disorder by the Chinese Psychiatric Association in 2001, continues to be seen as a matter that should belong to the patient, not the doctor. A homosexual doctor or sexologist is an oxymoron in China—one cannot be both judge and defendant in the same trial. Since sexuality studies experts need to present homosexuality as a mental health issue to the public, gay researchers cannot come out of the closet; otherwise their aura of objectivity will be compromised. Nonetheless, Cui also emphasizes that the phenomenon is gradually changing. While the beginnings of the field were defined by medical, sociological, and psychological approaches exemplified by such works as Li Yinhe's *Subculture of Homosexuality* (which she wrote based on interviews and surveys with gay men and lesbians) (1992), Zhang Beichuan's *Homosexual Love* (1994), Fang Gang's *Homosexuality in China* (1995), and Tong Ge's *AIDS Prevention for the MSM Community* (men who have sex with men) (2004), in more recent years the empiricist and quantitative emphasis gave way to more interpretive cultural analysis, such as Pan Suiming's *Sex Revolution in China* (2006), and Pan Suiming and Huang Yingying's *Evidence of the Success of Sex Revolution in China*.[7] The nascent field of queer theory in the PRC, heavily influenced by queer theory in Taiwan, represents a struggle with the medicalization and pathologization of sexuality.

Cui's analysis offers an answer to Damien's Lu's question: Why does China need queer theory? Mired in the nexus of political surveillance and medico-scientific knowledge, queer China suffers from a particularly pernicious form of sexual empiricism that requires the intervention of theory. More specifically, the political dilemmas of queer life in China call for a specific type of materialist analysis, which the queer Marxists examined in this chapter develop. As Cui points out, the PRC government conflates the issues of AIDS prevention and homosexuality. The state's understanding of homosexuality as a public health and social order concern is consistent with its modern legal framework, which prosecuted sex between men under "hooliganism" (*liumang zui*, disruption of the social order) rather than sodomy.[8] With hooliganism, Chinese lawmakers *desexualize* homosexuality by grouping it under a broader and more understandable category of social management. As long as queer activism remains constrained by the framework of public health, the *intelligibility* of homosexuality is predicated on the material funding of AIDS research and regulated by a surveillance network of national experts and international NGOs. In this context, Chinese queer theory enters an alliance with Marxist critique to challenge the distribution of resources (symbolic and material), as well as the monopoly of sexologists and educational experts in the production of knowledge for and about sexual minorities.

In addition to the economic constraints of AIDS and sexuality research, queer Chinese cultures face another unique problem that makes Marxist analysis extremely useful: the legacy of the Cold War. In the Chinas, the demand for empiricism is not only fueled by the rise of medical and psychiatric authorities in sexuality research, but also inflected by a persistent Cold War ideology that places a premium on the delivery and discovery of transparent information about the Other. In the United States, this ideology of the Cold War is responsible for the creation of area studies programs (and for their generally antitheoretical orientation), while the purging of theory in Chinese gender and sexuality studies programs can be seen as their perversely implanted counterpart. In his famous analysis of the three-world schema, Carl Pletsch argues that the division of the globe into three worlds in the postwar period entailed a division of intellectual labor in kind as well.[9] Whereas knowledge produced by the first world is institutionally divided by discipline (music, economics, political science, or psychology), knowledge produced by, for, and about the third world is categorized by language and area (China, Japan, Middle East, Africa, and Latin America). In other words, the preference for empiricism in China studies is always shaped by the ideology of the Cold War, although we are not always conscious of the connections. The antitheory stance of Chinese sexuality studies experts reinforces this division of intellectual labor between the gathering of raw materials in area studies and the production of universal or nomothetic paradigms in (queer) theory.

Since sexuality studies in China, in particular AIDS research, is materially mediated by a global network of NGOs, the formation of sexual knowledge reflects and refracts assumptions about China's accessibility to scientific inquiry. China's secrets as a postsocialist country and the secrets of its homosexuals are entwined in the popular imagination, forming two intimately related dimensions of the closet. Observing that social scientific research circumscribe Chinese queer theory, Lucetta Kam raises the important point that PRC's first-generation research-ers have all denied allegations of homosexuality against themselves—a phenomenon that Cui also observes in the interviews. Kam points out that PRC-based research projects on gender and sexuality fall into two categories: the first category of sociological studies focuses on the ho-mosexual population, such as Li Yinhe and Wang Xiaobo's *Their World: A Penetrating Look into China's Male Homosexual Community*. These studies are marked by a "heterocentrism and otherization of homosexuals" that not only "tells a lot about the positioning of the researchers and the re-lationship between them and their research subjects" but "reflects the overall power dynamics between the heterosexual majority and the ho-mosexual minority."[10] The second type of work consists of personal accounts, anecdotal evidence, and sociological interviews, such as Chou Wah-shan's *Beijing Tongzhi Stories*, and Wu Chunsheng and Chou's coedited *We Are Alive*. These works install the legal, medical, and academic experts in "the role of public spokespersons for the silent populations of lesbians and gays in China" and result in "a similar otherization of ho-mosexual subjects."[11] Kam's critique demonstrates that tropes of penetra-tion, unveiling, and unmasking dominate Chinese sexuality research. These tropes not only exoticize the homosexual subject as the Other, as Kam explains, but also reveal an important continuity between Cold War Orientalism and mainstream Chinese approaches to homosexuality. The historical irony is that contemporary Chinese sexuality researchers' language of unmasking and unveiling is indeed reminiscent of West-ern journalist reports and documentaries on North Korea and China in the 1960s and '70s. To the extent that the Cold War created the epis-temic preference for empiricist social sciences, a reconsideration of queer Marxist theory across the 1949 divide can also help us unlearn these Cold War bifurcations.

In this chapter, I consider the theoretical works of several PRC- and ROC-based queer Marxists: Cui Zi'en, Josephine Chuen-juei Ho, Ding Naifei, Liu Jen-peng, Wang Ping, and Ning Yin-Bin. While most of these writers reside in Taiwan, their works have become a shared resource and standard references for all critics writing in Chinese. Although queer Marxists have produced a shared body of knowledge across the straits, their insights and concerns are far from being unified: Cui, for example, theorizes the material conditions of possibility for queer expression in the age of China's entry into global capitalism, while Taiwan-based queer Marxists formulate a synthetic vision of the interconnections among sexualized labor, the discontents of capitalist modernity, and queer resistance to identity politics. From different locations in the two Chinas, these queer Marxists present a collective view on how gender and sexual differences may serve as a liberating force against global capitalism. A telling failure of capitalist modernity is the liberal pluralist creation of identity politics and minority discourses. Liberal pluralist critics assume that social change can be created only through formal correctives (such as legalized same-sex marriage) brought about by the state, and that the state embodies the will of the majority and adjudicates between the conflicting interests of identity-based groups. The starting point of liberal pluralism is an empiricist sociology of such competing groups in need of state management.[12] By contrast, queer Marxists regard liberal pluralism itself as a byproduct of capitalism, which has destroyed the totality of social life and replaced it with fragmented, atomized individuals. Against the capitalist reification of identities, Chinese theorists redefine queerness as a critical relation to power that is not immediately assignable to a preexisting group. For queer Marxists, the queer is not a synonym for homosexuality, but a material reminder of one's relation to an unequal structure of power, as well as a capacity to recognize the distance between the diversity of erotic desires, genders, identities, and intimacies in human cultures and the liberal pluralist reduction of such expressions into fixed categories under global capitalism. Consequently, queer Marxist writers reject the semantic splitting of "sex" into gender (as the proper object of feminism) and sexuality (as the proper object of gay and lesbian studies). The concept of queerness encompasses both sex as gender (female or male, anatomical or chromosomal identity) and sex as sexuality (act, pleasure, orientation, object choice). Recognizing the irreducible richness of human genders and sexual expressions provides a powerful ethical perspective on the postsocialist and the neoliberal states' technologies of social management in the Chinas.

Chinese-language queer theory has flourished since the late 1980s. In particular, Taiwan has been a wellspring of queer energy and innovation, spearheading sexual movements in Chinese-language communities. In the past two decades, scholars from mainland China, Hong Kong, and Taiwan have held numerous cross-strait queer conferences, producing such volumes as *Lianjiexing: Liang an san di xing/bie xinju* (Connections: Trans-Local Exchanges on Chinese Gender/Sexuality) (2010); "Beyond the Strai(gh)ts: Transnationalism and Queer Chinese Politics" (2010); *Xingdi Tujing: Liang an san di xing/bie qihou* (Changing Sexual Landscape: The China Turn) (2011); *Zhuanyan lishi: Liang an san di xingyun huigu* (The Personal Is Historical: Gender/Sexuality Studies/Movements in Greater China) (2012); and *Xin daode zhuyi: Liang an san xingbie xunsi* (New Moralism: Sexual Reflections in Greater China) (2013). In its content as well as historical routes of dissemination, Chinese queer theory is a collaborative endeavor created by PRC and ROC scholars; this theory, already geographically mobile and methodologically impure, also critiques nationalist and essentialist epistemologies from the perspective of queer transnationalism.

The "Chinese" in Chinese queer theory is not merely a location that must refer to the PRC, or a linguistic and ethnic marker that must have essentialist undertones. It also refers to the capacity of queer theory to engage questions of Chineseness in the context of the political standoff between the two Chinas. Indeed, much of queer theory in Chinese explicitly examines the intersections between sexuality, gender, and the quandary of two Chinas. The problematization of the signifier of China rests at the heart of Chinese queer theory, which is, from its inception, beset by a nomenclature debate. The story of Edward Lam's coinage of the term *tongzhi* in 1992 has often been told many times, although with significant variation of emphasis and detail.[13] Originally a political idiom in Chinese revolutions meaning "comrade," *tongzhi* was appropriated by Chinese sexual countercultures to refer to same-sex love. This appropriation of a state-sanctioned idiom by the oppressed is analogous to the parodic resignification of the insult "queer" into a means of self-empowerment in US history. In this sense, the function of *tongzhi* in Chinese is identical to the function of queer in English. However, because the Chinese example is explicitly tied to the revolutionary legacy of Sun Yat-sen and to Mao's brand of socialism, the Chinese use of the term as political parody also implies a distinctive attitude toward Chinese Marxism. Critics who are mindful of the connections between queer social discourse and Chinese Marxism often emphasize that it is no coincidence that the term *tongzhi* first gained currency in Hong Kong and Taiwan, where a cultural Marxism, decoupled from state ideology and bureaucracy, flourished in such a way that made it easier to imagine and articulate a queer Marxism.[14] Like *tongzhi*, the neologism *lala*, a common term for lesbians in Chinese-speaking communities, has a linguistic history that demonstrates the affinities between sexual and geopolitical concerns. Popular in Beijing and Shanghai circles today, *lala* was imported from Taiwan in the 1990s. The term originated from *The Crocodile's Journal*, a critically acclaimed novel by Qiu Miaojin narrated in the first-person voice of a lesbian character named Lazi. Both the term *lazi* (and its derivative *lala*) and the novel gained immense popularity in Taiwan and mainland China after Qiu committed suicide in 1995.[15]

In 1994 novelists and critics Chi Ta-wei, Dantangmo, and Lucifer Hung proposed "ku-er" in the journal *Isle Margin* as a transliteration of both "queer" and "cool."[16] Chi subsequently popularized the term "ku-er" in two seminal collections on queer theory (*Queer Archipelago* and *Queer Carnival*, both published in 1997). Another translation, "guai-tai" (queer/freak/mutant), was introduced in a special issue of *Ai bao* in 1994 and received sophisticated theorization in the works of Chu Wei-cheng and Chang Hsiao-hung, where the semantic specificity of the term allows for brilliant readings of a deflected but persistent desire for kinship in texts that appear to disavow or circumvent heterosexuality.[17] Other proposed terms for specific groups, self-stylizations, or nonnormative expressions as a whole include "tongren," "T/po" "piaopiao," "wangliang," "yaoyan," "kuyi," "wai," and "xie."

Nonetheless, no universal translation of the term queer proved satisfactory, and any proposal immediately raises the question of whether one is subsuming Chinese *tongzhi* under the Western category of queer. Accordingly, it has become obligatory for Chinese queer theorists to begin with an account of the conjunction of the Chinese and the queer: how does one justify the connection between Chinese same-sex relations and the English word queer? There are many reasons the nomenclature debate has become such an emotionally charged and controversial topic in queer Chinese studies. Two are particularly relevant to the claims of queer Marxist theory.

The first is the term's legal implications. Wenqing Kang points out that, historically, the Chinese government never persecuted homosexuals per se, because to do so would require the officials to first recognize their existence, which neither regime (before and after 1949) was willing to do. In 1997, the nonexistent legal category of homosexuality was "decriminalized." Following the pioneering work of Chinese legal scholars such as Guo Xiaofei and Zhou Dan,[18] Kang argues that homosexuality forms a paradox in the eyes of Chinese law because the state cannot oppress a population whose existence it denies.[19] Strictly speaking, in China there are no laws against homosexuality as such; rather, the modern Chinese state has historically handled the issue by the name of "hooliganism" (liumang zui), which, as mentioned previously, is a broad category of punishable behavior usually of a nonsexual nature, including loitering, public indecency, vandalism, delinquency, and gang fights.[20] Kang makes the important observation that homosexual behavior could be criminalized under such provisions—disruption of social order—but not as a sex crime. During the Cultural Revolution, homosexuals were classified as "bad elements" in the idiom of Chinese revolutionary culture. This paradox becomes even more problematic in the case of sexual contact between women, for which the law has no ready "analogy clause" linking it to rape or anal sex.[21] As Matt Sommer's work illustrates, what was criminalized under Chinese law through the Qing period was not homosexuality per se but jijian, "illicit anal sex," or sodomy.[22] The category of jijian did not address the issue of consent, and the definition of homosexuality as forced anal sex means that the system was incapable of handling other types of sexual activities between men, such as oral sex and mutual masturbation, and all relations between women. Therefore, Kang proposes that the much-lauded "decriminalization of homosexuality" in the 1997 Criminal Law of the PRC was a convoluted affair, especially since the term "hooligan" entered China's legal thought as part of its socialist modernization and nation-building program, quite ironically as the Chinese translation of Marx's lumpenproletariat.

The linguistic development of contemporary Chinese queer theory—the fact that both comrade and hooligan are borrowed from Chinese revolutionary vocabulary—suggests a suppressed connection between sexual struggles and Marxist intellectual practice. This point is worth stressing because a colossal body of contemporary queer studies in Chinese is fixated on nomenclature debates, asking whether it is culturally imperialist to equate Chinese *tongzhi* with Western *queer*, or to conflate Taiwanese and Chinese experiences under the same category of *tongzhi*. In my view, these nomenclature debates are best examined in relation to the incomplete character of Chinese independence in postwar history. The proliferation of sexual identities and categories in modern China has always been conceptually merged with the imperatives of national survival and sovereignty against a long history of Western encroachments that resulted in extraterritorial rights, concessions, unequal treaties, indemnities, and the sacking of the palace.[23] The current debates of *tongzhi* on both sides of the straits are animated in no small measure by the traumatic memories of colonial dismemberment, which produced acute anxieties over the right to national self-determination that manifest themselves as sinophobia and Oriental exceptionalism in queer discourses. Over the past two decades, a distinctive group of theorists in Hong Kong, Taiwan, and mainland China has formed a coalitional network around the arguments that Chinese *tongzhi* are not the same as Western queers. These scholars argue that by separating *tongzhi* from Western queers and by developing an account of the local specificities of *tongzhi*—or what I would describe as homosexuality with Chinese characteristics—we would successfully fend off the encroachments of Western queer theory and its cultural imperialism. The politics of *tongzhi* fills a nationalist need to develop a linguistic alternative to Euro-American queer theory by insisting on the impenetrability of Eastern material.

At the core of this argument is the hypothesis that, prior to Western colonialism and imperialism, China had a four-thousand-year record of tolerance and harmony when it came to same-sex relations. Consequently, both homosexuality and homophobia are Western imports. Building on stories about Chinese emperors and their male favorites (*nanchong*) recounted in Samshasha's *A History of Homosexuality in China* and Bret Hinsch's *Passions of the Cut Sleeve*,[24] Chou Wah-shan emerged in the 1990s as the most influential proponent of this view. Chou argues that China has a unique *tongzhi* community that cannot be conflated with "gays and lesbians" in the Western context because, while Western societies comprise of individuals, the basic sociological unit of Chinese culture is the family. For Chou, the English language has no equivalent of the Chinese tradition of same-sex erotic relations, tolerance, and harmony. Chou argues that the homo/hetero binary was a modern import, which the West imposed on other parts of the world by instituting distinctive forms of medico-scientific knowledge and taxonomies to consolidate its power.[25] While many scholars have criticized Chou's story of the transition from premodern tolerance to modern homosexuality and homophobia,[26] others have accepted Chou's argument for the existence of "a venerable tradition of homosexuality in China in contrast to the West."[27]

Many literary examples do attest to a tradition of alternative sexualities in premodern China. Giovanni Vitiello's The Libertine's Friend: Homosexuality and Masculinity in Late Imperial China, for example, delineates a unique form of "male romance" that arises from the crisis of literati masculinity in late imperial China. Vitiello uses both pornography and elite literature to reconstruct an alternative social history of male same-sex relations. He demonstrates that late imperial China developed a surprisingly malleable and distinctive culture that was constantly renegotiating the boundaries between homosociality and homosexuality, as well as differences in sexual roles and social statuses, in ways that are closer to Samshasha's, Hinsch's, and Chou's description than to that of their critics.[28]

But the question remains: should we read the unintelligibility of premodern sexual categories as their cultural normativity? Ding Naifei and Liu Jen-peng raise this question in their criticism of Chou, drawing attention to an "epistemic violence of silence" in the "order of things whereby some things are more speakable than others."[29] Sophie Volpp makes a related argument in Worldly Stage, which brings an equally rich and fascinating set of texts and historical concerns—such as the liaison between a cross-dressed boy and the King of Linchuan in Wang Jide's play Nan wanghou (Male Queen)—to bear on the relation between world and stage in late imperial China. Unlike Chou, Hinsch, or Vitiello, however, Volpp does not believe that the existence of such literature suggests a "vogue for male love" in seventeenth-century China, or that the ethnographic notation books on the "strange passions" of the southern custom of male cohabitation could be read as evidence of a new tolerance of male love. Instead, Volpp argues, these notation books "testify to the seventeenth-century interest in classifying lust, in cataloguing all its permutations" in accordance with the values of Confucian moral topography.[30] In addition to the vexed question of whether we should interpret the large body of homoerotic and homosocial literature from this period as evidence of a positive attitude toward homosexuality or as reflections of a desire to police sexual differences, critics also differ in their opinions on what counts as homoeroticism, homosociality, and homosexuality. Having published *Passions of the Cut Sleeve* in 1990, Hinsch argues in a much more recent book that the *haohan* (good fellow) figure in Ming fiction is a form of premodern homosociality as well, which is a view neither Volpp nor Vitiello is likely to accept.[31] Susan Mann further points out that scholars disagree on whether literary depictions of sexual relations between men indicate that such practices were considered normative among the literati only, or that the definition of normative sex between men was extended to the commoners as well.[32] Wu Cuncun similarly points out that the unique status of the leisured literati class justified male homoerotic sensibilities and turned them into a display of wealth, power, and "taste" in a culture that prohibited female prostitution.[33] These nuances render the hypothesis of a premodern Chinese tradition of tolerance and homoeroticism even less tenable.

Without contesting its historical validity, we can consider the political purpose this postulation serves for contemporary theory. The hypothesis of a premodern Chinese culture of homoeroticism before the advent of Western imperialism promises to make China historically unique and hence analytically impervious to the universalizing pretensions of queer theory. And yet, Chou's thesis also perpetuates a discourse of Oriental exceptionalism that attempts to solve the problem of Western universalism by reifying nonwestern differences. The postulation of an alternative Chinese sexuality outside queer theory functions as an ideological double-bind. In a field where China often becomes a relevant concern only as the producer of differences from Western queer theory, Chinese *tongzhi* studies often results in what Johannes Fabian has described as the "allochronism" of racial time.[34] As Fabian argues, modernity's colonial production of racial others operates through the "denial of coevalness."[35] This discourse translates the cultural differences between societies into degrees of development, producing an impression of a time lag between contemporaneous cultures. While the political use of cultural constructivist theories seems obvious,[36] the familiar stories about the "invention" of homosexuality in the West also tend to subscribe to an emanation model of modernity. This model presents homosexuality according to the definitions of the European sexologists as an origin for all gay men and women around the globe to emulate, whereas *tongxinglian*, *tongxing'ai*, and *tongzhi* are said to be translations, derivatives, or copies. A queer critique of heteronormativity thus comes into conflict with a postcolonial critique of allochronism. Certainly, a good way to denaturalize heterosexuality is to historicize the invention of the homosexual/heterosexual distinction, but the historicizing effort inevitably provokes debates about whether some human cultures are prehomosexual, prequeer, or altogether different from the West and hence either irrelevant or impervious to queer theory.

As discussed in chapter one, mainland China, Hong Kong, and Taiwan have each developed a globally visible and vibrant queer culture industry. An explosive growth of recent scholarship on the topic has clearly charted the sociological development of queer subcultures in these locations.[37] What remains underdeveloped is an account of their queer theory and intellectual contributions, which I offer in this chapter through a bifocal view of the discursive development of queer Marxism in mainland China and Taiwan. By writing this intellectual history, I seek to counter the prevalent perception that China lacks a recognizable queer theory of its own, or that any theoretical discussion in Chinese academic writing must be working with a Euro-American concept. An example from the veteran film critic Paul Pickowicz's work might illustrate the point. In a reflection piece on the development of Chinese film studies in the past thirty-five years titled "From Yao Wenyuan to Cui Zi'en," Pickowicz describes Cui's "bold films on gay sexuality" as the index of a new chapter of Chinese film history.[38] Compared to thirty-five years ago, much has changed—fieldwork in China is now possible, formerly classified archives are now accessible to researchers, and the marketability of Ph.D.'s in Chinese literature and Ph.D.'s in Chinese film has been reversed—but, for Pickowicz, the most important epochal change brought about by Cui Zi'en's generation is the status of theory in film studies. Observing that China has a unique history that has yet to produce a theoretical paradigm for film scholars who currently rely on Fredric Jameson and Edward Said, Pickowicz recommends, "We need to develop theoretical frameworks that are informed by Chinese realities, not western European or American realities."[39]

Pickowicz's impassioned criticism is directed, of course, at his graduate students and younger colleagues writing about Chinese film in English. But Pickowicz treats "Chinese realities" as a passive object and does not acknowledge the vast body of Chinese-language scholarship, theory, and paradigms of film studies. Cui, whom Pickowicz analyzes as a filmmaker, is also a prolific essayist and novelist, and precisely one of the intellectuals who have contributed to the development of a Chinese queer theory. In the next section, I trace the genealogy of Chinese-language queer discourses, focusing on the works of Cui Zi'en, Josephine Ho, Ding Naifei, and the Gender/Sexuality Rights Association, Taiwan. I characterize Chinese queer theory as a geopolitically mediated discourse that self-consciously reflects on the status of China within the powerful framework of sexuality. The status of China here refers to the theoretical problems of universalism and translation between the Chinas and the West, and within the two Chinas. Significantly influenced by Marxism but hybrid in its use, this theory contributes to global queer discourse by dislodging sexual difference from the domain of liberal rights. Instead, sexual difference is redefined as the historical conditions of thinking and writing about a gendered self. Chinese queer theory provides a unique perspective on the entanglements of cultural and material life by showing that legal, economic, and structural differences limit queer subjects' effective participation in public culture. In this light, queer writing is never simply a voluntary assertion of one's sexual belief in the public realm. Rather, queerness, in Chinese queer Marxism, becomes an occasion in life to explore the mutually constitutive nature of speech and power.

Cui Zi'en: The Communist International of Queer Films

Since the 1990s, Cui Zi'en has emerged as China's most iconic and controversial queer filmmaker, essayist, and novelist. Trained in classical Chinese literature but influenced by an eclectic range of intellectual resources from Confucianism and Buddhism to the poststructuralist thought of Deleuze and Derrida, Cui brings a unique, daring aesthetic style to Chinese cinema that often defies categorization. His work combines Christian liberation theology with a postmodern, carnivalesque subversion of gender and sexual categories that often puts him at odds with the Chinese Communist Party and mainstream cultural critics. The social subjects of his films and novels are not always homosexuals. They could be transvestites, voyeurs, boy toys, creepy uncles, gay-for-pay evangelists, bi-curious straight men, money boys, incestuous relatives, MTFs (male-to-female), insatiable sluts, dinosaurs, reptiles, and extra-terrestrials—in any case, subjects who are certainly "queer" and living at some critical distance from cultural norms and power. This deliberate mixture and range of social types in Cui's creative works is a political and performative gesture, whereby Cui expands the definition of "queer" from homosexuality to a wide range of nonnormative expressions and relations in the culture war against homonationalism. Provocative, perverse, and witty, Cui's novels and underground films brought about nothing less than a sea change for China's queer culture.

The immediate context for Cui's theoretical and creative interventions is the rise of the desexualized nouveau riche in China's gay communities. I argue that Cui's films are complex meditations on the historical moment of their production, and they cannot be treated as subtitled images at international film festivals with no regard for the Chinese political and intellectual contexts within which these narratives function as an intervention.[40] Furthermore, I argue that Cui's films must be analyzed together with his political essays and novels, whose combined effects create a coherent system of thought that is also a provocative queer theory. Cui's films are not merely fiction or entertainment—they are philosophical statements reminiscent of the fables, allegories, and aphorisms of continental philosophy, in contrast to the programmatic statements and propositions of analytical philosophy. Just as the continental philosophers often create philosophy by telling stories, Cui creates queer theory through his films, but the systematicity of Cui's theory is often lost from view without the aid of his expository prose. My analysis focuses on the dialectic of subversion and containment in Cui's creative and theoretical work, in which he expands and revitalizes a Marxist intellectual tradition by rejecting it. In particular, I explore Cui's works as a reimagination of the possibilities of human sexuality, creativity, and fulfillment under conditions of reified labor. In this sense, Cui presents an important theory of the liberating potential of sexuality for capitalism. In his films, Cui performs this theory instead of stating it: Cui purposefully creates jarring, dissonant film scenes that do not always cohere into a story. These broken scenes make a political gesture that brings narrative into crisis in order to prevent underground filmmaking from turning into mass entertainment, consumption, and identification for the queer middle-class. Here queerness cannot be celebrated in the name of a political idiom of tolerance, diversity, and pluralism; rather, queerness serves a critical tactic of intervention within a field of power that seeks to silence, erase, and assimilate all nonnormative expressions and desires.

Cui's underground filmmaking places an emphasis on spontaneity (turanxing) as an anticapitalist mode of creativity. In our interview, Cui argued that mass-produced works of art are often funded by foreign-infused, but state-controlled, capital, and that these films are marked by visually impressive special effects, celebrity glamour, professional acting, witty dialogues, and high entertainment value. Cui mobilizes the underground film as a political strategy to disrupt the connection between art, capital, and Americanization. Therefore, Cui's films are unscripted. He believes that working in an unscripted setting democratizes channels of creativity, and that doing so captures a different truth about China from the one presented on state-run television programs. Due to his conviction in the value of spontaneity, Cui has never adapted his own novels and short stories into films. Improvisation serves a triple political purpose: first, it frees the film from capitalism by dispensing with state-controlled resources and ideological slogans; second, it rebels against the traditional aesthetics of character development imported from Soviet realism and canonized by Chinese film schools in the academic tradition (Cui himself teaches at the Beijing Film Academy); finally, it prevents the queer viewer from identifying with the character and turning it into an object of neoliberal consumption.

Film scholar Wang Qi describes Cui as the "*enfant terrible* of contemporary Chinese cinema" for his "unconventional, rebellious contents, protagonists, and styles."[41] Indeed, Cui's films are outrageously playful, hypersexual, in-your-face, shocking, and perverse. His films have a deliberately unpolished look, constantly challenging Chinese viewers'

Soviet-conditioned, and now Hollywood-influenced, comfort zone and standards of aesthetics. In one famously scandalous scene from *Enter the Clowns*, the protagonist's father (played by Cui himself) unexpectedly becomes a woman. On her deathbed, Cui's character is upset that she never got to breastfeed her son, and demands to taste her son's own "milk" by sucking him off as a small compensation. The figuration of semen as the nourishment of life runs through Cui's films and, together with the death scenes, serves as an organizational device. *Star Appeal* (*Xing xing xiang xi xi*, 2004) builds on the theme of semen once more by playing on the homonyms of *xi* 惜 (cherish) and *xi* 吸 (suck). While the four-character phrase *xing xing xiang xi* normally means "kindred spirits" or "talented people who show appreciation to each other" in Chinese, Cui's homonymous title means "stars who suck each other's semen." *Mountains and Seas* (*Shan hai jing*, 2011) similarly pivots on the pun of *jing* (經／精 scripture/semen), showing off Cui's characteristically irreverent, refreshingly perverse sense of humor. In *Feeding Boys, Ayaya* (2003), men's milk is both a source of pleasure and a means of survival for China's subordinated laboring class. The story is centered on a number of young "money boys" who do not enter the profession under financial pressures, as is expected, but, instead, do so purposely to practice "Christian love" and the socialist ideal of serving the masses. For Zaizai and Xiao Jian, men are mammals who must return to their true nature and true mission in life, which is to nourish other men with their milk. This mission entails diligent and dedicated sex work, which the film represents as a normative, rather than socially transgressive, profession. Cui plays on the gap between the viewer's understanding of what is normal and the characters' own understanding. The film creates an alternate universe in which sex work provided by men for men goes unquestioned; in so doing, Cui draws attention to the constructedness of our own laws and social values. By thwarting the viewers' expectations of cultural normalcy, Cui performs an ideological reversal that calls into question two reified cultural assumptions of our time: how did heteronormative, cisnormative, and sex-negative values come to be regarded as normal in the first place, and how did they come to be intertwined with the ethics of labor?

In a brilliant reading of the film, Lisa Rofel points out that Cui "playfully satirized normalized work lives" by showing that society's "normalization techniques reduce and embed desire in a structured world of intensive labor extraction, one that produces a capitalist-inflected heteronormativity."[42] This unexpected mixing of labor issues and sexuality is a recurring theme in Cui's queer Marxism. Cui's films depict the blurring of all kinds of boundaries, including economic and sexual categories. Instead of representing a population we may call homosexuals, Cui's works detach homo-, hetero-, and polyamorous sexualities from individual identities.[43] Gender itself is fluid, as characters in his films habitually transform from one sex to another. Moreover, kinship relations are also destabilized. For example, in *My Fair Son* (2005), relations between father and son are eroticized—and graphically depicted. The story begins with a father's failed attempt to repair his relations with his distanced son. The reconciliation process is disrupted when the son develops a crush on the father's male assistant, Xiao Bo. As soon as the homophobic father realizes it, he banishes the male assistant from their life, a decision that irreparably damages his relationship with his son. But the next scene shows the father undressing and cuddling his naked son from behind. It is difficult to say whether the banishment of desire (Xiao Bo) is motivated by an effort to repair proper Confucian fatherhood, or by the erotic competition between the father and Xiao Bo for the son's affection. Cui crosses many boundaries between legitimate and illegitimate desires, sexual and nonsexual relations, and homophobic and homoerotic impulses. In *Star Appeal*, Cui narrates a sexual adventure between a human being and a Martian, with frontal nudity and simulated sex scenes. Cui elaborates the motif of intergalactic intercourse more frequently in his fiction. "Endanger Species Rule!" is a powerful short story depicting extraterrestrial dinosaurs who rape each other.[44] Their flow of desire, as well as unrestrained violence, allegorically expose the contingency of sexual regulation, which humanity has internalized as a historical necessity.[45]

Cui conducts these thematically deviant experiments with a degree of formal perversity, where the unconventional uses of camera angles, cinematography, and sound add another kind of disturbance to the viewer's comfort zone. As Wang Qi points out, Cui and Shitou (who is a prominent Chinese queer artist, actress, and independent documentary filmmaker as well) are two historical milestones in China's film history. According to Wang, Cui and Shitou change Chinese cinema with stylistic decisions such as "simultaneous sound recording, rejection of omniscient voiceover commentary, and dismissal of written scripts" that function as a deliberate gesture "against their previous experience with state-run television practices."[46] These directorial choices allow Cui and Shitou to "define their differences from the 'special topic' documentary serials (zhuanti pian)" produced by official channels.[47] Helen Leung observes that an "aesthetically violent language is evident in Cui's fondness for long shots with little depth of field, abrupt and rapid panning shots in place of cuts, and muted and claustrophobic lighting, as well as episodic and disjointed narrative structure. This visually demanding and, indeed, displeasing aesthetic has become Cui's authorial signature."[48] While these stylistic features may help capture what Wang describes as "an unofficial Chinese verité," critics and audience more used to commercially produced queer Chinese films such as *Farewell My Concubine* or *Permanent Residence* are likely to be disappointed by the rawness of Cui's work, thus missing the subtle links he tries to make between the material conditions of independent filmmaking and the anticapitalist potential of queer thought.

In our 2011 interview, Cui discussed at length why he chose independent filmmaking as his preferred medium of expression, and explained his belief in the political value of unpolished, unmediated videos. For Cui, independent film creates a dual refusal: the refusal of Soviet aesthetics that was codified in film school through the study of the "masters"; and the refusal of US capital, which has penetrated the market by co-opting the middle class of queer and queer-friendly consumers. To counter these forces, Cui mobilizes the material rawness of independent film as a political resource. Improvisation in his films, which are unscripted, decenters the authority of the director and democratizes the scene of creative exchange by allowing the agency of the actors to emerge. This choice redistributes the power relation between producer and actor, as well as between protagonist and supporting characters. The redistribution of power and agency in the storytelling process reconfigures the relation between the viewer and capitalism as well.

Cui's aesthetic theory explains his deliberate avoidance of linear narrative in his films. A clear example is the *Old Testament* (*Jiuyue*, 2002). The film consists of three different stories about a man called Xiao Bo that take place in different points in time.[49] The film's structure forces the viewer to momentarily contemplate on queerness itself as a story—as a struggle for visibility and equality, as a history of oppression that casts the self as a hero or a victim—and then to dispense with this process of cathected projection. Cui's film is carefully structured to prevent the viewer's identification with the main character, which Cui regards as the dominant mode of mainstream consumer queer Chinese films. The three segments are "semi-stories" or near-stories; that is, just as the narrative is about to cohere into a recognizable story to a viewer of the Hollywood generation, the film interrupts itself with the insertion of a chorus singing about death, and then switches scenes. The infusion of jarring nonnarrative elements within the film's narrative breaks the typical sequence of signification—our habitual mode of receiving and making sense of meaning in film. In the "Psalter—1981" segment, for example, Xiao Bo is a closeted man living with an adopted family. Xiao Bo is then forced to marry a woman. At this point, the story appears to be quite typical and even relatable—one may begin to think of the film as yet another sentimental tear-jerker about closeted gay men's struggles with familial expectations, as in Ang Lee's internationally acclaimed The Wedding Banquet (1993). Then a small chorus suddenly appears in Cui's film, though no explanation is offered for the narrative non sequitur. The chorus includes Cui himself singing a psalm about Xiao Bo's death, which further disrupts the neat separation of diegetic and extradiegetic realities most filmmakers would find desirable to maintain. In addition, the use of the chorus infuses Greek tragedy and Christian iconography into Cui's film, which makes it even more difficult for the Chinese viewer to identify with the story. The breaking up of the queer narrative by nonqueer and emphatically foreign elements also prevents the viewer from identifying the work as a "gay film" centered on a predictable coming out story. Cui's cheeky, unapologetically perverse style stands in sharp contrast to the melodramatic sentimentalism of mainstream queer Chinese feature films, which either emphasize unrequited or unspeakable love, as Stanley Kwan's Lan Yu (2001) does,[50] or a tragic-comic resolution of the conflict between same-sex desire and procreative obligations, as Ang Lee's The Wedding Banquet does.[51] Both trends present the modern homosexual as a victim of an unaccepting society, even when that victim eventually becomes a hero by overcoming these obstacles.

The independent film has neither commercial markets nor investors, and Cui's use of the low-budget underground film as a political statement, in a milieu where the interests of global capitalism dominate Chinese cultural production, presents a queer Marxist theory of freedom. Underground filmmaking becomes a genuine, nonstate-regulated form of proletarian art, unencumbered by the dictates of the market and stripped of the accouterments of fashionable postmodern gay glamour. Underground filmmaking offers a form of anticapitalist dispersal. It works against the mediation of labor by the interests of capital, democratizing the creative process and returning visual performances to nonalienated labor. The success and the performative aspects of Cui's low-budget films are well recognized by Chinese and international critics. Jonathan Hall describes Cui's film as a collection of "boys, girls, queer desires, and fantastic topographies" that "weaves a surreal tale from the materiality of low-budget filmmaking, never forgetting film's ability to visualize desire in ways both alluring and provocative," and in these "allegories of love, lust, and, transformation," desire is "a meandering movement between person, body, and gender" that "also coalesces into bonding and community."[52] Against China's rapidly rising pink economy, Cui's underground films imagine and foster a community—and a communism—that embody a queer Marxist critique.

If community-building is indeed one of Cui's political goals, as Hall suggests, why does Cui want to prevent the viewer's identification with his characters? Moreover, why does Cui seem to assume that identification with a story—if the film ever becomes a story—immediately implicates the viewer in neoliberal consumption? Cui's answer to these questions during our 2012 interview points to the particular history of queer struggles in China. For Cui, the present gay rights movement, which is based on an identity politics, constitutes another order of oppression and restriction. Cui does not regard queerness as a synonym for homosexuality, since homosexuality can be yet another identity category. For Cui, queerness rests on a capacity to recognize the distance between received categories and the diversity of erotic desires and modes of intimacy in human cultures. Queerness also marks a willingness to surrender the right to demand to know in advance what forms these relations might take. Queerness is an ability to be offended and edified in good and bad ways.

At the same time, Cui is also suspicious of the terms *ku-er* and *tong-zhi*, preferring the often pathologized *tongxinglian* (homosexuality) as a political idiom. Cui resists the tendency to characterize queerness as a postmodern, carnivalesque celebration of diversity and nonidentities. Cui wants his audience to remember mainstream society's understanding of homosexuality as a pathology and that "the revolution is not over." For Cui, the medico-scientific-sounding term *tongxinglian* preserves the stigma of the homosexual, upon which his films and fiction try to elaborate. Accordingly, his films are at once about self-identified gay and nongay subjects, but even in depicting gay characters, Cui always insistently connects them to themes and issues the majority of gay men and lesbians in China would not find relatable: a transsexual father/mother performing oral sex on his/her son, a confused father struggling with his desire for his homosexual son, money boys, AIDS, drugs, or aliens and dinosaurs. Cui works against the positive, desexualized image established by the gay movement in the past decade that emphasizes that homosexuals are "just like everybody else" except for what we do in our private bedroom in monogamy. Cui states in our 2012 interview, "My purpose of producing these films is to destroy the respectability of gays, rather than invoking sympathy for homosexuals as the downtrodden from mainstream society." For Cui, even the "queer" (*tongzhi*) movement has lost its political radicality (*yundongxing*) the moment *tongzhi* replaced *tongxinglian* as the common Chinese name for homosexuals. While recognizing the important milestones achieved in China, Cui also says, "I want to preserve the combativeness of the term homosexuality against this sanitized language of queer (*tongzhi*), which reduces it to a nonthreatening, depoliticized 'lifestyle.' The word homosexuality reminds us that we are pathologized by society and treated as a 'problem' (*wenti hua*), and we cannot afford to forget that." Cui believes that only by invoking the stigma of homosexuality can we preserve the progressive elements of the gay movement. The term homosexual emphasizes the socially constituted character of the gay subject, even if that subject has access to power, resources, prestige, and money. To be gay is to be part of an unequal structure of power, which the language of pride, tolerance, and celebrating diversity only obscures.

Given his differences with the Chinese Communist Party, in many ways Cui may seem to be the least likely candidate for the dispensation of queer Marxism. Indeed, Cui has criticized socialism as it is practiced in mainland China on numerous occasions. Cui is openly critical of the Communist Party and academics who hold appointments in the bureaucracy. His *Man, Man, Woman Woman*, a parody of the state-run China Central Television, is frequently cited by critics as evidence of the quarrels between Cui and the Chinese state authorities.[53] After coming out in the classroom in 1991, Cui was prohibited from teaching classes at the Beijing Film Academy, where he remains a tenured professor without teaching assignments. His relationship with the central authorities reached its nadir in 2005, when his efforts at organizing China's first Gay Pride were thwarted by the government. In Cui's recently published memoir, he recounts several experiences from his childhood in which his family clashed with state-directed socialism.[54] However, it is important to see that Cui opposes the bureaucratic use of Marxism and not Marxism itself, and that Cui retains and develops numerous ethical ideals and analytical tools of Marxism. In another interview, he states:

> Every time I travel to the United States and see these boundless, gigantic, extravagantly constructed private houses, I become afraid. No human being needs all that space. Public ownership of land of course has its problems, but human beings cannot give up the progress we made over private property just because a few problems we ran into with socialized land ownership. To me, communism is the courage to pursue a better future, to imagine a utopia, despite all the hardships and setbacks in the present.[55]

Here Cui characterizes socialism and communism as a futurity rather than a state policy. The imagination of communism as "the courage to pursue a better future" at once rejects the "actually existing Marxism" in the People's Republic and asserts the importance of Marxist ethics. In deconstructive terms, Cui's relation to Marxism functions as a productive failure. The famous Chinese film critic Zhang Xianmin seems to be of this view when he writes that Cui must be "a member of the capitalist class in terms of his unparalleled wealth of cultural knowledge, which he dispenses with reckless abandon."[56] Zhang is fully aware of Cui's contributions to proletarian visual culture, and his characterization of Cui as a capitalist in terms of the richness of his creative energy aptly captures the productive tensions between Cui's project and the historical narratives in which they are situated. For Cui, the contradiction is resolved, poetically, through the creative possibilities of film. In a public lecture titled "The Communist International of Queer Film," Cui proposes a parodic definition of the Communist International as underground video-piracy, through which viewers and artists like himself gain access to the works of Fassbinder, Visconti, and Bertolucci despite PRC censorship.[57] Through the underground circulation of such films as well as secret showings, the Chinese viewers form an alternative community and solidarity in ways disconnected from the communist ideology of the state. Conversely, Cui and his comrades can also export their underground videos to the West through venues such as international film festivals and, again, video piracy. For Cui, video piracy or free information sharing constitutes the real "communist international of China," a queer community of free association and property-pooling that out-communists the communists. Film, in other words, makes possible a queer Marxism in practice. Recognizing Cui's success in engendering a new kind of transnational, borderless intimacy through the dissemination of his underground film, Audrey Yue characterizes Cui as the embodiment of a "queer sinophone" cinema that creates a new kind of "mobile intimacy" between sign, image, constituency, and sexuality in order to emancipate the Chinese underground film from the dictates of China's neoliberal regime.[58]

Queer Dialogues with Marx: Josephine Ho's Sexual Revolution

Cui's emphasis on the possibilities and necessity of creating a nonstate version of Marxist, anticapitalist aesthetics places him in dialogue with the cultural theorists in Taiwan, who also adamantly refuse to let the official political identity of anticommunist Taiwan define them. In the ROC, Marxist thought is not ossified into a bureaucracy but, rather, historically prohibited until the lifting of the martial law in 1987. Many of ROC's radical cultural theorists of gender and sexuality came out of a reading group in Marxist theory during the height of the KMT (Kuomintang) regime under martial law, when intellectual dissidents were routinely persecuted and jailed by the authorities.[59] However, the most dramatic case of a sexual dissident's trouble with the authorities takes place after the end of KMT autocracy: the 2003 prosecution of queer

Marxist critic Josephine Ho, which is a historical event that ironically and uncannily embodies several analytical points she previously theorized about the nature of gender, sexuality, governance, and social power. My analysis of what has come to be known as the "zoophilia incident" in Taiwan, hence, also serves as an exemplary introduction to her complex queer Marxist theory.

In 2003, conservative women's groups and religious organizations in Taiwan brought a lawsuit against Ho, accusing her of spreading pornographic and obscene images in violation of the nation's laws (Criminal Code Article 235).[60] Their primary evidence was that the website of National Central University's Center for the Study of Sexualities, of which Ho was in charge, was found to contain hyperlinks to images of and information on zoophilia. None of these images was provided by the Center itself: they were all foreign (mostly US) websites such as discussion forums, sex education articles, and information sites. The only thing the Center provided was a hyperlink to these sites, on a page explicitly framed as educational information on the diversity of sexual practices across human cultures. The page was not specifically about zoophilia; it also contained information on homosexuality, transgender persons, BDSM, and other topics in sex education. In fact, just a simple Google search by an average internet user would yield more images on zoophilia than the Center's academic website would. Moreover, the hyperlink appeared on a specific section of the Center's educational contents, far from the Center's homepage and other introductory materials, which means it would be extremely unlikely for an uninformed reader to stumble upon these pages. Preposterous as it was, the case was accepted by the Taipei District Court. The plaintiff also sent a request to the Ministry of Education, demanding Ho's immediate suspension from Central University.[61] Major queer, labor, and socially progressive groups in Taiwan immediately came to Ho's support. The American Association of University Professors (AAUP) also issued a letter of support in 2005, recognizing that this case was a violation of the organization's mission of protecting academic freedom of speech worldwide. Other letters came from the World Association of Sexology (2003) and Hong Kong Sex Education Association (2003). Academics and activists also started an international appeal letter—and I happened to become the first signatory of that letter on July 7, 2003. The final published appeal list in 2004 contains signatures of

804 academics, social workers, and human rights activists from around the globe united in defense of Ho. After eighteen months of litigation, Ho was found not guilty by Taiwan's High Court.

As I will demonstrate further, the lawsuit against Ho was an ad hominem attack that turned a political disagreement within feminism into a witch-hunt. In order to purge sexual activism from feminism, conservative women's groups attempted to silence Ho, a "sex-positive" feminist, by inciting moral panic and mass hysteria about sex. We might ask, what does this incident indicate about the different understandings of sex in feminist and queer struggles? Moreover, how does Ho's work reveal a need to think about the difficult issues of zoophilia, pedophilia, teen sex, and sex work in a queer theory that the normalized discourse of gay rights threatens to assimilate? And how does Ho's invocation of Marx help her tackle these issues in queer and feminist theory?

In the postwar period, women in Taiwan attained a certain degree of political representation and empowerment. Annette Hsiu-lien Lu, for example, is a pioneering feminist thinker who wrote important treatises on the "new woman" (xin nüxing) that inaugurated the "new feminist movement" in the 1970s. Lu was elected Vice President of ROC in 2000 (and was reelected in 2004).[62] After Lu's "new feminist movement" (xin nüxing yundong) in the 1970s, Li Yuanzhen established Funü xinzhi, the Awakening Foundation, and the journal of the same name in 1982 to raise women's consciousness under the slogan of xin liangxing guanxi (new gender relations) in contrast to Lu's xin nüxing (new woman). The Awakening Foundation was instrumental in introducing several reforms bills to promote gender equality in the workplace. Enormously influential, the Awakening Foundation has inspired several other women's organizations, but the women's movement since the 1980s has also gradually become a "state feminism," meaning that Taiwan's leading feminists began to regard women's entry into politics as the only path for greater gender equality, and women's movements became subordinated to the dictates of the nation. Theoretically, state feminists are all essentialists who do not believe in gender constructivism because they believe that the promotion of women's political participation requires a united front of women's interests. Above all, the emphasis on electoral politics means that mainstream women's movements must cut all ties with marginalized, "unpopular," and potentially divisive issues such as sexuality. A conservative feminist, Lin Fang-mei, argues that the women's movement should concern itself only with issues that will appeal to the voting constituencies so that feminists can be elected to power and transform women's issues into concrete social policies.[63] In Lin's view, because women's liberation is sought through the welfare state, feminism must dissociate itself from radical movements that are not compatible with the directives of the state. Feminism in Taiwan, then, experiences a dilemma similar to gay normalization: in order to secure popular support, the movement attempts to craft a respectable image of women by purging sexual issues from its agenda. In this brand of feminism, a sense of proprietorship and entitlement emerges, one that gives certain individuals the right to define what legitimately counts as women's issues, who represents women's interests, and who belongs to the category of women. The attempt to protect the theoretical and political purity of women's issues from other agendas also refuses to examine the intersections of gender and other social differences, despite the fact that adverse conditions of women's lives are often precisely caused by labor migration, sexual discrimination, ethnic difference, languages, and class backgrounds. I suggest that the debate is not a contestation over the moral legitimacy of sexuality, as is commonly understood; instead, it is a consequence of the contradictory foundation of liberal pluralism. Mainstream feminists are constrained by the logic of political liberalism because their goal is to normalize women's issues by electing female politicians. As a result, mainstream feminists' intervention is limited to social issues that can resonate with the conservative electoral base, such as care for the elderly, women's personal safety from rape, childbirth, and childcare—though these can also be progressive issues if framed differently. Under the constraints of liberal pluralist electoral politics, mainstream feminists are either conservative or at best centrist, while truly progressive social movements are left in the hands of *nonstatist* feminists.

The rise of state feminism in Taiwan, then, reflects a highly politicized bifurcation between gender-based feminism and sex-positive feminism.[64] Ho's "zoophilia incident" indicates that feminism in Taiwan is beset with the problem of a chiasmic splitting of the term sex (*xing*) that Judith Butler describes in "Against Proper Objects": whereas for feminism, sex is that which one is (male or female), for gay and lesbian studies, sex is that which one does (sexuality).[65] The allocation of gender to the domain of feminism, and sexuality to gay and lesbian studies, repudiates feminist traditions of enhancing sexual freedom, as well as queer critiques of normative gender expressions and gender identities. As a sex-positive feminist, Ho incurs the wrath of conservative feminists precisely because she refuses the allocation of "proper objects" for feminist analysis and gay and lesbian studies. In Taiwan, however, another context underlies the split between gender-based and sex-positive feminisms: historically, sex-positive feminism in Taiwan is allied with labor movements, in particular with the ex-licensed prostitutes' movement and migrant workers' movements. Sex-positive feminism's attention to labor issues is one reason Marxism has become an indispensable intellectual resource for its theoreticians. Marxism has also provided useful tools for their critiques of state feminists during Taiwan's transformation into a liberal democracy.

Ho is arguably the most influential figure in Taiwan's sex-positive feminism. In 1994, Ho inaugurated the sexual liberation movement with the slogan, "I want orgasms (xing gaochao), not harassment (xing saorao)." Ho's new feminist slogan instantly catapulted her into heated debates.[66] In the same year, Ho received the "Woman of the Year" and "Woman Who Changed Taiwan" Awards. As Ho emerged as the most formidable theoretician of sex-positive feminism, a conservative backlash ensued, first from medical, psychiatric, and state authorities, and subsequently from mainstream feminists themselves.[67] As it turned out, "I want orgasms" became the watershed event that polarized the "women's rights" and "sexual rights" factions of Taiwanese feminism. Mainstream feminists, such as Liu Yu-hsiu, began to view Ho's vision as an impediment to the promotion of "women's rights" and "gender equality" in electoral politics, for fear that the voting public might not be ready to accept women's sexual liberation, even if it were willing to acknowledge women's rights to work.[68] The backlash from Liu and other conservative feminists eventually led to Ho's removal from the Taiwanese Feminist Scholars Association (TFSA).

The debate between Ho and state feminists corresponds with a Marxist critique of liberal formalism. Marx explains that human emancipation is not equal to the abstract rights sanctified by liberal pluralism. For Marx, substantive equality cannot be brought about by the mere creation of democratic institutions and parliamentary procedures, for the democratic state's formal emancipation from ethnic and religious particularities does not abolish the state's actual basis or investments in such particularities.[69] Marx argues that parliamentary freedom is actually the freedom of the elected bureaucrats from public scrutiny, misconceived as the freedom of the people through parliament.[70] To illustrate this point, Marx offers the example of religious freedom. Building on Bruno Bauer's observation that in the United States "the constitution does not impose any religious belief or religious practice as a condition of political rights," and yet the United States also remains in reality the preeminent country of Protestant religiosity where "people do not believe that a man without religion could be an honest man," Marx distinguishes between the freedom *of* religion and the freedom *from* religion, arguing that the rhetoric of the separation of church and state actually protects Christian dominance by making it legally impossible for the subjects to criticize the actual alignment of church and state.[71] Following Marx's distinction between the freedom of religion and the freedom from religion, we might say that Taiwan's state feminists and female politicians have proclaimed the doctrine of "two-gender co-rule" (*liangxing gongzhi*) and introduced the formal freedom *of* gender, but these politicians have not created the freedom *from* gender. Men and women are legally and formally equal in Taiwan, but there is no equality for those who seek freedom from normative categories of gender, such as transgendered and transgendering persons, intersexed individuals, effeminate gay men, butch and femme (*T/po*) lesbians, single women, women who choose not to bear children, sex workers who do not believe that sex should only occur under the sanctity of monogamous marriage, and numerous other communities who live and work at a critical distance from the idealized notion of womanhood, which state feminists take to be the basis of the gender equality movement. The discourse of "women's rights" and "two-gender co-rule" in Taiwan reverses the terms of patriarchal domination while leaving its social organization intact. A queer discourse is not tantamount to the empowerment of sexual minorities; rather, it is a historical response to the rigidity of identity categories that liberal pluralism creates. In Taiwan, the state feminists' conception of the social whole as the competition between empirically existing minority groups (men and women) not only misrecognizes the operations of power, but also naturalizes the state as a legitimate apparatus adjudicating between these competing groups.

Ho explicitly draws on Marx's concept of freedom and on his critique of liberal pluralism in her works, which encompass a wide range of topics: feminism, queer theory, gender/sexuality education, sex work, youth, transgenderism, censorship, global governance, psychoanalysis, globalization, depression, and the antinuclear plant movement. In her writings on sexuality, Ho combines insights from Marxist cultural analysis with psychoanalysis and queer theory to demonstrate that, contrary to state feminists' claims, gender and sexuality are inseparable in feminist analysis, because normative gender is consolidated through normative sexuality. Moreover, normative gender is predicated on an unequal distribution of economic and symbolic resources between subjects of different genders, a process that Marxism can help illuminate. Ho's most important theoretical work in queer Marxism is *The Gallant Woman*. Published in 1994, *The Gallant Woman* is an innovative work in cultural materialism that reveals the logical and historical relations between capitalist modernity and sexual repression. The book's title is a wordplay on the homonyms *haoshuang* 豪爽 (gallant, unruly; truthful and unaffected) and *haoshuang* 好爽 (feeling good, having an orgasm), which allows Ho to reinforce her theoretical argument that the women's subordinate status in society (their inability to become gallant women) is connected to the repression of their sexuality (their inability to enjoy orgasms). Ho's work shows that a tactic of sexual shaming reinforces women's subordinate status in social, emotional, and professional contexts. This shaming conditions women to accept their subordination, first, by making women feel ashamed of their bodies and their sexual desires while maintaining deference to men. Whereas sexual aggression is considered a sign of masculinity and a desirable quality for men, women are taught to protect their bodies lest their value on the marriage market drop. The suppression of women's ability to express and assert their sexual desires forms the emotional nucleus of a structure of unequal power and agency that perpetuates itself. Ho points out that a traditional critique of patriarchy is insufficient because gender under capitalist modernity is much more complex than the domination of one group by another. Women, too, internalize this psychic structure of shame and misrecognize it as a material matter that involves differential salaries, social roles, and opportunities. Ho's queer critique is also a Marxist critique in that her theory describes women's auto-commodification of their bodies. Ho shows that the mechanisms of social control and gender inequality have deeper roots in economic and material forces. Therefore, to rebel against such structures, women must unlearn sexual shame and become active agents in relationships and life.[72]

The 1990s of Taiwan were overshadowed by an uninterrupted series of high-profile stories of the rape and murders of women. The murder of Bai Xiaoyan was the most grisly event in the series. In 1997, Taiwanese entertainment celebrity Bai Bingbing's sixteen-year-old daughter, Bai Xiaoyan, was kidnapped, raped, tortured, mutilated, and murdered by a gang of criminals. During the ransom negotiations, the criminals cut off Bai's finger and took pictures of her naked body after raping her, and then sent those to the family. They also murdered additional victims, including police officers and a plastic surgeon (after demanding him to perform facial reconstruction surgeries), held a South African military attaché and his family hostage, and raped additional women. While the criminals were still at large, the Taiwanese media leaked photos of the teenage victim's naked and mutilated body. The event became a national trauma, and concerns about women's safety became a dominant social issue.

In the immediate years before the Bai-incident, Taiwan's sensationalist media released multiple stories about male perverts lurking in women's public bathrooms. Ho wrote her major theoretical works in this milieu of acute social anxiety about sex. While conservative women's groups quickly mobilized to condemn these bathroom voyeurs, exhibitionists, and the male population in general as oppressors of women, Ho saw the problem in women's own internalization of oppression. With "I want orgasms, not harassment," Ho urged women to develop self-defense skills instead of fearing men and their sex. *The Gallant Woman* was a historical rejoinder to the conundrum of a conservative feminist theory that represented women as a group in need of state protection and intervention. On the one hand, there was a clear need to devise social policies and programs that would ensure women's safety. On the other hand, the events also fostered a general phobia of sex, and portrayed men as naturally predatory, and women as hopeless victims who needed the management, protection, and discipline of the state in order to function and survive in society. These connections between the repression of women's sexuality and the liberal welfare state brought Ho to Marxism.

The Gallant Woman shows that capitalist modernity is reproduced through the illegible and disempowered presence of certain sexual modes of being. In turn, gender hierarchy between men and women takes on a quasi-economic character of profit and loss. Ho emphasizes the centrality of sexuality to modern culture as a whole, and exposes the pervasiveness of moralistic teachings, the unchallenged authority of medical and educational professionals, and the near-universal internalization of sexual repression. Moreover, she builds her argument from a wide array of concrete and telling examples, such as the design of public bathrooms in Taiwan and the narrative logic of heterosexual erotica, demonstrating not only how culture constructs sex, but also how sex constructs cultures.[73]

The Gallant Woman describes the nature of sexual repression in Chinese culture from the patriarchal thinking of Confucianism to the conditions of capitalist modernity. Ho argues, in a de-biologizing move, that women's oppression is not rooted in anatomical differences but in an economic logic of exchange (*jiaohuan*) that constitutes women as losers in every scenario. Ho points out that women lose in sexual exchanges because they are taught to perceive sex as a punishing and negative experience unless it takes place in a monogamous heterosexual marriage. Here, Ho offers more concrete examples than Gayle Rubin's well-known analysis of "sex-negativity" on a similar point. As Rubin puts it, sex is "bad" unless it takes place in a specific, exonerating context: "The only adult sexual behavior that is legal in every state is the placement of the penis in the vagina in wedlock."[74] Ho formulates a specific theory of the dynamics of gender and sex negativity in Confucian society by describing how women come to internalize the requirements of patriarchy as an exchange in a zero-sum game: "A woman whose body is seen by a man loses, but if she happens to look at a man's naked body, she also loses."[75] This economic logic requires a socially reinforced distinction between "fallen women" who "lose" their virginity before marriage, and "respectable women" who only perform the same act in "exchange" for a lifetime of economic security. Men are winners in both scenarios. Here, Ho shows that women do not obtain equality through the acquisition of rights (suffrage) alone; rather, women's equality becomes possible only when women begin to see and treat themselves as active agents in decision-making processes. Such a transformation requires a psychic revolution that begins with women's reclamation of their own bodies. Women must become *haoshuang*, gallant beings confident enough to demand erotic pleasures.[76]

In Ho's analysis, sexuality is not analytically or politically separable from gender. Rather, sexuality and gender are mutually implicated in each other. This implication is not a liability, but a productive tension that has political uses. Crucially, Ho is not a determinist, and gender does not immediately equal ineluctable oppression. The radical nature of her theory lies in her reading of sexuality as a form of agency, and in her insistence that sexuality is precisely the means by which women overcome the "gendered vulnerabilities" imposed by capitalist modernity.[77] Ho's culturally specific analysis focuses on the dynamics of unconscious acculturation under capitalist exchange instead of a binary structure of male dominance and female oppression. For Ho, women become "winners" not by reversing the structure of power, but by becoming active subjects of desire. Ho's theory of sexual revolution shows that gender is not a given or inalterable facticity, but a process, a series of cultural contestations, and if women's oppression originates from the effects of acculturation rather than a biological necessity, then culture can be unlearned and revolutionized. Sexuality provides the site of agency for the unlearning and relearning of culture that Ho terms "sex revolution," a concept that forms the basis of her queer Marxist theory.[78]

In *The Gallant Woman*, Ho does not argue for the importance of queer issues to the feminist project from the perspective of coalitional politics. Her analysis of the necessary intersections between queer and feminist interests is not based on arguments about altruism, victim solidarity, or the liberal doctrine of respect and tolerance for individual differences. Instead, queerness signifies a different social configuration of bodies and desires that disrupts and denaturalizes capitalism's instrumental constructions of good versus bad sex. Ho suggests that women can become liberated by aligning themselves with the disruptive force of queers. Like "bad women" who have multiple affairs and partners, queer people provide a valuable education to gallant women because these social subjects are the material reminder of the irreducible richness and diversity of sexual expressions in human cultures. Their existence reveals the constructedness and arbitrariness of the institution of heterosexual procreative monogamy that women are induced to view as their destiny.[79] Precisely what constitutes the queer subject in Ho's writing oscillates from examples of extramarital relations, incest, S/M, to a wide range of other types of sexual conduct that cannot be categorized in terms of any binary models. However, even when Ho is writing more locally on the topic of homosexuality, she emphasizes that the "lesbian" is not a self-same subject. For Ho, the "woman-loving-woman" or "woman-identified-woman" imposes a perilous homogeneity that renaturalizes "true love" or "identification" as the prerequisite for a legitimate connection between human beings. The "woman-loving-woman" in 1960s' and 1970s' lesbian feminism, Ho argues, should be replaced by the "woman-licking-woman," "woman-rubbing-against-woman," "woman-fucking-woman," "woman-seducing-woman," and other possibilities.[80]

The analysis of the auto-commodification of the "self-respecting virgin" in *The Gallant Woman* is clearly indebted to Marx's critique of *homo economicus* or the subject of rational expectations. Ho's advocacy of "sex for sex's sake" as the means for a revolution of culture in *The Gallant Woman* prefigures her more explicitly Marxist analysis published three years later, where Ho develops, through a rereading of Wilhelm Reich, a theory of the contradiction between the forces and relations of erotic production.[81] Ho argues that this overdetermined contradiction produces conditions that are conducive to revolution, but revolution is not a structural inevitability: "Revolution is only possible, but not necessarily inevitable, even when points of resistance are already in place. It would take active intervention and discursive codifications to bring forth a revolution."[82] For Ho, revolution is not a messianic future. Similarly, culture in her theory is necessarily made and remade through human intervention. This reading of culture-as-process allows her to theorize the usefulness of sexuality to feminist struggles, which cannot be reductively viewed as the natural unfolding of an Asian neoliberalism.

The implications of this theory are profound. Ho offers a theory of sexual revolution that resists the liberal pluralist view of homosexuals as a new ethnicity. Instead, she recasts gay men and lesbians as a kind of queer tutelage for women. *The Gallant Woman* offers a powerful reinterpretation of queerness as a structure of exemplarity, a scene in which ethical, political, or familial predicaments that are relevant to men and women alike are worked out. We can therefore characterize queerness in Ho's work as an open invitation for (heterosexual) women to rethink their own positions of power by becoming involved in the dilemmas and consciousness of other erotic social agents. Ho's theory of sexual revolution is derived from Freudian Marxists (in particular Wilhelm Reich) who insist on the totality of the social (conceiving society as an indivisible whole) and on the possibilities of sublimation and transference (arguing that the relations between society's individual elements may take on a different appearance and be misrecognized).[83] Although repression may initially appear to be primarily sexual, it indexes a deeper level of gender inequality, which is why sexual liberation is a necessary step in Ho's feminism. Moreover, repression also indicates the inhibition of energies that can be redirected to other uses. This view of repression has its roots in Freud, but it is also a psychoanalytic adaptation of the labor theory of value developed by Marx, Adam Smith, and David Ricardo. Marx understands society to be a living organism linked by a series of economic, transformative activities which individual agents never fully recognize. When twenty yards of linen become a coat and, eventually, come to be exchanged for a loaf of bread, the value of the original quantum of labor expended in the creation of the linen remains identical despite the fact that it has taken different forms, but the social relations between the plantation worker, the tailor, and the baker are obscured.[84] Marx's point is that the same value sustains the livelihood of social agents in domains of economic activities that appear, at first, completely unrelated. Because money effectively monopolizes the function of universal exchangeability, the actual constant in the equations, labor-power, is erased from view. The labor theory of value insists that the value of a commodity is not determined by the immediate producer, but, rather, by the (infinitely delayed) aggregate of labors that makes it possible for any particular producer to live, work, and manufacture the commodity for social exchange.[85]

In Ho's Freudian-inflected version of the labor theory of value, sexuality is conceived of as a fraction of energy (nengliang, Chinese equivalent of German Trieb and drive or instinct in English). This energy, like the quantum of value in Marx's labor theory, is both indestructible and transferable. Freud offers an array of metaphors to describe these translations (displacement, condensation, sublimation, and transference), with specific descriptions of how each mechanism works.[86] These processes do not change the essence of the energy, but they do conceal its origins. For Marx, a fundamental structure of misrecognition is essential for class society, which allows both the dominant and the laboring classes to regard a deeply unequal relationship between human beings to be an equitable and transparent exchange of things.[87] The nexus of Freud and Marx helps Ho develop a holistic theory of the transformative powers of a sexual revolution for society at large.

Ho's view in *The Gallant Woman* closely aligns with Yin-Bin Ning's work on the emancipatory power of sexual pluralism.[88] Ning argues that unpaid sexual labor in a heterosexual marriage is analogous to the surplus labor of the proletariat; therefore, by demanding money for their labor, prostitutes reveal the inherent contradictions in the modern family and reverse the ideological workings of that institution.[89] Ning develops Marx's distinction between use value and exchange value to argue that the social movement to criminalize prostitution conflates the particularities of labor (the sexual nature of the occupation) with the universal exchangeability of labor-power.[90] Similar to Ho's conception of queer sexual difference as a form of agency, Ning's theory refuses to see queerness as the identity of a people. Rather, Ning describes sexual difference or perversity (*biantai*) itself as a cultural resource (*wenhua ziyuan*) that people can mobilize for sexual and nonsexual purposes.[91] Therefore, Ning offers a strong counterargument to the conception of queer people as a *minority*, which is the political doctrine of a liberal politics that seeks to integrate sexual diversity into the dominant order on the principle of diversity.

Ho and Ning's queer Marxism is a significant historical alternative to standpoint theory, the tradition within certain leftist discourses that project women, the homosexual, the proletariat, or some other subjects as a privileged standpoint that renders the contradictions of capitalism visible. Rather than describing oppression, Ho and Ning offer examples of how Marxism and structuralist analysis can help articulate a nonidentitarian approach to the insurrectionary energies of the erotic. Like Cui, however, Ho and Ning are not orthodox representatives of the reception of Marxism in their country. In the 1990s, several influential Chinese introductions to the Marxist-feminist debates appeared in Taiwan. The Marx that arrived in the Cold War anticommunist context of Taiwan was, in a manner of speaking, damaged goods. In an award-winning collection edited by Gù Yanling, Huang Shuling describes "Marxist feminism" as a degenerate version of "utopian socialism." Huang explains that Marxist feminism equals the nationalization of women's private property, collective childrearing, coercive assignment of women to factories, and the state's unquestioned authority over women's labor and bodies.[92] According to Huang, the errors of Marxist feminism have already been made evident by the discredited practices of the Soviet Union and the People's Republic of China. Fan Qing's contribution on socialist feminism in the volume presents Marxism as a gender-blind historical materialism that attempts to subordinate women's needs to those of class struggle.[93] In the Cold War context, Ning and Ho's work on "sex revolution" also represents an effort to deliteralize revolution and to reclaim revolution from the state.

Ho's queer Marxism participates in the tradition of cultural materialism, which offers theoretical reflections on the relations between a society's economic base and ideological superstructure without necessarily arguing that culture is determined in the last instance by the economic base. Her queer Marxism also participates in the tradition of dialectical criticism, which consists of writings that reconstruct apparently contradictory or antithetical forces in society into a logical whole. Marxist dialectical criticism's influence on Ho is discernible in her analysis of the issue of global governance. In two important essays, "Queer Existence under Global Governance," and "Is Global Governance Bad for East Asian Queers?" Ho analyzes the contradiction between the global nature of modern surveillance network and its irreducibly local, concrete effects. Ho characterizes Taiwan's regime of sexuality as a new form of global governance created and sustained by supranational bodies such as the IMF and the United Nations, international women's conferences, women's NGOs, religious organizations, and a global discourse of human rights.[94] Amorphous and deterritorialized, this new regime of power is global in its reach, but it is able to co-opt concrete state-powers to punish deviant sexual expressions within national borders. Because of Taiwan's precarious nation-state status, the feminist state is structurally induced to adopt conservative and even repressive policies to promote an image of Taiwan as a liberal democratic, and hence legitimate, nation-state in the international community. The contradiction between the global and the local means that queer resistance in Taiwan confronts a transnational vector of power that is difficult to challenge through legal reforms on a domestic scale. Religious and women's NGOs in Taiwan are able to persecute sexual minorities with the current level of ideological persuasiveness and material support from the state because their work is compatible with a global hegemonic moral discourse centered on the United States.[95] The contradiction between global governance and national emancipation indicates the limits of an emancipatory politics tethered to the fortunes of the nation-state. This contradiction also tells us that structural crises do not automatically produce a new form of consciousness.

Queer Minority Discourse and Reticent Poetics

Like Ho and Ning, the Gender/Sexuality Rights Association Taiwan (G/SRAT) brings a queer Marxist perspective to combat the liberal pluralist conception of minority rights. Founded by feminists who were expelled by the Awakening Foundation for supporting the ex-licensed prostitutes' movement, G/SRAT is the official name of Queer & Class, an advocacy group that works on the interstices of labor and gender/sexuality issues. The existence of G/SRAT provides an instructive example of how a labor movement could proceed through an interrogation of gender. From the start, G/SRAT's work is deeply informed by the theoretical debates in feminism, Marxism, and queer theory about the relation between labor and naturalized notions of gender. In their work, the members of the Association—Wang Ping, Chen Yurong, Ni Jiazhen, Jiang Jiawen, and Ding Naifei—emphasize the impossibility of thinking about gender outside the contexts of class and power. For G/SRAT, gender is not a person's universal or immutable essence, but a relation to the world that is inflected by and imbued with other contingencies—class, education, location, language, nationality; consequently, the subject of the group's activism is not "women" but prostitutes, female factory workers, migrant workers, single mothers, T's and po's ("butch" and "femme" lesbians), feminine and masculine gay men, adulterers, bisexuals, transgendered persons, people living with HIV/AIDS, students, betel nut beauties,[96] and migrant workers. G/SRAT identifies as one of its main goals "the creation of new discourses about gender," namely the transformation of the category of gender itself: "For gender to be a useful category for thinking and activism, gender cannot remain in the static, binary definition of "female/male."[97] G/SRAT's efforts in transforming the concept of gender have had a discernible impact on Taiwanese political culture. An example is the wording of two legal changes in Taiwan, the Gender Equality Employment Law in 2001 and the Gender Equity Education Act in 2004. Initially proposed as "Nan nü gongzuo pingdeng fa cao an" (literally the "equal employment for men and women"), the Law was finally legislated as "liang xing gongzuo pingdeng fa" (literally "equal employment for the two sexes") in 2001 in response to G/SRAT's activism. The language shifted from the conservative understanding of gender as "men and women" to the relation between the sexes. Similarly, the Gender Equity Education Act ("xingbie pingdeng jiaoyu fa") was originally named "liang xing pingdeng jiaoyu fa" (literally the "bill for the education on the equality of the two sexes") but the phrase "liang xing" ("two sexes") was eventually replaced by "xingbie" ("gender/ sexual difference") in order to accommodate other gender and sexual expressions, such as transgender.

G/SRAT's work in Taiwan shows that a queer intervention does not have to be restricted to the political empowerment of homosexuals; rather, it can also bring about concrete social changes on legal, cultural, and material levels through the unlearning of gender categories. While mainstream women's groups remain committed to the legalization of "women's rights," for G/SRAT, gender is not synonymous with the category of women, and progressive social change cannot rely on a static conception of gender as male/female.[98] Instead, gender is the material and discursive contestation over these categories themselves. In addition, these categories' apparent immutability is sustained by distinct state apparatuses. Human freedom, of which gender and sexual freedom is part, cannot be realized through state measures. Rather, freedom can only be reimagined and constructed through democratic dialogues among nonstate actors in civil society. In the midst of the clamor for legalized same-sex marriage, G/SRAT marched to *oppose* the institution of marriage at Taipei Pride 2012, proposing the alternative slogan of "pluralism of relationships" on their banner against "marriage equality." G/SRAT understands that marriage should be made available to those who desire it, but the current gay movement merely seeks to extend heterosexual privileges to same-sex couples without critically questioning and transforming such privileges. A queer Marxist perspective, by contrast, critiques marriage as an economic institution designed to protect the interests of monogamous couples. The ideology of the family, romance, fidelity, monogamy, and childbearing ensures that privileges and material wealth are selectively passed down from one generation to another. From a Marxist point of view, the idealized, romanticized, and religiously sanctioned notions of monogamous coupledom is a historical product of the rise of private property. Monogamy allows men to pass their private property to their offspring by first ensuring their sexual monopoly over individual women so that the children will be their own.[99] In the context of Taiwan, many urgent redistributive justice programs and social reforms are blocked by the movement to legalize same-sex marriage. Wang Ping, G/SRAT's Secretary General, uses Taiwan's governmental housing subsidies for married couples as an example to illustrate this point. Wang points out that many gay couples are demanding legal recognition to participate in the government's housing subsidy program, and many gay couples believe that their inability to access such benefits is an example of sexual discrimination. But the government's housing subsidy policy also excludes single heterosexual men and women who cannot, or choose not to, find marriage partners. The government developed the program because it recognized that capitalist globalization has intensified Taiwan's economic stratification, to the point that it is practically impossible for a single person to purchase housing in the greater Taipei area. Unable to devise an effective economic program to counter the forces of capitalism, the government instead resorted to a social policy that benefits married heterosexual couples.[100] The demand for same-sex marriage in this particular case fails to recognize the real economic problems of income disparity, inflation, unemployment, and the concentration of wealth and power in the hands of the few. Instead of arguing for social reforms and greater redistributive justice, proponents of the marriage equality movement accept an obsolete institution that tethers economic rights to the historical requirements of childbearing, monogamy, and procreation. By contrast, a queer Marxist movement should strive to open up the range of legitimate forms of association, union, and intimacy: a woman who enjoys a casual sexual relationship with a man should not be coerced by housing or tax benefits to turn their relationship into a marriage; conversely, two sisters living together and providing emotional and financial support to each other should not need to present evidence of sex for society to consider them to be in a legitimate relationship with legal entitlements.[101]

In the work of G/SRAT's theoretician, Ding Naifei, queerness refers to a wide range of abject beings rendered inarticulate and unrecognizable by the stigma imposed by a social hierarchy of labor. By attending to the historical factors that attributed to the contiguity between labor and sexual stigma, Ding's work makes a significant departure from the liberal philosophy of substantive personhood that characterizes the homosexual as a self-affirmative entity. The dual emphasis on sexual and class issues makes Ding one of the most original thinkers in Taiwan's critical arena, since her work demonstrates, through historical research as well as critical analysis, the mutual embeddedness of the stigma of sex and the stigma of labor. This mutual complicity is the condition that inaugurates the queer subject. Queer subjects in Ding's work include bondmaids, concubines, polygamists, polyamorous persons, prostitutes, red shoes, and obscene "things" from the Ming period to contemporary Taiwan and Singapore.[102] Precisely because the queer is not a visible quality of sex, but a sedimented *effect* of an invisible but resilient historical institution, Ding's analysis also radically alters our opinion on the nature of social exclusion. We should recall that Ding is writing against the entrenched tradition of state feminism and marshaling stigma as an anti-essentialist form of collective disempowerment that does not lapse into an ontological category. As with Spivak's deconstructive reading of the subaltern *as* a negative accounting (the entire Indian population minus the elite), the queer in Ding's works cannot be defined in advance as a preexisting group (women or homosexuals) by the state. The subject of stigma is, rather, a negativity and an absence, a historical process of exclusion without positivistic contents. In an early essay, "Parasites and Prostitutes in the House of State Feminism," Ding characterizes the queer as the unwanted rats and flies in the feminist classroom that, much to the annoyance of feminists, persistently return.[103] The rats and flies that keep coming back in the face of power in Ding's theory are not mere intellectual abstractions but actual movement strategies in

Taiwan, such as the (G/S)rats that feminism failed to exterminate, and the ex-licensed prostitutes who pestered the Mayor with guerrilla tactics learned from flies (蒼蠅隨行/娼影隨行).[104]

Liu Jen-peng and Ding Naifei develop an immensely influential theory of "reticent poetics" in a number of works.[105] Liu and Ding use "reticent poetics" to explain the unrepresentability of queerness within a political and cultural framework that appears to be tolerant, queer-friendly, and even feminist.[106] The intellectual source for Liu and Ding's concept of "reticent poetics" is not Western queer theory but Chinese philosophy: Zhuangzi's writing about "wangliang" 罔兩 (the shade of a shadow, often translated as Penumbra). In one of Zhuangzi's parables, a crowd of Penumbrae is intrigued by Shadow's movement with the sun, but Shadow refuses to explain its Attendance or dependence upon Substance. This refusal performatively produces the unknowability of the source of Penumbrae's question and displaces the mode of interrogation onto the Form of the Substance, which is not part of the Penumbrae's question.[107] Against the sociologist Chou Wah-shan's observation that Chinese societies have always been tolerant of homosexuality, Liu and Ding use this revealing non sequitur in Zhuangzi's parable to develop a persuasive argument that reticence or tolerance is precisely what produces the unintelligibility of the queer. Shadow's focus on Form is a rhetorical displacement that effectively disables an analysis of the process of hierarchization—that is, how Substance, Shadow, and Penumbrae are established as different positionalities in an indivisible hierarchy in the first place. Penumbrae do not seek to "come out" (xianshen) or to be represented and tolerated, but Shadow persistently misunderstands their questions. This theory of "wangliang" and "reticence" differs from the theory of women's oppression, which often implies that women must be presented as "victims" in order to have any claim to political rights at all. Women's emancipation is then problematically predicated on the denial of women's agency. Against this view, Liu and Ding argue that the "cultural tolerance" Chou refers to constitutes a form of oppression rather than liberation because it is dependent on the melodramatic presentation of the suffering of the homosexual subject.

For Taiwan's mainstream feminists, women's shared experience of oppression defines the ontological coherence of women as a social category—where oppression is understood largely as the absence of legal protection in the workplace and education. Because feminism is premised upon a common gender, and the commonality of that gender is derived from oppression, mainstream feminists such as Lin Fang-mei and Liu Yu-hsiu argue that sexuality has to be removed from the feminist agenda, citing the logic that the image of the sexually liberated woman undermines the legitimacy, progress, and respectability of women's issues, which the liberal state is just beginning to recognize. Since the presumed goal of feminism is the creation of state machineries capable of furthering women's legal rights, state feminism must suppress the internal differences among women in order to make women's plight resonate more with a largely patriarchal society. Hence mainstream feminists like Lin and Liu either believe that patriarchy cannot be transformed, or they argue that its transformation has to be postponed. Criticisms of Ho's politics of sexual liberation include charges that Ho "wants to fly before she learns how to walk," that her vision is cartoonish, Disneyesque, utopian, irresponsible, disconnected from reality, and that sexual autonomy is a luxury for "bourgeois women" that should not be attempted by lower-class women who do not have the material basis for such rights. For feminist critic Lin Fang-mei, Ho's "gallant woman" is a cartoonish, unrealistic figure similar to "superman or batman," and Ho's queer Marxist theory is reminiscent of a "TV commercial for shampoo, stockings, and tampons" that is best reserved "for the promotion of condoms, love hotels, and disco clubs."[108] Conservative critics presume that feminism can only progress if its claims are consonant with the values of mainstream society. As a politics founded on a desire for acceptance, mainstream feminism is mirrored by the liberal view of homosexual as a minority analogue—"people just like everybody else"—and by the liberal use of this analogy as the *basis* for justice considerations. Queer Marxists, by contrast, use the unassimilability of the queer to reveal that the heterosexual framework is a contingency that passes as natural and universal. Moreover, state feminism relies on a philosophical notion of womanhood as a universalizable singularity. The normalizing operation of state feminism not only seeks to purge sexuality from the domain of gender politics, but also asks different women to "fit" the social model of the virtuous woman by renouncing their sexuality. In short, the theoretical disagreements between mainstream feminists and queer Marxists concern sexuality's relevance and instrumentality to the feminist cause, and the usefulness of a unitary notion of womanhood. Because Lin Fang-mei does not regard sexuality to be a feminist issue, she pejoratively characterizes "sex radicals" like Ho and the women fired from the Awakening Foundation as "parasites" who use "women's resources" to do sexuality-based work.[109] Ding's "Parasites and Prostitutes in the House of State Feminism" is a response to this charge. Again, Judith Butler's critique of the semantic splitting of sex into gender (as the proper object of feminism) and sexuality (as the proper object of gay and lesbian analysis) helps explain the battles in Taiwan as well."[110]

As a queer Marxism, Taiwan's progressive sexual theory was critically informed by the 1997 ex-licensed prostitutes' movement and other labor struggles. In "Stigma of Sex and Sex Work," Ding shows that mainstream feminists' inability to recognize sex work as "work" issues not from a transcultural fear of sex, but more specifically from the successful transplantation of the premodern class stigma of the maid and the little wife. This premodern class stigma transforms into the symbolic debasement of the modern prostitute, whose labor is not recognized as labor, but is immediately seen as exploitation because it is performed outside the sanctity of the heterosexual monogamous marriage. In *The Gallant Woman*, Ho makes a related point about a new "work ethics" centered on the social engineering of women's lean bodies.[111] Ho suggests that women are induced to increase their productivity and become more competitive on the job market by altering their bodies through dietary control, but this desire is sustained by an enormous amount of social resources committed to advertisements and beauty products that are financed out of the surplus labor of the more productive new woman. Ho explains that her emphasis on the materiality of social reproduction is a resistance to the "neo-Marxist tendency to reduce the reproduction of capitalism to ideology and politics," which overlooks the fact that ideology, even as false consciousness, is produced at an economic cost borne by the social agents themselves rather than the state apparatus.[112] Both Ho and Ding raise, from different materialist perspectives, the question of sexuality's relation to the reproduction of society.

Insofar as the prostitutes' movement cannot be understood outside the context of the women's movement, and insofar as transgender lives are contesting *gender* norms, neither can be summarily reduced to "a sexuality" that is part of a sexual pluralism. Indeed, queer Marxist theory is not exclusively concerned with sex and sexuality: it is also a critique of gender and gender-based oppressions—the diagnosis of gender identity disorder, the presumed correspondence between gender identity and biological sex, the regulation of hair length, uniforms, and educational content in women's schools, and coercive or unwanted operations on intersex children. Queer theory contains an analysis of a social mechanism that subjects individuals to harassment, even death, as a result of feminine or masculine self-stylizations. Not all effeminate men or butch women are clamoring for sexual rights or the recognition of erotic behavior. The question of gender normativity does not immediately constitute the victims as a "sexual" minority because social punishments are meted out before any sexual act comes into view, and in ways that are quite independent of normative or non-normative sexualities. We may conclude that queer bodies are situated in struggles against a persistent *dualism of gender* that functions as a cisnormative regulatory ideal between one's biological sex and one's gender identity.[113] The critique of the imposition of normative gender attributes on different bodies can be distinguished from the research on sexual conduct in human culture, but these questions demonstrate that gender and sexuality commonly concern feminism, gay and lesbian studies, and queer theory. If queer theory cannot operate without a theory of gender, we must remember that feminism in Taiwan must also include "sexual questions" such as the harassment of women, women's reproductive rights and bodily autonomy, and pornography. The disagreement between sex-positive and sex-negative feminists is actually a misnomer, for it involves not so much a different attitude toward sex, but, rather, a chiasmic attribution of gender to women and sexuality to queers. The rhetorical success of this conceptual separation has to be explained in terms of the problems of the liberal pluralist model of personhood. It is a historical result of liberal pluralism, in other words, that gender comes to be viewed as a category that can be defended but not problematized or pluralized, while sexuality must be affirmed in the plural and celebrated as "alternative" or dissident configurations. In order for mainstream feminists to present sexuality and feminism as analytically distinct, sexuality has to be seen as the domain of an entirely separate *people* with no necessary or logical bearing on gender.

Queer Marxism's challenge of liberal pluralism then also poses a fundamental challenge of the personification of sexualities on a theoretical and political level.

A Marxist Theory by Non-Marxists?
Revolution in/of the Queer Subject

In the first volume of *Capital*, Marx offers a theory of abstract labor as a kind of social power that at once homogenizes individuals and places them into discrete identity groups and ineluctable classes. How and why does abstract labor hold individuals together in a binding social totality while creating distinctions between them? Marx explains that abstract labor reproduces society first by reproducing the conditions of social production. Marx's labor theory of value holds that the value of a commodity is the sum total of the original value of the raw materials, a fraction of the value of the instrument needed (the means of production), and the value of the labor-power expended in the production of that commodity. However, unlike Ricardo, who defines value as the quantum of labor embodied in each particular commodity, Marx understands the value of labor-power from the point of view of the reproduction of society. Value is therefore not determined by the particularities of articles of utility or by the endless possibilities of different concrete labors that individuals perform, but by abstract labor, the aggregate production of commodities in society as a whole. This correction Marx makes to Ricardo is essential to later feminist readings of domestic labor *as* labor—which includes certain "immaterial aspects" such as childbearing and emotional repair—labor in the properly Marxian sense, since value in Marx is defined not by the intrinsic properties of a materially existing commodity, but by the cost of social conditions that are required for the production of that commodity and for the reproduction of the laborer who works on that commodity.[114]

A consideration of the value of labor-power must therefore begin with the category of "socially necessary labor (time)," which does not refer to the average of productivity at the current level of technical development (as is commonly understood), but to cultural ideas of what constitutes an acceptable desire and what constitutes a proper means of satisfying that desire, or what Marx calls the historical and moral elements of society.[115] The value of a commodity is the amount of human labor expended to create it, but the value of the commodity of human labor-power is determined by moral and discursive operations outside the capitalist reproduction scheme. These operations require a maintenance cost from the social body and constitute part of the cost or value of labor-power. In order for capital to reconstitute itself, it must reproduce the productive forces (the laborer), the raw materials and the machinery, *as well as* the moral and intellectual conditions that allow capitalist production to exist in the first place. From an individual point of view, in the expanded reproduction scheme, the capitalist only sees a portion of capital recommitted to the production process at the end of each production cycle, and the capitalist understands reproduction to involve only the renewal of manpower, machinery, and raw materials. From a social point of view, however, at the end of each cycle of the labor process, a portion of surplus value is appropriated by the system itself to reproduce the existing relations of production. This central idea in Marx is the foundation of Althusser's famous formulation that the reproduction of capital is both the reproduction of the material forces and the reproduction of "the social conditions of production" that include the church, the family, the police, the army, and the school—or what he calls the ideological *state* apparatuses.[116]

The idea that abstract labor reproduces society first by reproducing state apparatuses explains why G/SRAT, an organization ostensibly committed to the advocacy of gender diversity, has also insistently participated in antiwar, anti-imperialist, and labor movements. G/SRAT recognizes that these events and material forces create the social conditions of gender expressions, and that sexual freedom will never be obtained through a local struggle without a confrontation with the fundamental mechanisms for the reproduction of social power. G/SRAT has organized and participated in the Minority-Against-the-War movement in 2003, which protested the Taiwan government's support for US military actions; the Personal Information Protection Alliance in 2002, which was formed to oppose the passage of a bill that would allow the state to collect citizens' personal data in the form of a "Health IC Card." During the 2004 presidential election, G/SRAT and other progressive organizations launched the famous "one-million-invalid-ballot" (*bai wan fei piao*) campaign, calling on the populace to reject both the "Blue" and "Green" candidates by purposefully invalidating their ballots. Recognizing that "democracy" has become a political tool and reduced to ethnic tensions, the movement sought to return electoral politics to a rational and democratic debate in civil society. As G/SRAT's Chen Yu-Rong and Wang Ping have argued, the current political standoff over the cultural and political identity of Taiwan—whether Taiwan is "Taiwanese" or "descendants of the Yellow Emperor"—has usurped and deflected transformative energies originally invested in other social issues, rendering sexuality- and gender-related questions politically unspeakable.[117] They strive to show that a critique of the state has now become a prerequisite for all meaningful gender- and sexuality-based struggles in Taiwan, since the dominant debate on Taiwan's political status has radically impoverished our imagination of what is political. We can extrapolate from G/SRAT's movement strategies that queer struggles require organized resistance to the workings of state apparatuses. If the queer is not another identity category, but a strategy for the transformation of state apparatuses, queer theory also needs Marxist theory, for it is in Marxism that we find the most useful tools for such analyses.

The perceived mutual exclusivity of gender struggles and sexual struggles is a political consequence of the liberal pluralist assumption of "woman" as a nonpluralizable gender and queer as nonsingularizable sexualities. The homogenization of women is fundamentally dependent on the evacuation of sexuality from women's lives, which is then phantastmatically reassigned to queers as sexualities. Marx's analysis of the reproduction of labor-power as the reproduction of a social division is crucial to the understanding of the relation between stigmatized social practices and gender norms in queer Marxism. The apparatuses designed to ensure the reproduction of society along asymmetrical lines are called, in Althusserian terms, state apparatuses that include women's NGOs, the church, and the family, although these "state" apparatuses are not directly controlled by the government. The Marxist insight that the reproduction of a state requires the reproduction of such apparatuses offers a critical explanation for a historical alliance between labor and sexual concerns in Cui, Ho, Ding, and other queer Marxists.

The bifocal view in this narrative of queer Marxism in the two Chinas also highlights the difficulty of correlating sexual politics to developments of socialism. Both traditions—to the extent that they can be dichotomized—emphasize the need for sexual and gender analysis to resist economic determinism; in turn, these theories offer critical tools for the dialecticization of biopolitics and materialism. The poststructuralist critique of Marxism as a dogmatic elevation of economics to a monocausal determination of social life overlooks the importance of the *dialectic* in Marxist thought, which queer Marxists in the Chinas analyze through readings of queer creativity, sex work, state feminism, queer subject-formations, and civil society. In Marx, this dialectic between materialism and biopolitics is captured by his notion of the "double-character" of the commodity of human labor-power. Labor-power is a special commodity that is reproduced through material and cultural means. His description of the transformation of labor-power into a commodity under capitalism does not imply the primacy of the economic, but is itself a critique of the cultural assumptions of that primacy.

Although queerness is a controversial category in Chinese theory, it is generally accepted that sexuality studies entails a transformation of power relations and identity categories in a culture. A familiar queer argument is that identity-based movements—feminist or gay and lesbian or otherwise—often reinstate the very terms of power that they seek to overcome by naturalizing the conditions of their injury.[118] Whether informed by the Marxist notion of social structuration, deconstructive criticisms of linguistic referentiality, or psychoanalytic readings of the unconscious, varieties of queer theory continue to find the opaque, incomplete, or barred subject of desire a useful notion for political contestations. A queer subjectivity is an instance of capitalism's failure to discipline desire into fixed identities. This failure can be mobilized to create a more self-reflective and expansive model of radical democracy. Queer theory then commonly distinguishes between the transformation of the categories through which political representation is sought, and efforts to secure rights for those already constituted as subjects by those categories.[119] Queer theory, in other words, requires that we change the subject, before Marxism requires that we change the social. In queer Marxism, queer sexual identities or positionalities do not necessarily refer to homosexuals; rather, these subjects include prostitutes, Filipino maids, factory workers, pedophiles, and high school students. The systemic relation between these seemingly unrelated positions can only be restored by a critique of the historical workings of capitalism. Cui's creative works, Josephine Ho's and Ding Naifei's social theory, and Wang Ping's activism are all examples of a hybridized queer Marxism that connects queer struggles to critiques of capitalism and neoliberalism. Diverse as they are, these theories demonstrate the urgency, and productivity, of rematerializing queer studies.

CHAPTER 3

THE RISE OF THE QUEER

CHINESE NOVEL

When and why did people start telling stories about gay men and lesbians in Chinese? The question of Chinese queer literature's origins is important for at least two theoretical debates: the invention of homosexuality and queer identification. Since Foucault, critics have been accustomed to describing the homo/heterosexual definition as a modern Western invention, an "event whose impact and whose scope we are only now learning how to measure."[1] The conception of "homosexuals as a species," Foucault argues, was unique to the history of the modern West, which radically separated it from former understandings of same-sex sexual relations such as pederasty in Greek culture.[2] As Sedgwick explains it, whereas previously "every person was considered necessarily assignable to a male or a female gender . . . [now every person] was considered necessarily assignable as well to a homo- or a heterosexuality, a binarized identity that was full of implications, however confusing, for even the ostensibly least sexual aspects of personal existence."[3] With Foucault's, Sedgwick's, and Halperin's works, the argument that homosexuality was first invented in the modern West has become widely accepted. The corollary of this argument is that the invention of homosexuality had never occurred elsewhere, or that it did only as a consequence of coming into contact with the West. This question has led many critics in Chinese gender and sexuality studies to plumb the large body of erotic literature in premodern China for literary images, anecdotes, and linguistic details that could be used to historicize the invention of homosexuality in China. For critics who disagree that erotic texts in premodern Chinese literature indicate a preexisting homosexual identity, the advent of the modernist queer novel in the twentieth century supplies the best evidence that there was no such thing as "homosexuality" in premodern China. Critics who hold this view then argue that this development was intimately tied to the appearance of neologisms such as *tongxing lian* and *tongxing ai*, which first entered the Chinese language through translations of Western sexological writings in the Republican period (1911–49).[4] For Foucauldian critics in China studies, the fictional appearance of fully ontologized homosexual characters in the 1980s indicates an epistemic shift that can help us appreciate the difference between premodern forms of same-sex desire and modern concepts of homosexual identity, sexual orientation, oppression, and self-affirmation in Chinese culture.

The cultural history of queer identification is another important reason to consider the origins of queer literature. Every person who grew up gay before the information revolution might remember feeling alone in the universe at some point.[5] While all literature represents, shapes, and constructs the life of a society, queer fiction, in particular, provided a site of identification that helped queer adolescents make sense of their entangled emotions and imagine themselves as part of a collectivity—even if they read the books in secret and in isolation from one another—before more organized modes of community-building, safer venues for social networking, and more accessible media representations became available with the passage of time.[6] The rise of modern gay and lesbian fiction in Chinese is a crucial event we need to understand to reconstruct the affective history of a culture, as intangible as that topic may sound.[7] This literary history provides important clues to the key turning points in the collective self-making of modern gay culture.

Both of these questions—identity and identification—refer to complex social processes that are intimately connected to the literary problem of "character." I argue in this chapter that a distinctive aesthetic apparatus for representing fully ontologized homosexual male characters appeared in Chinese literature first in the 1980s, that this apparatus was first developed by Taiwan-based Chinese authors, and that this literary development occurred as a result of their queer engagements with Chinese Marxism. The last point distinguishes my analysis from Foucauldian histories of sexuality in China studies: while my approach accepts that significant epistemic changes occurred in twentieth-century

Chinese cultures with implications for queer identity and identification, I argue that these changes did not take place primarily as a result of translations of Western knowledge. Instead, I emphasize the agency of Chinese cultural producers, as well as the importance of situating their works in the historical context of Chinese queer writers' responses to Marxism as both a communist bureaucracy and an indispensable intellectual resource.

By highlighting the problem of queer literary characters in the period before the relaxation of cross-strait relationships, I am also staking a claim for the significance of the forgotten years of the 1980s for queer literary history. Indeed, queer Chinese studies scholars work almost exclusively on the 1990s, the era when tongzhi wenxue—a self-stylized queer literature—emerged in the PRC and the ROC. Readers of contemporary literary criticism cannot escape a euphoric feeling about the 1990s as a moment of queer heteroglossia, carnival, subversion, efflorescence, and free play. Most commentators on the tongzhi wenxue in the 1990s in the Chinas characterize it as a rupture with the past.[8] Certainly, the emergence of tongzhi wenxue was revolutionary in many ways. Readers familiar with PRC censorship laws may be surprised to find Lin Bai's One Person's War (Yigeren de zhanzheng, 1994), which describes a young woman's autoerotic activities and same-sex desire while growing up, and Chen Ran's Private Life (Siren shenghuo, 1996), which contains a scene of an erotic encounter between an eleven-year-old girl and a woman in her twenties. Several PRC works from this period gained international fame through film adaptations: Zhang Yuan's East Palace, West Palace (Donggong xigong, 1996), written by Wang Xiaobo and adapted from Wang's novella, became a critically acclaimed milestone in Chinese queer cinema in 1996, while the hauntingly beautiful story of Bei-Tong's 1998 internet novel Beijing Comrades (Beijing gushi)[9] gave birth to Stanley Kwan's critically and commercially successful film, Lan Yu (2001).[10] Across the straits, Chu T'ien-wen—who was already arguably the most well-known Taiwan-based contemporary writer in international circles—published her Notes of a Desolate Man (Huangren shouji, 1994), a novel about a gay man's poetic meditations on love, life, sexuality, and loss, during the same period. Notes won prestigious prizes in Taiwan and was translated into English in 2000. Its success crystallizes the electrifying cultural energy and undercurrents in the 1990s' tongzhi *wenxue* created by Lin Bai, Chen Ran, Wang Xiaobo, Cui Zi'en, Qiu Miaojin, Chen Xue, Hong Ling (Lucifer Hung), Chi Ta-wei, Liang Hanyi, Lin Junying, Cao Lijuan, Wu Jiwen, and many others.

While the achievements of the 1990s' *tongzhi wenxue* writers are numerous and formidable, they are often too quickly assimilated into a narrative of emergence that stands in sharp contrast to an earlier era of homosocial richness found in late Qing and early Republican texts. Building on the long tradition of erotic literature from the Ming dynasty, fiction from the Qing period features countless examples of homoerotic relationships. Between Jia Baoyu, the polyamorous protagonist of *The Story of the Stone*, and the boy actors and patrons in *The Precious Mirror for Ranking Flowers*, the Qing dynasty seems to be a prolific font of creative homoerotic energies that is only later interrupted by the turmoil of twentieth-century wars and revolutions, before the resurgence of such literary interests in the 1990s again brought these themes to the fore. By bypassing the 1980s, the standard history of queer Chinese literature implies that communism (and anticommunism) have suppressed the creativity of queer writers; hence, only after the advent of liberalism in postmarket reform PRC and postmartial law Taiwan did queer writers again find a voice and a place in the literary arena.

This chapter discusses Chen Ruoxi's 1986 queer Marxist novel, *Paper Marriage*. By emphasizing the forgotten years of the 1980s in the history of queer Chinese literature, my intention is not to offer a revisionist account in the narratives of queer identity and identification, but to suggest that Marxism and communism have also served as creative sources for queer thinking. While emphasizing the limits of identity and identification as models for constructing queer literary history, I will also propose an alternative reason to consider queer literature: historically, queer writing also embodies anticapitalist thinking. While queer literature no doubt engages questions of identity, it also produces new forms of solidarity, political analysis, and countercultures that are useful for a new geopolitical reading of capitalism. For its provocative imagination of how the injustice of the international division of labor creates an occasion for an unexpected union of two human beings of incompatible sexual orientations, I consider Chen's *Paper Marriage* to be an exemplary work of queer Marxism in the two Chinas. Indeed, no contemporary writer represents the perspective of the two Chinas better than Chen, a Taiwan-born native who immigrated to the PRC in support of Mao's new China. Insofar as her queer stories came out of her encounter with Maoism while living in the PRC during the Cultural Revolution, her fiction shows a critically queer engagement with Chinese Marxism that, I argue, provides the epistemological foundation for the emergence of modern queer subjectivities in Chinese. The novel's rich insights into the interpenetrations of economic and sexual injustices chart a cognitive strategy for unlearning the cartography of the Cold War. These insights and experiences from the 1980s indicate that identity and identification are always intertwined with geopolitics, and that queer literature and sexuality, in turn, provide a powerful framework for contesting consequences of capitalist modernity.

The First Queer Novels

The first two Chinese queer novels, Pai Hsien-yung's *Crystal Boys* (*Niezi*) and Chen Ruoxi's *Paper Marriage* (*Zhihun*), were written in the 1980s. Both were published first in Taiwan, although they were widely circulated and consumed in Hong Kong and mainland China as well. Pai Hsien-yung's *Crystal Boys* (*Niezi*), published in 1983 in Taiwan and in 1988 in mainland China, is commonly recognized as the first modern queer novel in Chinese. This reputation is due to the fact that *Crystal Boys* is the first *canonical* novel to explicitly represent male homosexuality as its main theme—as opposed to earlier works that contain recognizably homoerotic undertones (such as Yu Dafu's writings) or underground works with limited circulation; indeed, *Crystal Boys* is the first full-length novel in Chinese to achieve canonical status because of, not in spite of, its homosexual themes.[11] Prior to *Crystal Boys*, the 1970s saw the publication of several important "mass novels" concerning homosexuality, such as Guangtai's *The Man Who Does Not Want to Be Married* (1976), Xuan Xiaofo's *Outside the Circle* (1976), and Guo Lianghui's *The Third Sex* (1978), although these works are generally considered pulp fiction and never made the kind of impact that Pai's and Chen's works did. A close friend and a classmate of Pai's at National Taiwan University, Chen Ruoxi wrote *Paper Marriage* (*Zhihun*) three years later than *Crystal Boys*. Like Pai's work, *Paper Marriage* was immediately considered a masterpiece, and enjoyed a wide readership in both Taiwan and mainland China.[12] I focus on Chen's work in this chapter because Chen Ruoxi criticism is much less developed in English compared to the scholarship on *Crystal Boys*, although it is worth noticing that the plot of *Paper Marriage* has been made famous worldwide through a loose cinematic variant—Ang Lee's critically acclaimed 1993 feature film, *The Wedding Banquet*.[13] *The Wedding Banquet* receives extensive scholarly discussion in major studies of queer Chinese cinema, such as Song Hwee Lim's *Celluloid Comrades*, and in this sense *Paper Marriage* has also been indirectly canonized as a milestone of queer Chinese culture in English-language criticism. In Chinese scholarship, *Paper Marriage*'s status and impact are undisputed. In *The History of Homosexual Literature*, Mao Feng characterizes *Crystal Boys* and *Paper Marriage* as two foundational texts that introduced a "new humanism" in modern Chinese literature, one that brought not only visibility but also sympathy to a formerly taboo topic.[14] Chu Wei-cheng describes *Paper Marriage* as the forerunner of a new phase of queer literature (1983–93) that began to represent homosexuality as a "social problem."[15]

While critics commonly recognize Chen and Pai as the first authors to make homosexuality an object of high aesthetic representation in modern Chinese literature, little has been said on the connection between their literary efforts and the development of modernism and cultural Marxism in Taiwan. This movement began with the founding of the literary magazine *Modern Literature* (*Xiandai wenxue*) in 1960 by a group of students at National Taiwan University that included Chen Ruoxi, Pai Hsien-yung, and Wang Wenxing. The first parts of *Crystal Boys* were published in *Modern Literature* before the complete text appeared in book form. These students translated the canon of Western modernism (Joyce, Woolf, Faulkner, Camus, Thomas Mann, Beckett, and Kafka) into Chinese and published similar experiments of their own in the magazine. As a result, they are described as foreign-influenced modernists at odds with the *xiangtu* ("nativist" or "rural") writers, who are represented by Chen Yingzhen, Yu Tiancong, and Huang Chunming and historically associated with the journal *Literature Quarterly* (*Wenxue jikan*), a main competitor with *Modern Literature*.[16] The disagreements between the two groups focused on whether literature should follow the aesthetic principle of "art-for-art's sake," or serve as a vehicle for "art-for-life's sake" in its representations of rural life, the lower classes, and social responsibilities. Among the many charges hurled at *Modern Literature* were critiques of its wholesale acceptance of Western aesthetic forms and its lack of attention to socially marginal subjects.

The main figures in the *xiangtu* movement, in particular Chen Ying-zhen, were heavily influenced by Marxism. In 1968, Chen Yingzhen was arrested and sentenced to ten years of imprisonment for publishing journalistic essays and fiction that depict the plight of the rural class, and for participating in a reading group on Marx, Lu Xun, and Marxist authors. The official charge against Chen and other members of the reading group was the spread of communist propaganda.[17] The other members of *Wenxue jikan* were also implicated, for which reason Chen's arrest is also called the "Wenji Incident." Therefore, the debates between *Modern Literature* and *Literature Quarterly* were not simply intellectual disagreements; rather, they were part of the local intellectuals' protracted cultural struggles to work out the relevance of Marxism in anticommunist Taiwan. Although *Modern Literature* became the first venue to provide a literary contemplation on the subjectivity of the modern homosexual character, it is important to note that writers in the modernist group embraced that figure as a response to the challenges posed by the *Literature Quarterly*'s affiliations with Chinese Marxism. In part, these writers created the figure of the persecuted modern homosexual to refute the charge that modernist writing showed no concern for those living on the margins of society. The creation of the modern homosexual was therefore not merely a reflection of a newfound cultural identity or an epistemic change; it was also a result of a dialogue with Chinese Marxism, an answer to the Marxist critique of the depoliticized nature of modernist literature through an example of humanism's and modernism's capacity for representing social differences. Although Pai is not himself a Marxist writer, both he and Chen Ruoxi were heavily influenced by the Marxist critique of the *Literature Quarterly* group, but preferred the aesthetics of modernism and chose to represent the downtrodden from the perspective of sexual difference instead of economic disparity. In this sense, Pai and Chen's project of constructing the homosexual figure in high modernist Chinese literature embodied a dialectically constituted queer Marxism.

The modernist imagination of Chen and Pai converted a vast domain of aberrant sexualities in human cultures—what we might term homosexuality, prostitution, cross-generational love, polygamy, and S/M—into a manageable and describable typology.[18] Insofar as their subject is sexual stigma rather than male homosexuality, Chen's and Pai's literary works are queer rather than gay, articulating a vision consonant with the political arguments of the queer Marxist theorists discussed in chapter two that queerness is not an identity but a constellation of social positions and power relations that the category of homosexuality fails to describe. As is well known, *Crystal Boys* is not just the first modern Chinese novel about same-sex love but also, and equally importantly, a moving depiction of male prostitution, sexual awakenings, and erotic experiences outside the purview of the heterosexual family.[19] Liu Jun, Pai's biographer, comments that "through *Crystal Boys*, Pai successfully legitimated the existence of homosexuals, proving their humanity to society. Pai performed a cultural translation: Li Qing and his friends transform from sons into bad sons and then finally into sons again, and in this process Pai hints at the possibility that homosexuals can be understood by and integrated into mainstream society."[20] Following Liu, we could say that Pai's novel is and is not about homosexuals. It may be more accurate to say that Pai is more interested in depicting the friction between human sexual diversity and the requirements of the Confucian procreative heterosexual family. Li Qing's exile from his biological family and his discovery of a second family—the "queer nation" (*wo men de wang guo*) of young male prostitutes who are similarly banished from their networks of biological kinship—deconstructs the very idea of family from a queer perspective. This perspective does not valorize homosexuality per se; rather, it highlights the intersections between all kinds of nonnormative experiences and expressions, such as male prostitution.

Crystal Boys hence contains vestiges of the same kind of resistance to liberal pluralist solutions of social conflicts through identity politics theorized by the queer Marxists in chapter two. More significantly, however, both *Crystal Boys* and *Paper Marriage* are transnational tales that are centrally concerned with the geopolitics of the Cold War. As such, these texts also offer an opportunity to rethink the relation between Marxism and queer cultures, and contribute to the development of queer Marxism. It was no accident that queer Chinese literature emerged in the critical years of the 1970s, when the Cultural Revolution, as a failed attempt to regulate Chinese cultural expressions according to the requirements of industrial socialism, provoked a rethinking of queer Marxism. Chen's and Pai's seminal representations of alternative sexualities did not emerge in a historical vacuum; rather, queer modernist literature came into being in the context of an international political discourse that conflated China with communism and presented both as "global problems." In one of the earliest treatments of Chinese literature available in English, C. T. Hsia identifies Pai's writings as one of his three examples of a collective "obsession with China," a characteristic Hsia attributes to all literature from Taiwan during this period.[21] Hsia's interpretation is continuous with a long-standing tendency to read Pai's works, particularly *Crystal Boys*, as political allegories. Pai's *Crystal Boys*, whose Chinese title (*Niezi*) literally translates as "bad sons," has been interpreted again and again as an allegorical representation of the tensions between mainland China, the authoritative, unrelenting father figure, and the renegade province of Taiwan, the bad homosexual son.[22]

Popular in the 1980s and '90s, these allegorical readings were motivated by a desire to sanitize a gay novel written by a highly respected author by reinterpreting its homosexual contents as coded messages for loftier themes such as anticommunism. While the allegorical readings no longer hold sway, their ubiquity in Pai Hsien-yung criticism until recent years highlights the difficulty of interpreting modern sexual discourses outside the political geography of the Cold War, which continues to circumscribe the writings of queer authors of varying origins. Whereas Pai was born in Guilin, China and did not relocate to Taiwan until 1952, Chen is a native Taiwanese who had never set foot in mainland China prior to her Cultural Revolution experiences. This anomaly shows that while Marxism was a common concern to early modernist queer Chinese writings, these connections apply to Chinese authors born inside and outside mainland China. Whether pathologized as obsession, misread as national allegory, or identified as fatherland and origin—the signifier of China fueled the imagination of a generation of queer writers and carried an emotional weight that could not be explained away as a psychological aberration. As my discussion of Chen's personal transformation from ardent Maoist to famed cold warrior below will show, Chinese Marxism has an overdetermined and heterogeneous relation to the birth of queer sinophone creativity. Chen's desire to destabilize the identities of Chinese Marxism has a distinctive influence on her representation of queer relationships. Conversely, queer feelings helped Chen reevaluate her relationship to communist China, transforming its ideological signification from an admirable classless society to red scare, and then from red scare to a positive understanding of cultural roots, emotional ties, and shared beliefs that sustain life in the sinophone world.[23] Chen's creative journey offers an exemplary instance of queer Marxism, a transformation of Marxism from communist bureaucracy to a critical method of reading the social field of power.

The Marxist Roots of Modern Queer Writings

In the current scholarly field, Chen is almost never identified as a queer writer. One simple reason is that Chen Ruoxi wrote her novel one full decade before the *tongzhi wenxue* movement, which partially explains her exclusion from the canon of modern Chinese queer literature. The more important reason, however, is the political reception of her work during the Cold War era. Before *Paper Marriage*, Chen was first and foremost known as an internationally acclaimed anticommunist writer who launched her literary career through the "China question."[24] In 1966, Chen, a native Taiwanese, made a shocking decision to "repatriate" (*hui gui*) to mainland China in support of Mao's Cultural Revolution. In her recently published autobiography, Chen emphasizes that she made that decision while she was studying in the United States, not in Taiwan, and that her romanticization of Mao's China was a reaction against rampant capitalism in the United States. She was inspired by many of the 60s' radical movements against the failures of capitalist democracies: the antiwar movement against US imperialism in Vietnam, the free speech movement, the beginning of the environmental movement with the publication of Rachel Carson's *Silent Spring* in 1962, and, finally, Taiwan's White Terror in 1964.[25] Chen was also greatly affected by the sexual liberation movement that started in Berkeley—the setting of *Paper Marriage*—which convinced her of the necessity of articulating sexual struggles to other political horizons such as the antiwar movement. In the United States, Chen began participating in a Marxist reading group that radicalized her politics. This history shows that Marxism and queer sexuality have always been intertwined in her imagination, and that her eventual turn to Maoism and queer subcultures was animated by the same political passion. Insofar as Chen discovered Marxism—or rather, Mao's China—in the United States, and insofar as this discovery turned out to be the historical condition for the emergence of the homosexual subject in modern Chinese litera-ture, Chen's aesthetic project serves as an example of the multilayered, transnationally mediated nature of queer Marxism.

Chen repatriated to China with radical socialist longings. Her first day in Mao's China, however, quickly revealed the gap between her uto-pian vision and the actual political practice of the PRC. She was humili-ated at Customs: her collection of western literature was confiscated as "imperialist ideology," her collection of classical Chinese literature was declared "remnants of feudal decadence," and, finally, a cherished pic-ture she took of two shirtless male aboriginal peasants was tossed away as "pornography."[26] This traumatic incident convinced her of the dan-gers of a Marxism devoid of an understanding of human sexuality. Years later, when Chen began writing *Paper Marriage*, her goal was precisely to reclaim both Marxism and sexuality from their distorted use in the PRC bureaucracy and to argue for their mutual compatibility.

In 1973, Chen became disillusioned with Maoist politics and, after some struggles, obtained permission to leave communist China. Like Arthur Koestler and other "ex-communists" had done for Stalinism, Chen quickly became a bona fide interpreter of the "real China" to West-ern observers. In the opinion of the influential China historian Frederic Wakeman—who taught at the University of California, Berkeley and served on advisory boards for the US government—Chen's fictional sto-ries gave the West "an insider's voice" from the "lost years" of Chi-nese historiography.[27] Chen published a series of short stories in the 1970s based on her experiences in China. In 1978, a collection was published in English, titled *The Execution of Mayor Yin and Other Stories from the Great Proletarian Cultural Revolution*.[28] Although some of her earlier works (including *Spirit Calling* and *The Old Man and Other Stories*) have also been translated into English, *The Execution of Mayor Yin* remains Chen's most famous work to date in international circles. Marketed in English as stories "from" (not "about") the Cultural Revolution—a word Chen never used in the Chinese original—*The Execution of Mayor Yin* presents Chen as a survivor of what Howard Goldblatt describes as "a society gone terribly wrong."[29] As an "authentic native" whose fictional writings were largely interpreted as historiography and reportage, Chen alone "comprised a significant part of what Western readers knew about Mao's Cultural Revolution."[30] Perry Link praises Chen for providing "unique windows into a mysterious China," "the first signs the outside world had of the catastrophic failure of the Maoist experiments of the 1950s and 1960s."[31]

Whereas Chen's Cultural Revolution stories explore a China shrouded in Oriental inscrutability, distorted by communist irrationality, and badly in need of social scientific explanations, her queer novel continues this documentary interest but transforms its object into the homosexual secret.[32] After the queer novel's protagonist learns of her homosexual husband's sexual history, Chen has her character scream with excitement, "I have discovered a new continent!" (54). The language of "discovery" emphasizes the gap between the heterosexual narrator's life experience and the narrative object of homosexuality, whose secrets the novel brings to light in a manner similar to the Cultural Revolution stories. Written in the first-person voice, *Paper Marriage* takes the form of a fragmentary diary of a heterosexual woman. This unusual narrative framework creates the impression of an unbiased sociological observation, skirting traces of novelistic mediation and artificiality. The reader in turn becomes the story's unintended recipient, who may have discovered the diary in another place and time. More specifically, the diary-form of the narrative presents itself as an objective, unmediated record of a heterosexual female woman's encounters with the homosexual community in an anthropological scene of "original contact." Indeed, the structure of the diary-novel conveys the impression of a first-person witness account similar to Chen's Cultural Revolution stories. This continuity indicates that the emergence of modern queer subjectivities has important and often unacknowledged roots in Cold War Orientalism, and that the same group of writers responsible for shaping an entire generation's perceptions of communist China has also played a key role in the production of new sexual knowledge. In this sense, the legitimation of homosexuality as an object of high literary interest was historically predicated on Chen's cultural authority on communist China, while both conversations contained important critiques of liberal capitalism.

Strictly speaking, *Paper Marriage* is not a gay novel, since its primary narrative focus lies on the transnational love between a heterosexual woman from the PRC and an American gay man. By presenting a loving partnership that crosses boundaries of sexual orientation and national affiliation, Chen develops an alternative form of "cultural communism" that deconstructs the relationship between Marxism and homosexuality. Chen shows that queer sexuality is not diametrically opposed to communism, since queer sexuality compels a rethinking of human community, intimacy, and connectedness. Rather than serving as a synonym for homosexuality, queerness for Chen refers to the recognition that human bonds, intimacy, desires, alliances, and sexual encounters always exceed identity categories *and* geopolitical boundaries. Chen's work exposes the failures of sexual categories—heterosexuality or homosexuality—as reliable indices of human fulfillment and attachment, while contesting the ethicality of the institution of citizenship. Her work indicates an intimacy between the queer critique of sexual identity and the Marxist critique of national borders. The brilliance of Chen's queer Marxism lies in her ability to demonstrate the mutual dependency between these two forms of ethical inquiry.

To develop her queer Marxist critique, Chen deliberately chooses a transnational setting. Although Chen herself was born in Taiwan, the literary characters of *Paper Marriage* are American and mainland Chinese rather than Taiwanese. The protagonist, Pingping, is originally from Shanghai, while the story takes place in Oakland, Berkeley, and San Francisco. The story's setting is not unlike the author's own background as a displaced, diasporic person with life experiences in Taiwan, mainland China, Hong Kong, Canada, and the United States. Sean, Pingping's American homosexual husband, expresses a transcultural fascination with China that inflects and reshapes the queer narrative. After he becomes ill with AIDS, Sean plans a projected (but never realized) trip to China with Pingping. The dream of China quickly becomes the "only force that keeps [him] alive" in his battle with AIDS (228). In fact, for Sean, the history of communist China and the future of the queer community are allegorically identical. He believes that the Red Guards are the counterparts of the radical student activists and sexual dissidents of 1960s' Berkeley, and he posits a homology between the Cultural Revolution and the future liberation of homosexuals (67–68). In Pingping's own view, however, China is negatively associated with poverty, overpopulation, and communist persecution of intellectuals (217).

The arc of the story as a whole does not indicate which interpretation of Chinese Marxism is correct. The oscillation between utopian and dystopian projections makes it difficult to fix the queer novel's relation to China, but the real interpretive difficulty posed by this novel involves our habitual tendency to read literature as a reflection of a nationally and territorially defined culture, where culture is in turn understood as a certain stage in a global "history of sexuality." The novel's ability to use the political signifier of China to foreground the mutually constitutive relation between political economy and sexuality makes an important contribution to queer theory. The types of discourses produced by Chen's inaugural queer novel do not map onto discrete cultures that are isomorphic with juridical territories. Rather, her attention to sexual matters shows us how borders are crossed and transgressed at all times, how rules of kinship are unstable and fraught with internal contradictions, and why new and unanticipated alliances need to be forged in transnational or nonculturally specific ways.

As a historical artifact from the 1980s before the coinage of "tongzhi" and other contemporary queer discourses and political movements, *Paper Marriage* stands as a surprisingly early example of an interventionist tactic for new coalitions and imaginations across political divisions. If the history of the queer Chinese novel does not reflect a unilinear development from same-sex eroticism to a modern homosexual identity within a strictly national context, it becomes important to ask what exactly is instantiated by this queer, but heterosexual, romance between a gay man and a straight Chinese woman. Why was this foundational queer novel about male homosexuality written by a woman, and why is it set in America rather than the PRC or the ROC? To a reader who expects literary history and national history to be congruent, this work will appear as a triple impersonation—an inauthentic report by a Taiwanese woman on the psychology of a homosexual man in the voice of a mainland Chinese woman. Similarly, a reader in search of a gradually unfolding modern and self-affirmative gay and lesbian identity in the Foucauldian sense will be troubled by the novel's punishing attitude toward AIDS and nonmonogamists. A nationalist critic will have trouble reconciling the novel's progressive politics with its reactionary portrayal of Pingping's quest for a green card in her pursuit of the American dream. Indeed, this perplexing novel is queer in multiple senses, posing (as good literature tends to do) more questions than answers.

By presenting one of contemporary Chinese literature's first homosexual stories as a transnational encounter, Chen's novel raises the question of whether there is a history of sexuality to be written for China. Foucauldian historians of sexuality do not always acknowledge that the construction of homosexuality as an embodied identity requires, first and foremost, the construction of a location. In Chen's work, the modern homosexual is created through a "discovery" of America and China as contrasting locations. America is presented as a land of economic opportunities and sexual decadence, where a curious "lifestyle" called homosexuality and material wealth coexist, whereas China is imagined in contradictory and heterogeneous ways: as the utopian future of queer people; as shared beliefs and rituals uniting populations in the ROC, PRC, and the Chinese diaspora in America; as communism; and as a culture of food. Through the marriage between heterosexual woman and homosexual man, China and America dialectically define each other's conceptual borders. Here, Chen stages queerness as a revolutionary practice that connects these two distant locations and makes them intimate again. Unlike her earlier anticommunist fictions, *Paper Marriage* characterizes queer desire as precisely what disrupts the Cold War binary opposition between Chinese communism and American capitalism. This transnational tale allows Chen to present queer feelings as a powerful framework for the analysis of the material institutions that organize birth-accidents into citizenships and rights. *Paper Marriage* is not a celebration of the free union of two people of incompatible sexual orientations in a social vacuum. Rather, *Paper Marriage* delineates important historical reasons queer struggles can also become anticapitalist thinking. The injustice of the economic disparity between China and the United States is the primary cause for Sean and Pingping's paper marriage, but the system of transnational migrant labor also produces an unexpected alliance between these individuals whose sexual orientations alone would have brought them together. Sean and Pingping's union is a private solution of the problem of the international division of labor that deprives Pingping of the right to work in the United States on account of her birth in a different nation-state. The system is also, of course, heterosexist in nature, which dictates that only persons who happen to be born within a US territory, or else married through a heterosexual union to those who were, are entitled to the privileges of citizenship. With their "marriage of convenience," Pingping and Sean stage a protest against the institutions of heterosexual marriage and citizenship at once. The novel presents an argument for the intersections of queer feelings and antinationalism, showing that the confluence of the two can produce new forms of solidarity, political analysis, and countercultures that are best termed queer Marxism.

The diary-novel of *Paper Marriage* encompasses details in Pingping's life from her marriage to Sean to his death from AIDS. While working as an undocumented immigrant at a Chinese restaurant in California, Pingping experiences sexual harassment by her boss. After Pingping rejects his sexual advances several times, her boss reports her to the Immigration and Naturalization Service (INS) in retaliation. Pingping receives the deportation letter immediately. While literally standing at a crossroads, she thinks about the disgrace of her impending return to Shanghai, where she was once forced to live in a crowded dormitory with other women factory workers (217). Sean, an American man she has met only once through her Chinese friends, miraculously drives by at this point and offers to marry her for free. Assuming that the fake marriage will "last half a year at most" (13), Pingping starts living with Sean and meeting other gay men and lesbians, including Sean's promiscuous boyfriend, who eventually infects Sean with AIDS. The beginning of the novel emphasizes Pingping's ignorance of and curiosity about gay people and their lifestyles. While Sean is out clubbing, Pingping takes an uninvited tour of Sean's bedroom. Much to her disappointment, Sean's room is not "decorated with pictures of naked men and strewn with men's sexy lingerie on a pink bed sheet as she has imagined" (17). Other discoveries and self-corrections ensue. Over the course of the novel, Pingping comes to understand the complexity, range of preferences, and internal differences in the gay community. She learns that some are monogamous and others polyamorous, and that gay life is inflected by differences in gender, class, color, nationality, political views, masculine/feminine self-stylizations, preferred sexual positions, dietary regimen, and religion (206). "Sean's article in defense of monogamy in *The Advocate* made me ponder the complexity and diversity of human nature. In my eyes, he is a liberal, even a radical; but to his own kind, he becomes a conservative" (128–29).

The immigrant narrative—a material tale of labor and survival—takes a surprising turn and becomes a queer narrative. Pingping's need of a green card becomes an unexpected introduction to the queer community. In the first part of the novel, Sean appears as a highly exoticized and strangely benevolent American character. His American citizenship promises to be the solution to Pingping's dilemma, and the relationship between the two characters signifies a misrecognition of the structural roots of overdetermined problems. Sean's offer to marry a Chinese immigrant he barely knows, a highly improbable act of generosity, further accentuates the sociopolitical context of queer desire, placing the novel in the context of late Cold War Sino-American political relations and representing America as both the cause of an injurious exclusion and the means for overcoming it. As unrealistic as this plot development may sound, the arrival of the benevolent (American) homosexual character on the Chinese literary scene is a significant event, since Chen's formula departs from earlier negative stereotypes and representations that associated homosexuality with cross-dressing, prostitution, suicidal tendencies, and gender identity confusion. The romanticism of the homosexualized allegory of postwar American aid is countered by the bleakness of the AIDS narrative in the second half of the novel. Reflecting what Gayle Rubin has called "the domino theory of sexual peril," the novel draws a punitive equation between sexual promiscuity, homosexuality, and AIDS.[33] The sharp change in tone has perplexed many critics, who have characterized Paper Marriage as the embodiment of a strange kind of "sympathetic homophobia."[34]

The inclusion of the AIDS plot, however, can also be seen as a strategic resolution of the tension between cultural particularism and legal formalism. AIDS offers a convenient ending for the novel because Chen needs to create a morally acceptable plot that will allow Pingping to pay back her emotional and material debt to Sean. Sean's assistance to Pingping in her plight as an undocumented immigrant cannot be represented as simply gratuitous in a novel written in the late Cold War years, when it was increasingly clear that Taiwan was materially and politically dependent on the United States for its continued existence (just as Pingping is on Sean). By afflicting the male protagonist with a fatal disease, Chen allows the two to switch roles—the patron becomes the patient, while the refugee becomes the savior. The relation then becomes a "fair trade" between Pingping's able-bodiedness and Sean's

American citizenship.[35] Originally, Pingping is the unassimilable alien, the embodied cultural particularity of China seeking to be admitted into the universalism of America. By the end of the novel, her character exposes the emptiness of this distinction.

Chen begins the novel by setting up China as a sinophone lifeworld of shared customs and beliefs among the Chinese immigrants. China is represented as a close-knit social network of friends and families (laozhong), marked by a constant exchange of gossip, food, cash, and letters between Shanghai, Taipei, Hong Kong, and San Francisco. Pingping's introduction to Sean is explicitly represented as the benefit of her social capital in the diasporic Chinese community, in which the need for survival overrides the political differences between Taiwan and the PRC. Although several of the minor characters are from Taiwan and Hong Kong, Chen groups all of them under the sign of cultural China defined in contrast to America as a relatively fixed set of rituals, family ties, and social values.

The unitary notion of China is felt in the rhythms of everyday life—the preparations of food, clothing, and different forms of manual labor and emotional attachment. The novel's concern with China manifests itself in its strategic choice of the wedding ceremony as the opening chapter. Because a heterosexual wedding, as Sedgwick shows, is a highly idiomatic, ritualistic, performative, and therefore culturally specific institution, the choice to begin the novel with a wedding allows its two dominant questions—what is China and what is a queer relationship—to come into view simultaneously.[36] The wedding scene then makes it possible for the novel to introduce an assortment of idioms that define cultural China, starting with food, while placing the question of the relationship between Pingping's queer marriage and cultural China at the center of the narrative. Both homemade Chinese food and professional catering are provided at the wedding, but Chen emphasizes that "no one touched the restaurant food" because of the superior taste of Chinese cooking (2). We learn that Pingping's aunt (Guma) disapproves of the sham green card marriage, but she "smiles for the first time since the Minister pronounced them husband and wife" when an American guest compliments her on her dishes (2). The paper marriage scheme, which begins after all with Pingping's racialized labor at a Chinese restaurant, comes full circle as the novel reinforces the connection between China and food with the addition of a host of gastronomically inspired details of Chineseness: for example, the Chinese invention of tofu is mentioned twice (25, 112). Pingping's pride in tofu is contrasted with her outrage at Sean's misunderstanding of soy sauce as a Japanese invention, a mistake she attributes to the problem of the Chinese national character: "No wonder he thought soy sauce was first made by the Japanese. We Chinese have never learned the power of advertising. Many of our inventions have been put on Japanese labels and sold as their own. . . . When are we Chinese going to learn to promote ourselves?" (220). The striking emphasis on Chinese specificity suggests that Chen's queer novel is shaped by a historical need to give an account of what cultural China means, if only in stereotypical terms. The important analytical question then arises: why is this inaugural novel about queer feelings and identifications so invested in giving an account of China?

After introducing the Chinese as a people with a special connection to the culinary arts, Chen quickly turns the wedding ceremony into a scene of gift-giving "the Chinese way," namely in cash. After the ceremony, Auntie and Cousin try to force three hundred US dollars and a jade bracelet on Pingping, which results in the usual polite protests, tears, and remarks about the protagonist's dead mother. The jade bracelet Pingping puts on in this opening scene turns out to be only the beginning of a series of objects and labels that will cement the link between her gender and her Chineseness against her will. To further develop the theme of cultural differences, Chen has Pingping commit a faux pas. When the minister asks her if she will take Sean as her lawfully wedded husband, she answers "yes" in English instead of "I do." The signifying elements of the ceremony's hyperbolic Westernness—the exchange of wedding vows, the Christian church, the minister's pause at Pingping's nonstandard wedding vows—are followed by scenes that are hyperbolically Chinese.

For her INS interview, Pingping decides to wear "something feminine," which earns her an offensive compliment from Sean: "You look very pretty in American clothes" (143). To Pingping, the characterization of her "feminine" outfit as "American" clothes misidentifies a self-stylization of gender as cultural mimicry. Pingping, however, does not try to correct Sean's confusion of her gender self-stylization with reified cultural difference. Instead, she considers the mistake itself to be representative of a certain culture: the American national character: "Like *most Americans*, Sean thinks that China has never evolved past the era of Blue Ants. But prejudice and ignorance cannot be dispelled overnight.

I decided not to correct him. Instead, I tried to act like an American—when someone pays you a compliment, don't try to be modest; just say 'thank you'" (143, emphasis added). While the colorful stereotype of China as a yellow peril of millions of blue ants working under the red flag is used to explain a general failure of American culture, the Americanness of this mistake is contrasted with Pingping's self-perception of the Americanness of her own response. Pingping, too, mistranslates the discussion of gender into the problematic of culture.

While *Paper Marriage* is a foundational queer novel in Chinese literature, its historical mission of constructing the homosexual subject is constantly interrupted by a desire to say what is Chinese and not Chinese. That desire, in turn, is complicated by labor issues, which create a productive tension that defines Chen's queer Marxist practice. Indeed, the amount of textual attention to the comparison between American and Chinese cultures and their "modes of production" in a text that purports to be concerned with homosexuality is striking. The novel attempts to define cultural differences through categories of primary labor and subsistence—food, language, clothes, and shelter—whereby Pingping's gender and sexuality become inextricably bound up with these concerns.

Chen employs the vehicle of the fake marriage plot to connect the themes of labor and sexuality. Fearing that their communications might be under INS surveillance, Pingping decides to withhold the "truth" about her marriage from her own family in China, while Sean is too distanced from his own divorced parents (which is a common stereotype of Americans in Chinese fiction) to mention his new marriage to them. These strategic decisions on the part of the characters allow the novel to construct binarized responses from the respective parents of the newlyweds. Both Pingping's parents and Sean's mother eventually find out. Assuming that his daughter has actually "married a foreigner" and "forgotten her roots so soon," Pingping's father writes an angry letter accusing her of "bringing disgrace to the entire family" (87). By contrast, when Sean's mother calls and finds out that she is speaking to a woman who self-identifies as "Mrs. Murphy," the American mother is overwhelmed with joy (19). Pingping writes: "American parents are so forgiving. When they find out their sons got married without inviting them to the wedding, instead of getting angry, they ask you if you are willing to accept a belated wedding gift" (20)—which turns out to be a microwave. The microwave returns to the first scene of food, but denotes a different organization of labor and temporality: whereas the novel's opening scene connects Chineseness with the preparation of food (Guma's cooking) and with Pingping's racialized labor at the restaurant, the microwave encodes Sean's mother's Americanness by associating it with prepackaged food and thoughtless consumption in the compressed space and time of modernity.[37] It is hard to say whether Sean's mother's deliriously happy reaction indicates the differences between American and Chinese cultures, as Pingping assumes, or actually her homophobic celebration of her son's conversion back to heterosexuality. Pingping's own interpretation leans toward the former, which she further emphasizes by noting Sean's mother's failure to speak Chinese correctly: "She said, 'Welcome to the Murphy family, Bing Bing.' She can't pronounce 'Pingping'" (20). For Pingping, the question of Sean's homosexuality repeatedly becomes an occasion to reflect on her own Chineseness.

The creation of stereotypical Chinese characters—laced with sentimentality, family values, ethnocentrism, and secret kitchen recipes—is, however, deconstructed by the novel's attention to queer matters. Pingping's queer union disarticulates the linguistic and social elements that the novel compresses into the signifier of China. As the novel progresses, China's claim to distinctiveness is overridden and negated by the advent of AIDS. World-shattering and border-erasing, AIDS returns a narrative that began with cultural incommensurability to the vulnerability of the human body prior to its cultural markings. After her Chinese friends discover that Sean is HIV-positive, their stereotypically Chinese qualities suddenly disappear. Pingping's decision to stay married to Sean alienates her from her friends in the Chinese community, who are uniformly anxious to distance themselves from anyone living with an AIDS patient. The food-loving, communally living, blood-related, and family-oriented Chinese characters begin to disavow their "blood-is-thicker-than-water" connections to Pingping. The ease with which a supposedly unshakable solidarity falls apart in the second half of the novel offers a sharp contrast to the initial representation of Chinese culture as a unique kinship structure of mutual obligations and shared history.

This contrast is even more striking on the level of the novel's structure. The essentialist construction of Chinese culture through tofu, soy sauce, and family values is undermined by defecting Chinese characters who abandon Pingping and, by extension, the novel's self-Orientalizing project as well. Once those characters stop treating Pingping as "family" because of her connections to a person living with AIDS, they are immediately removed from the plotline. The strategic and precise excision of the Chinese characters from the novel at the transitional juncture between Orientalism and Pingping's awakening queer consciousness reveals the constructedness of Chineseness. The Chinese characters are elaborately constructed, but they also prove to be surprisingly disposable. Chen's textual organization offers more insight into her historical concerns with Chineseness than the novel's manifest thematic issues do. In the second half of the novel, Chen's characters are developed in relation to Sean's illness. Sean's American friends—Julian and his estranged mother—begin to assume a greater role. The criterion for narrative inclusion changes from a particularizing language of cultural affinity (China) to a universalizing language of human life. A communal solidarity through long-distance or diasporic identification with China is undone by its own terms. The last minor Chinese character to disappear from the novel is Mable, an "ABC" (American-born Chinese). Mable's betrayal is particularly disappointing to Pingping, because Pingping believes that ABCs embody the "synthesis of American and Chinese virtues" (225). The strategic positioning of the most Americanized Chinese character as the last one among the laozhong to exit the novel ensures that the textual disappearance of these characters is keyed to their degrees of Chineseness or Americanness.

The seemingly essentialist construction of culture in the first half of the novel turns out to be a narrative ruse to expose the fragility of cultural essentialism, which the novel critiques by representing AIDS as a queer issue with which the Chinese characters fail to sympathize.[38] *Paper Marriage*, in other words, deliberately creates an expectation of an essentialist discourse of China in order to thwart it. Pingping's odyssey from persecuted illegal immigrant to permanent resident is represented, temporally and causally, as the unlearning of her heteronormative assumptions about the institution of marriage. Initially, both Pingping and Sean assume that a marriage, or the family, is the site where procreation, sexual pleasure, shared bank accounts, jointly filed taxes, emotional repair, companionship, and social obligations line up perfectly with each other. By the end of the novel, Pingping obtains her green card as planned, along with an unexpected real husband. She realizes that love between two human beings, sexual object choice, and financial responsibilities do not always have to converge, as the institution of heterosexual marriage dictates. She begins as a homophobic character wishing to "convert" Sean back to heterosexuality and help him recover from "his addiction to that kind of sinful lifestyle" (45). By Sean's deathbed, she has learned to disaggregate love, support, and emotional bonds from her partner's procreative choice, gender, and sexual orientation. The queer novel therefore has a dual focus: it is both a story of an immigrant who sheds her Chinese nationality through a marriage in a legal sense and a story about a heterosexual person who sheds her homophobia through the same marriage in a spiritual sense. If this landmark queer text collapses Pingping's nationality and heterosexism into one and the same transformation, the desire this novel narrates, and the histories that gave rise to it, cannot be facilely translated back into a calculus of the presence and absence of a modern Chinese homosexual identity. Rather, it is a textual instantiation of the mutual transformation of the discourse of China and the discourse of sexuality.

Chen's refined literary technique manifests in the studied casualness of her prose. *Paper Marriage* begins with Pingping and Sean's exchange of Christian wedding vows and ends with Sean's death. Its narrative structure is an ironization of the marriage vow, initially taken by a heterosexual immigrant and a homosexual man to "cheat the immigration system." At the beginning of the novel, Sean and Pingping promise to take each other as husband and wife until "death do them part." After Pingping receives her green card, Sean offers to divorce her so she can find her own romantic prospect, but the discovery of Sean's HIV-positive status convinces her to stay in the marriage in order to take care of Sean. Then, she falls in love with the dying gay man. The death of Sean from AIDS is also the death of the novel, that is, the termination of the fictional diarist Pingping. After his death, Pingping is overcome with her loss and grief. Her writing voice ceases, and the paper marriage—that is, the novel *Paper Marriage*—comes to an end. In other words, Sean's death is the demise of Pingping's fictional persona, the moment where the "I" and *Paper Marriage* finally part company. The unexpected literalization of the economically motivated lie, "till death do us part," makes the paper marriage the only true marriage in the book.

Chen clearly intends for *Paper Marriage* to serve as a queer-materialist critique of the institutions of heterosexual marriage and citizenship. Pingping and Sean's queer marriage turns out to be more meaningful and more fulfilling than any "real" marriage in the eyes of the law or procreative heterosexuality. Sean confirms the emotional truth of his queer marriage. On two different occasions, Sean tells his friends that he is truly glad he is finally married (141, 178). Here, Chen's novel offers a surprisingly early argument for unconventional marriages that prefigure contemporary queer theories of the need to dissociate procreative heterosexuality from domestic partnership.[39] It demonstrates that any two (or any number) of human beings who choose to cohabitate and share their rights and obligations can enjoy a fulfilling relationship, whether they are same-sex partners, sisters, friends, or relatives.[40] Sean and Pingping do not intend to be married in the conventional sense, but their marriage turns out to be more real and more meaningful than the ones based on sexual exclusivity, sanctioned by religion, and idealized by the media. In contrast to the unintended but successful union between the gay man and the heterosexual woman, Chen deliberately includes a panorama of failed relationships in the story and spends a great deal of time developing their details of discord. These include failed marriages (Rongfang), estranged married couples (Pingping's cousin), a woman's disappointment in dating a younger man (Pingping's friend Shangguan), divorce (Pingping's ESL [English as a Second Language] classmate from Hong Kong and Sean's ex-wife May make their first appearances in the novel as divorcées; Sean's mother Patience is married three times), and even domestic violence (Jean is abused by her alcoholic husband). In the end, Sean acknowledges Pingping as his true wife—not just legal or convenient, but "beloved." The very last scene in the novel is a conversation between Pingping and her lawyer after Sean's death, in which Pingping tries "futilely" to explain her "real relationship to the deceased," who has left all his worldly assets to his "beloved wife." The lawyer responds coolly that he is "only capable of answering questions related to the law," and "Sean's will is entirely legal" (372–73). The novel ends on a poignant note, drawing the reader's attention to the distinction between the "legal" meaning of the marriage, which is now imposed upon Pingping (together with Sean's assets and the privileges of American citizenship) despite her protests, and the "human," inexplicable meaning of marriage in Pingping's life. The novel ends, in other words, with the failure of language in the face of a heterogeneity effect that can only be called "queer." The ending of the story is, of course, the terminus of another event—our reading of a tale called *Paper Marriage*. Pingping's inability to explain the titular event also signifies another order of textual silence, the impossibility of narrative closure. Is the novel about the economic inequality between citizens of different nationalities or about homosexuality? Does it endorse or critique heteronormative privileges? By making the novel's ending coincide with Pingping's linguistic failure, Chen characterizes "paper marriage"/*Paper Marriage* as a richly ambiguous idea.

The association of the queer with unspeakability is, finally, reinforced by the insertion of an enigmatic episode before the formal ending of the novel. The very last diary entry, which takes place after Pingping's meeting with the lawyer, is a short note on the unexpected suicide of Pingping and Sean's friend Julian. The novel explains neither the motive of the suicide nor the event's relevance to the main plot. Pingping concludes that she can only mourn the premature passing of their friend in silence, and gives up the diary-keeping for good. The novel ends with pain, inarticulateness, and enigmas, leaving the reader with a profound sense of the emptiness and meaninglessness of the immigration law its principal characters have been combating since the beginning of the tale.

A Queer Discovery of Geopolitical Differences

Stylistically, Chen's diary-novel turned out to be a formative precedent for several influential queer Chinese novels, including two groundbreaking, scintillating works—Qiu Miaojin's *The Crocodile's Journal* (1994) and Chu T'ien-wen's *Notes of a Desolate Man* (1994), both of which take the same narrative form, a first-person diary of the protagonist. This model's influence is also discernible in Lin Bai's *One Person's War* (1994), Chen Ran's *Private Life* (1996), and Bei-Tong's *Beijing Comrades*. Chen Ruoxi's stylistic choice also hearkens back to important literary predecessors such as Jean Genet's *The Thief's Journal*. The confessional mode narrative frame Chen helped popularize for queer literature dispenses with third-person omniscient narration and creates the poetic impression of "language overheard." The privileged mode of modern Chinese queer writing emphasizes motifs of confession and secrecy, which are derived in part from a long-standing perception of China as a form of interiority shrouded in real and metaphoric barriers—the Iron Curtain,[41] the Forbidden Palace, the Great Wall,[42] socialist policies of delinking from world trade, and the imperial attitude of the Qing Court toward the West.

In Chen Ruoxi criticism, scholars consider her prose style an integral component of her thematic interests. Chen's use of a candid stream of consciousness, delivered in a simple, straightforward prose, has been cited as part of her unique ability to unveil the realities of a mysterious Communist country. Fan Luoping notes that Chen's fiction has an evocative power that produces the reality it represents through a characteristically plain, unadorned style.[43] Expressing his admiration for Chen's ability to translate the experience of victimization into literature, Yang Hanzhi describes these stories as a "dagger made of flesh and blood"; Wei Ziyun similarly calls them a "testimony of blood and tears."[44] Some critics, however, insist that Chen's queer novel and her Cultural Revolution stories embody different styles. Yang Changnian, for example, considers *Paper Marriage* to be "fiction," while the Cultural Revolution stories are "realism." As a result, Yang claims that *Paper Marriage* is an inferior work compared to her "earlier brilliance."[45] In David Der-wei Wang's opinion, Chen "has not written a great work since *The Execution of Mayor Yin*," but precisely for the opposite reason: her depiction of the Chinese diaspora in America is of journalistic interest (*xinwen xing*) rather than aesthetic interest (*wenxue xing*).[46] For Wang, *Paper Marriage* contains too much realism.

In many ways, *Paper Marriage* is an heir to the exposé literature on Chinese communism. Significantly, the Cultural Revolution itself is mentioned several times in the novel. The first bonding moment between Sean and Pingping is a conversation on the similarities between the 1960s' countercultures in the United States and the Cultural Revolution in China (65–68). Sean, like the novel's author herself in the 1960s, likens Mao's Cultural Revolution to the sexual liberation movement in Berkeley. Pingping is attracted to this interpretation of the Cultural Revolution as a sexual revolution, and dissident sexuality itself as a revolution in culture. A shared interpretation of queer feelings as "revolution" allows these two people, born on different sides of the Pacific Ocean, to imagine themselves as belonging to the same history. The most significant representation of the Cultural Revolution, however, is the novel's metafictional dialogue with another diary. As Pingping recounts in her diary, her brother Yihe was persecuted by the Communists during the Cultural Revolution because of a diary:

> When our house was confiscated during the Cultural Revolution, Yihe's diary was seized and transcribed for all to see. Because its contents were too rich and too real, not only did the diary get Yihe into trouble, poor Mom was denounced as having "ideas of the capitalist class" and "encouraging children to become rich and powerful." My own diary only talked about the weather and other trivia so it was tossed away . . . but I was so scared and scarred that I decided to never keep a diary again (46).

On the wedding night of her marriage to a homosexual for a green card, Pingping is "so depressed" that she cannot help but break her own promise and start another diary, a project that accompanies her throughout her marriage (45). By characterizing *Paper Marriage* as a product of a compulsion to write, a compulsion that reverses and overrides a scarring experience from her childhood during the Cultural Revolution, Chen uses the novel's diary-form as a *mise en abyme* device to link Pingping's queer life to the trauma of the Cultural Revolution. The novel's interest in the political event, however, exceeds the critique of the Communist Party. It is, quite specifically, a representation of a reading process—the decoding of a diary within the framework of a diary. The Red Guards read both Pingping's and her brother's diaries, but decided that only the latter was of value to the political reeducation of the masses. Pingping remembers the Cultural Revolution as an act of interpretation. In her own diary, Pingping reads and comments on the fate of the two early diaries, and proposes her own interpretation of the political significance of these life-altering events. Just as the Red Guards have interpreted her first diary, *Paper Marriage* also invites its reader to interpret, decipher, and participate in this entwined story of modern homosexuality and Chinese communism.

The metafictional links between Yihe's diary and Pingping's diary emphasizes that both Chinese Marxism and homosexuality are social texts that require interpretation and analysis. Chen's interest in interpretation is perhaps one reason for the multiplicity of textual objects that populate this novel. Yihe, for example, never makes an actual appearance in the novel, but remains a disembodied character who is only remembered on account of the diary incident and whose presence is only felt through a host of textual objects—letters he writes to Pingping (*jia shu*), art supplies, care packages, and Pingping's memory of the exposed diary from the Cultural Revolution era. In metafictional terms, the existence of the brother's diary is a consequence of Pingping's relationship to a gay man. Pingping's traumatic memory of Chinese communism gives birth to a desire to recuperate the lost object of words (Yihe's diary was "confiscated" and her own was "tossed away") through a different kind of linguistic construction, her diary about a gay man. By emphasizing the textuality—that is, the discursively constructed nature and unstable meanings—of both Chinese Marxism and homosexuality, Chen also suggests novel ways for synthesizing their social histories.

The story of the rise of queer Chinese literature is an exemplary dialogue between Marxism and sexual modernities. Chen's writings demonstrate how the category of the queer can transform and expand the political meanings of Chinese Marxism. In turn, Chen's commitment to Marxism heightens her awareness that queer sexuality is as much a labor issue as a gendered one, producing in *Paper Marriage* a powerful analysis of the intersections of the immigrant's plight and its encounter with sexual difference. Historically, Chen's novel also marks the limits of Marxism, standing at a critical juncture when an older binary opposition between communism and capitalism ceases to be an effective rallying point for progressive Chinese intellectuals. The story of Chen's career suggests that the complexity of human sexuality offered an important alternative basis of leftist thought in the years of late Cold War, when Marxism no longer stood as a clear explanation of the organization of power and inequality in the world. As intellectuals began to reject the metanarratives of class struggle and national liberation, queer sexuality provided the language and imagery through which to explore a more complex and interconnected world. In the 1970s, Chen's disillusionment with the Cultural Revolution produced the anticommunist stories in the *Yixianzhang* series for which she became famous. In 1986, her topic was now homosexuality, which she saw as a kind of "social excess" entwined with a more complex organization of political power, national borders, and cultural ambiguity. Her novel demonstrates not only a renewed dialogue between Marxism and queer thinking, but also the infinite possibilities of their reconfiguration.

CHAPTER 4

GENEALOGIES OF THE SELF

As mentioned in the previous chapters, liberalism in modern Chinese political debates has a specific meaning that stems from the Cold War understanding of Taiwan as "Free China," that is, what the PRC would have been if it had not adopted communism. PRC policies in the 1980s— Deng's market reforms, the end of official socialism, and the liberalization of the PRC economy—were strongly shaped by the government's perception of Taiwan's economic modernity, which had attracted global attention since the 1960s with reports on the ROC as an "East Asian Economic Miracle." During this period, Taiwan achieved extraordinary growth rates and accelerated industrialization despite a history of colonialism, devastating wars, and a scarcity of natural resources. As implied by the word *miracle*, liberal political theory suggests that the newly industrialized countries (NICs) of Asia, unlike most countries in Southeast Asia, Latin America, and Africa, have somehow escaped the laws of colonial underdevelopment, which in turn shows that the real cause of poverty in the third world is not the history of Western imperialism, but the economically backward countries' own lack of willingness to modernize. The kernel of this ideology is that China, like Taiwan, can become a modern and affluent society as long as it is willing to adopt democracy and market capitalism. In orthodox economic theory, Taiwan's high growth rates in the postwar era demonstrate the merits of export-led developmentalism over import-substitution models.[1] The concept of miracle asks us to forget history's effects on the present and offers a powerful rationalization of liberalism.[2] The global characterization of Taiwan as China's economic miracle, in fact, corresponds to the model minority myth in US domestic politics, both of which are designed to deny that racism and colonialism have any lasting effects on those determined to succeed.[3]

How did Chinese queer writers intervene in this global construction of liberalism as miracle? In this chapter, I argue that queer culture is not a product of liberalism's promotion of human diversity; rather, it comes into being as a social critique of the liberal fable of self-invention. Far from being complicit with liberal pluralism, queer culture offers powerful conceptual tools for analyzing the systemic reproduction of inequalities. By revealing the structural principles in social formations that liberal apologists describe as meritocracy and equal opportunity, queer writers enter an alliance with the Marxist critique of bourgeois individualism. While insisting that identity categories, such as gay and lesbian, are discursively constructed and internally heterogeneous, queer writers also show that the critique of identity politics does not mean that social positions are fluid and freely chosen. Rather, being queer—living at some critical distance from normative organizations of gendered and sexual life—provides a necessary perspective on the systemic reproduction of unequal access to social resources. Against the liberal myth of the self-fashioning bourgeoisie, this queer perspective offers a *genealogical critique*, one that restores the historicity of the self to view.[4]

A paradigmatic instance of this queer Marxist genealogical critique is Xiao Sa's work in the 1970s and 1980s. Xiao is a prominent Taiwan-based Chinese writer best known for her explorations of gender and economic modernization. In this chapter, I offer a reading of Xiao's fiction as a queer intervention in the neoliberal fantasy of Taiwan as China's economic miracle. In her *Song of Dreams (Rumengling,* 1980), Xiao develops a queer Marxist "genealogy of the self" that shows the actual determinations of desire by a US-controlled zone of commodities. Xiao rewrites a Chinese tradition of feminine literature (*guixiu wenxue*) into a queer narrative of layered temporalities, contradictory desires, and conditioned experiences. This queer narrative presents the "self" as having multiple origins and genealogies against the neoliberal myth of the self-made middle class. These genealogies critique the neoliberal discourse of economic miracle as well as the unitary conception of women's experiences. As the title suggests, Xiao self-consciously inscribes herself in the tradition of Chinese *écriture féminine* that begins with the eleventh-century female poet Li Qingzhao, who is most famous for her *ci* poem by the same title, "Rumengling."[5] But while the tradition of feminine writing Li inspired depicts the bliss and woes of women's domestic life, Xiao rebels against this tradition by celebrating women's recalcitrant sexuality against the moral imperatives of the heteronormative family. In her depiction of women's rejection of procreative heterosexuality, Xiao outlines a queer politics that mobilizes the negative space of the socially unintelligible, the marginalized, and the aberrant against the sentimental and redemptive values of "reproductive futurism."[6] As is the case with the other queer Marxists considered in this book, Xiao's work is queer in the expansive sense of the word: although the novel does contain a minor male homosexual character, its primary thematic concerns lie with the heterosexual female protagonist's initiation into and rebellion against the institution of heterosexual marriage while she transforms from a penniless social outcast into the president of a housing corporation through sheer determination, risk-taking, and luck. In tracing the unruly movement of desire, Xiao also unearths the genealogies of the self. Every time the narrative of the protagonist's upward mobility verges on a liberal fable of self-making, the novel interrupts that fantasy by bringing the story back to the protagonist's ghostly encounter with the social regulations of her gender and sexuality from a past she is desperate to forget. Xiao's queer critique of the presumed telos and trajectory of heterosexuality emphasizes the regulatory effects of gender and sexual norms. Here, queerness provides a powerful framework for outlining the historicity of the self against the economic fable of the self-determining individual. In drawing attention to the effects of gendered pasts on the present, Xiao disorients the libidinal horizon of the middle-class subject.

Song of Dreams intervenes in the debate about the costs and nature of Taiwanese modernity by exploring the connections between two different kinds of miracles, Taiwan's transformation from an agricultural former colony to the center of global finance and industry in a mere decade, and the narrative dissolution of the institution of heterosexual marriage and patriarchy. In both dimensions of the narrative, Xiao takes pains to show that the miraculous appearance of freedom and development often conceals the dark side of modernity. While neoliberal policymakers explain Taiwan's economic miracle as a national achievement of the people's hard work under Kuomintang (KMT) leadership, the novel exposes the actual determinations of the Taiwanese bourgeois subject by a zone of commodities dictated by American interests. In creating a story about a woman's escape from heterosexual marriage to a polyamorous life, Xiao also emphasizes that desire is inextricably linked to social survival, such that there is no self without a history. We can, in other words, never write a genealogy of the gendered self without considering its relation to the material constraints of capitalism.

Contemporary criticism generally presents Xiao as a feminist writer. However, Xiao's own writing career demonstrates that the category of women's literature is an unstable construction shaped by factors unconnected to gender. Prior to 1986, Xiao was known as one of the most powerful realist writers in Chinese literary circles; during this era, her literary fame was not yet determined by her gender. Xiao's transformation into a feminist icon was the result of a highly publicized scandal involving a celebrity, Loretta Hui-shan Yang. Following Xiao's meteoric rise to literary prominence in the 1970s, several directors adapted her works into films. In the 1980s, Xiao started collaborating with her husband Zhang Yi, an up-and-coming director, and produced screenplays for several award-winning films with Yang as the leading actress. The most celebrated product of the "golden triangle"—as the team of Zhang, Xiao, and Yang came to be called—was *Kuei-mei, a Woman* (Wo zheyang guole yisheng, 1985), which received the Golden Horse Best Film Award. Euphoric news stories about the golden triangle, however, came to a dramatic halt in 1986, when Xiao published a "Letter to My Ex-Husband" in the *China Times*, exposing an affair between Zhang and Yang. The scandal instantly became the object of fervent media attention. Critics noted the historical irony—in *Kuei-mei, a Woman* and *This Love of Mine* (Wo de ai, 1986), both of which were written by Xiao and directed by Zhang, Yang plays a heroic wife who keeps the family together despite her husband's extramarital affair. In real life, Yang turned out to be "the other woman." For all her talent, Xiao could not write the script of her own life. *This Love of Mine* premiered the same month the "Letter to My Ex-husband" was published, and the media furiously condemned Yang and Zhang's hypocrisy. Under public pressure, Zhang and Yang left the film industry at the peak of their careers and cofounded *Liuligonfang*, the internationally acclaimed studio of Chinese glassware today. In the meantime, the "Letter to My Ex-Husband" turned Xiao overnight into a feminist writer—a cultural spokesperson for women everywhere weathering the shackles of marriage, limited economic alternatives to marriage, and the social shame of divorce.[7]

Xiao's "Letter to My Ex-Husband" came to be viewed as a new feminist manifesto in the conservative years of Taiwan's martial law era, during which "private" matters such as divorce and sexuality were rarely discussed in public, especially by women.[8] In a lecture titled "The Social Consciousness of Xiao Sa and Her Works," Ye Sifen (at Taiwan Technology University) characterizes Xiao as "a feminist and an inspiration to our generation . . . who has walked out of the shadows of a failed marriage and rechanneled her trauma into a creative success."[9] As the Rushdie affair did for *The Satanic Verses*, the highly publicized affair between Yang and Zhang created such intense public interest in the overtly political messages of Xiao's works that it derailed inquiries into their formal aesthetic complexity. Xiao's multifocal literary project, exploring themes ranging from urbanism to youth delinquency, was irrevocably eclipsed by her newfound reputation as an emotionally battered woman and an embattled feminist, and her writing began to be read and classified as a reflection of a generalizable phenomenon of women's consciousness. Xiao's fiction appeared in both Chinese and English anthologies on women's literature, and Xiao was accordingly canonized as a "woman author."[10] Since then, virtually every available study on Xiao discusses her work in relation to her gender and her divorce. Sheng Ying, for example, considers Xiao to be one of the three most important Chinese women writers (the other two being Jiang Xiaoyun and Lung Ying-tai) who ushered in a distinctive style of feminine writing.[11] Fan Luoping suggests that Xiao created a "new feminist literature" (*xin nüxing zhuyi wenxue*) that revolutionized Taiwan's literary terrain, hitherto dominated by a "feminine-sentimental" (*guixiu wenxue*) tradition.[12] International critics follow this description, often casting Xiao, as Fatima Wu does in an important article, as a woman writer principally concerned with "the topic of abandoned women—the woman's emotional state during a marital crisis and her destruction or recovery after the separation or divorce."[13] Here, Xiao's biographical divorce and her literary project are fully conflated with each other under the general sign of "a woman's emotional state."

Under what historical circumstances did such disparate, heterogeneous themes as divorce, sentimentality, extramarital affairs, gender inequality, urbanization, care for the young, and sexuality come to be regarded as the "experiences of women"? The cultural transformation of Xiao's writings into the embodiment of a feminist standpoint rests on a unitary conception of women that suppresses the heterogeneous, critically queer energies of her texts. Feminist standpoint theory argues that, by nature of their disadvantaged positions in society, women form a distinct social group with shared values and interests irrespective of their class origins, political identifications, and gender expressions. The idea of women's literature presupposes a fictive unity of one's chromosomal makeup, anatomy, reproductive capacity, desire, identity, object choice, experiences of disenfranchisement, and familial relations.

Against the historical reception of Xiao as the voice of women's consciousness, my analysis shows that her writings are actually grounded in a queer temporality that disrupts the presumed continuum between gender, sex, and desire. While Xiao is certainly interested in women's sexuality, desire, and marriages, she does not represent these issues in order to naturalize a normative expression of gender; rather, she does so to problematize it. The numerous stories in which Xiao discusses the institution of marriage present it as an unwelcome social contract imposed upon women, who are forced by the material conditions of the labor market to enter monogamous heterosexual marriages. It is therefore more accurate to regard Xiao as a queer author whose texts critically question the relation between femininity, anatomical genders, and economic opportunities. In *Song of Dreams*, her most ambitious philosophical exploration of the fictive ideal of gender, Xiao suggests that gender is a form of becoming, and that one becomes a woman only to the extent that she is perceived as a desiring subject in socially acceptable ways. The text contains many different objects of desire including men, commodities, and the "self"—desire is often the desire to be desired in specific ways. But in each scenario, Xiao emphasizes that desire places one in a matrix of social power beyond one's recognition and control. The text rebels against the disciplinary mechanism that produces an illusion of natural continuity between women's gender, heterosexual desire, economic roles, and familial life—and so, it is difficult to say that the subject of Xiao's writing is "women." On the contrary, Xiao deploys a wide array of characters and situations to represent internally contradictory roles women are supposed to assume and conflicting notions of femininity.

One element distinguishes Xiao from other queer and feminist writers who interrogate, rather than represent, the meanings of gender. For Xiao, the internally heterogeneous nature of womanhood is thinkable and representable only through the analysis of global capitalism, and the discontinuities between gender and sexuality are intimately related to the fragmentary conditions of human existence under capitalism. Through the impersonal, systemic social history of commodities, Xiao shows capitalism's desynchronizingation effects in concrete situations. In developing this line of thinking, Xiao brings a queer Marxist perspective to bear on the category of women by presenting commodities as the real protagonists in a personalized social history. In so doing, she also produces a nuanced text that illuminates the intimate and mutually constitutive relation between gender and the East Asian economic miracle. Before we can properly comprehend her feminist intervention in the literary history of the two Chinas, therefore, we must first examine the materialist dimension of Xiao's interpretation of culture.

Xiao's Realism

Xiao's critique of gender is continuous with her critique of capitalism, which she develops by expanding the practice of critical realism in the peripheries of global capitalism.[14] Born Xiao Qingyu in Taipei in 1953, Xiao is one of Taiwan's most prolific and prodigious luminaries in the '70s and '80s. In 1972, she published the first collection of her short stories, *Chang di* (*The long dike*), to critical acclaim at the age of twenty, while still a college student. Internationally, Xiao is best known for "My Son, Han-sheng," a short story about the generational gap between a middle-class couple and their adolescent son.[15] Many of her works have been translated into English, including "The Aftermath of the Death of a Junior High Co-ed," "The Colors of Love," "My Relatives in Hong Kong," "Second Honeymoon," "Old Mrs. Kuo's Distress," and "Floating Leaf." "My Relatives in Hong Kong" has been translated into German as well.[16] These stories explore the problems of materialistic culture, class relations, youth delinquency, the consequences of gentrification, and the disparity between town and country. In a realist style, Xiao dissects the changing values of society, developing a literary optic for reading the convulsive rhythms of capitalism in distinct locations.

From the 1970s to the early 1980s, Xiao received numerous literary awards for her realism, including the prestigious United Daily News Literary Prize (1979, 1980), the Chinese Writers' and Artists' Association Award (1981), and the China Times Literature Award (1984). In the words of veteran writer and cultural critic Sima Zhongyuan, Xiao is a "female literary genius" (cai nü) whose literary style is "natural and realistic, without a trace of artifice and pretense, marked by a lyrical richness that simply flows."[17] On awarding Xiao the 1979 United Daily News Literary Prize, the selection committee praised Xiao's work for its "impeccable language" and its "realist effects," which "touch the heart so powerfully that it feels like the story must be real."[18] In addition to being a realist in the aesthetic sense, Xiao is also known for her exploration of materialism. In a note to the English translation of "The Aftermath of the Death of a Junior High Co-ed," Anne C. Carver and Sung-sheng Yvonne Chang write: "Hsiao [Xiao] Sa's stories typically explore the motivations and consequences of the socially-conditioned behavior of ordinary citizens and offer insightful analyses of contemporary social problems. Her stories hold great appeal for contemporary readers in Taiwan, particularly for those who feel apprehensive about the prevailing materialism and opportunism of today's urban society."[19] In the introduction to another collection, Eva Hung characterizes Xiao's work as a unique description of "'a perfect love experience' in exchange for the women's 'nest-eggs'—an apt symbol of the commercialization of human relationships in a material culture."[20] These critical comments situate Xiao's work closely within the type of a materialist analysis of culture associated with Marxism. Xiao's deconstruction of heterosexual desire in Song of Dreams, therefore, is not an abstract expression of womanhood; rather, it continues and builds on her earlier critique of capitalism in her realist fiction, and must therefore be situated in the tradition of queer Marxism.

Song of Dreams makes a unique contribution to queer Marxism by rewriting the genealogy of heterosexual desire as a story of commodities. This approach emphasizes the interrelations between the workings of capitalism and the multivocal signification of gendered life. By showing that commodities structure desire, Xiao grounds the genealogies of the gendered self in the contradictions of the world capitalist system in the neocolonial periphery. The libidinal plot of Xiao's text, which includes a wide range of romantic and sexual encounters, refracts the economic history of East Asian modernization. Xiao's treatment of marriage, love, and family relations in this seemingly depoliticized novel provides a realist lens through which she dramatizes the otherwise unfathomable structural forces of international capitalism as an individuated, and gendered, embodied experience. Repeatedly, her characters ask what it means to be part of a spatially and temporally fragmented world as they embody and encounter capitalism's social contradictions. The libidinalization of capitalism's structural principles is not an unmediated reflection of global commodification, but a locally grounded effort at achieving a historical understanding of human sociality under intense economic modernization.

Song of Dreams

Originally serialized from November 1980 to April 1981 in *Zhonghua Supplement* before appearing in book form in July 1981, *Song of Dreams* (*Rumengling*) is a critical social history of Taiwan during the era of the official discourse of the East Asian Economic Miracle (1960s–1970s). It tells the story of Yu Zhen, a woman who rises from humble beginnings to become the president of a large housing development corporation. The narrative focuses on Zhen's inner transformation as she throws off the shackles of marriage to attain financial and sexual independence at the dawn of Taiwan's period as an economic miracle. This journey captures the transient moments and alienation of modern life. By representing a woman's struggles with society's expectations of a continuous, logical transition from adolescent love to heterosexual marriage, *Song of Dreams* constructs the story of Taiwanese modernity through the unfolding of queer temporalities.

Zhen begins as an unhappy provincial teenage girl whose family suffers from poverty and a lack of education. After Zhen's parents find out that she is pregnant by Huang, her high school boyfriend, Zhen has a properly queer experience to which many gay and lesbian children can relate: her parents disown her. Ostracized and disenfranchised on account of her sexuality, Zhen, like the queer children Chris Nealon describes as "foundlings," articulates a queer disaffiliation from the demands of the family.[21] Initially, Zhen marries her boyfriend in the hope of reinscribing herself within the network of proper kinship. However, once her daughter is born, she again questions her place in a heteronormative family defined by procreative sexuality. Led by a conflated desire for sexual experimentation and Western cosmopolitan glamour, Zhen abandons her husband and daughter and begins an affair with Allen, an American soldier stationed in Taiwan. The affair turns out to be only the beginning of a cascade of nonnormative relationships, which distances her even further from the monogamous heterosexual marriage that launches the novel. In this way, *Song of Dreams* delineates an elaborate exit from a heterosexual marriage, which stands as a failed model of human sociability and a repressive origin from the perspective of the novel's narrative logic. By beginning with a failed heterosexual marriage, *Song of Dreams* inverts the typical ideological catharsis of the marriage ending of domestic fiction, whereby the romantic union of the couple effaces the political and economic differences that propel the novel's plot. As a dystopian, rather than wish-fulfilling, text about heterosexual marriages, *Song of Dreams* also serves as an example of what Elizabeth Freeman terms erotohistoriography, the production of an alternative understanding of the past through a rearrangement of bodily pleasure and historical consciousness that disrupts the chrononormative organization of human bodies toward maximum productivity by way of a "wedding complex."[22]

Xiao presents desire as an intractable, primal force that provides resistance to the assimilative pull of patriarchy. Desire dislodges the docile subject from her roles as wife or mother, exposing the contradictory effects of capitalism's reduction of women to reproductive organs. After Zhen's parents disown her for her pregnancy, she moves in with her in-laws. Since Zhen's pregnancy prevents her effective participation in the chain of capitalist reproduction, she attempts to generate a minimum income by taking on a variety of odd jobs she can perform at home—such as cutting stencils—but she remains completely financially dependent on the Huangs, who only give her the coarsest and cheapest food. This economic context underlies her sexual transformation from mother to polyamorous woman. Zhen's affair with Allen results from the simultaneous seduction of his whiteness and delicious chocolates: before she meets Allen, she has never seen Western-packaged chocolate, candy, bubble-gum, and potato chips. The novel describes her fascination with these objects, which she incessantly brags about to the Huangs, much to their annoyance. Zhen's former and current selves collide at the site of the material disparity between Chinese food and Western commodities. But Zhen experiences the most striking disparity between East and West in bed:

> [After their first night together, Zhen realized that] there was a world of difference between Western men and Chinese men. To be more precise, there was a world of difference between Allen and Huang. If Huang was a man, then Allen was a beast. But Zhen lusted after this beast, who gave her pleasures she never knew existed, filled every vein in her body with excitement. (131)

The affair with Allen introduces Zhen to a US-centered zone of commodity exchange. It also introduces her to sexual desires she has never known. After Allen, Zhen begins accumulating a long list of suitors, mentors, companions, and playthings: her affair with the American soldier is followed by Lin, a married man who leaves his wife and children behind in the countryside to start up his own business in housing development in Taipei. Zhen becomes Lin's lover and business partner. After their relationship falls apart, Zhen takes over the company and becomes a successful entrepreneur in her own right. Financially comfortable now, Zhen suffers from the problem of the nouveau riche until she meets Liu, a cultured upper-class man twice her age. Under Liu's tutelage, Zhen begins acquiring the cultural capital of the bourgeoisie—famous artworks, high-class manners, and friendships with important socialites in an attempt to become part of the cultivated elite. After Liu passes away, Zhen takes a younger, muscular man named Luo as her lover and financially supports him. By the end of the novel, Zhen succeeds in securing everything she longed for in her childhood—beauty, wealth, status, power, prestige, professional success—but longs for the human connectedness that she once enjoyed when life was simple, before Taiwan's economic miracle transformed the cityscape beyond recognition. Despite her economic success, she realizes that a person is not a unitary being, but a palimpsest of layers and layers of incompatible selves.

The narrative of Song of Dreams is dynamic rather than descriptive; the text presents Zhen's movement away from the heteronormative model of human intimacy—from Huang (premarital sex, teen pregnancy, and a dysfunctional marriage), Allen (interracial relationship, love triangle, cohabitation without marriage), Lin (affair with a married man, mixing money with love), Liu (cross-generational, also extramarital), and finally to Luo (pure carnal pleasure and reversed traditional gender roles). This dynamic movement constitutes a queer temporality that underlies Xiao's social critique of the dehumanizing effects of economic modernization. Combining the traditional realist idioms of property acquisition, entrepreneurship, and commodity consumption, the novel tells a unique tale of middle-class self-transformation. Zhen's moral boom-and-bust thus chronicles Taiwan's capitalist transformation, bringing a gendered linearity to bear on the problem of the treadmill effect of capitalist reproduction.

In *Song of Dreams*, Zhen is simultaneously a fully embodied character and an empty vehicle for the true subject of the novel: the changing moral values of the 1950s, '60s, and '70s. In order to tell the story of epochal differences, Xiao foregrounds the commodities each decade consumes. The timeline of the story moves elliptically, sometimes skipping years in a single page, but each era is anchored in a distinctive type of commodity that seduces, embarrasses, and defines Zhen. Modernization changes Zhen's relation to the commodities in each phase of her life. In turn, a story about an ordinary woman's life also becomes a record of modernization. By creating a commodity-centered narrative, Xiao brings a belated answer to the famous question Marx once posed: What would commodities say if they could speak?[23] As a personalized presentation of the contradictory development of the periphery and the core, *Song of Dreams* captures the social history of commodities in Taiwan's boom decade. Stretching from the 1950s to the 1970s, the novel reads less like a personal drama than like a social documentary of artifacts, offering a poignantly lyrical montage of details from lost histories that include women's fashion, street life, songs, advertisement, arts, and commodities. Like Walter Benjamin's *Arcades Project*, Xiao's novel finds in the ruins of history the possibility of documenting, representing, and critiquing bourgeois existence. In the epilogue, Xiao describes her own work as a depiction of the "changing values in society in the decade of Taiwan's economic miracle" (343). Without naming her object of representation, Xiao simply begins the novel with a deictic: "That year (na-nian) a go-go dance and miniskirts were in fashion" (1). Zhen's miniskirts and go-go boots are soon replaced by bell-bottoms, swing coats, gaudy accessories, and purple eye shadow with which she dances to soul and R&B at American-owned nightclubs in Taipei. Commodities demarcate eras, dramatizing the embeddedness of subjectivity in the historical time of capital. The plethora of commodities that populates this text—the steaks, Hepburn haircut, price of orange juice, the advent of the radio and television, bamboo chairs, miniskirts—provides a kaleidoscopic view of the changing history of Taiwan.

Song of Dreams presents a unique upward mobility narrative that combines the historicity of the self with the problem of the East Asian economic miracle. The novel forces the reader to ask, to what extent is the "I" an effect of social norms and powers beyond one's recognition? The arc of the plot shows the process whereby the self metamorphoses from a source of subjective perception into an object of reflection. But *Song of Dreams* is more than a Bildungsroman, as Xiao is as interested in telling a dramatic story—one might even say urban legend or fairy tale—about a small-village girl as she is in capturing an objective snapshot of the story of Taiwan with minimum authorial mediation. In Xiao's aesthetic practice, the libidinal plot is intimately, perhaps hopelessly, bound up with the socioeconomic reality of society, and there is no easy way to separate a pure subject from external reality that is not, in the final analysis, an optic illusion of bourgeois individualism. Xiao addresses this tension between agency and structure when she explains the ending of the story:

> While *Song of Dreams* was serialized in *Zhonghua Supplement*, many people asked me how the story was going to end. . . . When I started working on the novel, I had no intention of turning it into a legend, so in a way, the ending does not matter that much. It is simply a story of a woman from the age of seventeen or eighteen to thirty some years old. . . . This is a topic I have always wanted to write about: how fast and drastically everyone's values and worldviews changed in Taiwan in the past two decades under rapid economic development.[24]

The claim that "the ending does not matter that much" follows the aesthetic principle of realist photography—the chopped off figures and buildings on the edges of the picture convey a sense of spontaneity in contrast to the carefully, but artificially, planned composition of a Pre-Raphaelite oil painting. On the other hand, the libidinal plot necessarily demands catharsis and closure. The text refuses the trajectory of our cathected desire, opting instead to retain the impersonal forces of history. Xiao's text thus challenges the moral finality of the structure of the traditional novel. Whereas the ending of the traditional novel, by virtue of its position, typically implies a moral attitude on the ethical dilemma or central conflict that drives the story forward, Xiao refuses to allow Zhen's struggles with class inequality and gender normativity to dissipate into a symbolic resolution that brings pleasure and catharsis to the reader. Instead, such struggles are real and continuous, and by disavowing the possibility of overcoming such contradictions, the novel also serves as a reminder that we are part of the political dilemma it delineates. In so doing, Song of Dreams develops a critique of the liberal conception of human freedom from historical determinations, rejecting the idea that discrimination against women and minorities does not really exist, and that the lower class only suffers from its own lack of motivation. The forceful joining of these two miracles in the text—the miraculous ascendance of Taiwan as a powerhouse in the industrialized economy of the Pacific Rim, and the miraculous self-reinvention of Zhen as a woman without history—plays one neoliberal fantasy against the other. Song of Dreams presents the confusion and conflation of two senses of fortune: wealth and luck. In such fantasies, both Taiwan and women become model minorities who can override the historical laws of subjugation and rise to the top of the socioeconomic order through sheer hard work and determination.

Instead of providing narrative closure, Xiao's genealogies of the self foreground process and reflexivity. The novel accomplishes this goal partially through a recurring image of the mirror. Song of Dreams begins and ends with mirrors, both real and figurative ones. In the first few pages of the book, Zhen is introduced to the reader as a narcissistic but insecure girl in the countryside who spends hours in front of the mirror. The heavy narrative descriptions of Zhen as reflected image present her as a passive object at a point of the story where we expect to meet an active protagonist. Beginning with reflected images and an ironic disjuncture between Zhen's self-perception and her characterization, the novel also invites the reader to form a judgment and incorporates it into the narrative chain of signification. While doing so, Song of Dreams also presents the problem of reflexive desire through the image of the mirror, drawing attention to the fact that Zhen's desire is to be seen—and desired—in a fashion that her current economic status does not allow. Xiao's textual organization mocks her protagonist's comic combination of vanity and parochialism with several scenes rendered in vivid detail and with finesse. The first scene has Zhen spending hours in front of "a small hand mirror" in her "dimly–lit room" with a "make-shift makeup kit: an eyebrow pencil bought with money she saved up, half a tube of lipstick from her mother, and the retired powder stick from Hong. Do not be fooled by the simplicity of tools: the eyebrow pencil can double as an eyeliner, and the lipstick substitutes for a blush as well" (2). After eventually deciding on a "vermillion miniskirt paired up with a white school uniform not yet embroidered with her class number," Zhen puts on her "almond kernel necklace and almond kernel bracelet" and makes a "standard pose in a go-go dance," "feeling immensely satis-fied with her chic look" (2). The disappointing party only serves "cheap watermelon seeds" next to "two whirring electric fans" while she is ex-pecting "air conditioning, juice, hors d'oeuvres, and handsome college students driving sports cars" (3).

Xiao develops several details to show that Zhen experiences mate-rial destitution and cultural disenfranchisement simultaneously in order to emphasize, in a queer Marxist fashion, that the material and the cultural are not fully separable, and that material inequalities have gendered and psychic dimensions. Zhen's first gaze into the mirror in the opening pages soon becomes another scene in which Zhen imag-ines herself to be the protagonist of a Western romance novel. The fan-tasy is initiated by a date with a university student from a wealthy family who speaks fluent English and "dreams about becoming a diplomat after graduation" (9). After exchanging letters for months through a newspaper dating service, Zhen and the university student decide to meet. Although Zhen does not know how to eat a steak and has nothing of substance to talk about at dinner, the first date ends relatively well. However, the bourgeoning romance comes to an abrupt end after the student secretly follows Zhen home to her "four-ping-size house [142 sq. ft.] that has nothing but a square dining table and four bamboo stools . . . and a rusty bicycle that her father put inside at night, for fear that their neighbors might steal it" (21). In her depiction of this short-lived relationship, Xiao dramatizes the contradiction between the world economy's core and the periphery through a series of commodities (in-cluding information commodities and educational capital). The con-versations between Zhen and the university student involve Dadaism, existentialism, hippies, drugs, and Freud (12–13). Xiao depicts Zhen's provincialism by underscoring her inability to participate in this conver-sation about Western culture. Xiao then suggests, through the mouth

of Zhen, that differentially valued forms of cultural knowledge become a source of "psychological persecution" (16) for non-foreign-educated Chinese. While Zhen feels victimized by the premium placed on Western knowledge, she is also herself overcome by an inescapable desire to become just like her persecutor, wondering to herself: "Isn't the protagonist in all the novels she read always a smart and pretty university student who carries a pile of untranslated, English-language textbooks with her wherever she goes? Zhen fervently believed that, as long as she could pass the examinations and enter the university, she too would be entitled to romance" (28). Here, the consumption of knowledge displaces the commodities of fashion, but the libidinal plot has already begun to crystallize.

By connecting "a pile of untranslated English-language textbooks" to a woman's entitlement to "romance" in Zhen's world in this inaugural episode, Xiao suggests that Zhen's awakening as a self-reliant social climber begins with her conflation of her access to the cultural capital of the West with the norms of femininity and desirability. Seeing capitalist America as the source of "romance," Zhen rebels against her mother's conservative ideas of fashion, preferring short skirts in an attempt to become more "modern." Soon, she runs away from the life she was prescribed:

> She always felt that fate was unfair to her. Her life was full of disappointments. This party was not at all what she wanted, but it was so crudely forced upon her. Her house, her source of survival, was crammed together with other houses haphazardly constructed for the commoners in the new residential quarter.[25] . . . Looking at her own silhouette, Zhen was suddenly overcome by self-pity. She refused to believe that she was destined to be buried among these petty characters of the slum, and she knew that one day she would finally escape this crammed, lowly house and its patched-up, torn-down, and embarrassingly cheap furniture. (7)

The image of the "silhouette" presents another kind of mirror that helps define Zhen's project as the transformation of the self, and the novel as a genealogy of the self. Insofar as the self is only thinkable in relation to an Other, the problem of the self is also a problem of desire. By filling these opening scenes with mirrors, shadows, and qualitatively differentiated commodities such as the "untranslated, English-language textbooks" and "cheap furniture," Xiao also emphasizes that the genealogy of reflexive desire is necessarily circumscribed by structurally regulated flows of commodities and resources in the world.

After Zhen successfully escapes the "life she is born into," Xiao develops the mirror metaphor further into an elaborate episode of an encounter with one's past self. One day, Hong, a friend from Zhen's provincial hometown, reappears, but the friend has changed beyond her recognition:

> A woman with the Hepburn hairdo walked out of the car, still speaking simple, broken English with the foreign man with blue eyes and sandy-brown hair in the car. What really attracted the entire village's attention was her dress—she was wearing a semi-transparent fishnet blouse that barely covered anything. Underneath the see-through fishnet blouse was a red-flower patterned bikini on her luscious body. "Look, a hooker!" Zhen said to the baby daughter in her arms, laughing. (107)

The language of "look, a hooker!" presents Zhen as a gazing subject, for whom Xiao's sardonic tone invites the reader's external scrutiny. Xiao uses Zhen's pejorative response to create an irony of situations, drawing attention to the fact that later Zhen becomes exactly what she despises—the "shameless" woman wearing clothes that "barely cover anything" and dating the same American man, Allen, who is, at this point, Hong's boyfriend. This irony emphasizes the theme of reflexivity in the genealogy of the self. After the "hooker" takes Zhen back to Allen's fancy apartment and treats her to "bubblegum, chocolate, American cigarettes, American wine, and an assortment of goodies bought from the GI club" that Zhen has never even heard of (110), Zhen thinks to herself, "I might be poor and only have tattered clothes to wear, and no time for makeup between laundry and diapers, but at least I am married, and my child is not a fatherless bastard. And I would never sink this low and shamelessly live with an American soldier I am not married to!" (111). Within weeks, Zhen becomes another Hong. "She walked in and out of restaurants and clubs, dancing, drinking, and frolicking, with her head held up high and her face beaming with pride" (124). Here, Xiao again creates an ironic distance between her protagonist and her thoughts, transforming Zhen from a psychological essence into a social type. In so doing, Xiao captures the tension between moral and economic values with cold precision.

The novel ends with Zhen gazing at her pregnant teenage daughter, the return of the repressed. The daughter functions as another mirror, reminding Zhen of the past she is unable to escape despite her material success. Indeed, Zhen realizes that she has failed to break free of a tragically repetitive past and shame from which she once thought money and her now glamorous life would have barricaded her. In this context, Zhen's is an antihumanist story, one that caricatures the myth of the self-making (wo-)man by having that figure appear momentarily to be the architect of her own destiny, only to immediately succumb to the dehumanizing effects of the inexorably juggernaut of economic modernization. In a different sense, the novel also depicts her rags-to-riches story as a "miracle," as the story of a Chinese Horatio Alger who is capable of upward economic mobility without state-engineered correctives. Although both humanist and antihumanist readings are possible, neither prototype properly defines the novel's narrative interest; rather, the novel's primary object of representation is the tension between structurally determined exploitation and its miracle discourse. This polarization of the novel's narrative interest emphasizes both agency and structure in its presentation of upward mobility, offering a literary instantiation of Marx's axiom: "Men make their own history . . . but not under circumstances chosen by themselves."[26]

Miracle Discourse/Americanism

The emphasis on commodities is therefore not random; rather, the commodity narrative serves as a literary device that emphasizes the structural determinations of subjectivity over and against a neoliberal ideology of freedom. The discourse of commodities helps delineate Taiwan's incorporation into a postwar US-dominated security zone. Lurking in the background of this ostensibly depoliticized novel is the consistent presence of social venues created by American military operations in Taiwan, otherwise known as the culture of the Seventh Fleet. American militarism in the Asia-Pacific functions as an occluded presence in the novel, a deliberately created "white space" on Xiao's social canvas that radically alters the aesthetic composition of the text through its generative silences. The question never asked is why American soldiers were stationed in Taiwan at the time, a fact that the characters in the book treat as a nonissue. The occlusion of the question creates a "pink elephant in the room" effect, one that draws more attention to the presence of American military in Taiwan than would a direct representation of imperialism in traditional socialist realism. Xiao's "negative space" is part of an intentional design, which is discernible in the strategically chosen setting of the story in sites and scenes that are emblematic of American military power during the 1970s. Many of the key events take place in the American GI-club, where lower-class soldiers traffic in local girls. Another site of cathected desire in the novel is Tianmu, the famous enclave for Taiwan's expatriate community and members of the US Armed Forces, where the Taipei American School and the first department stores in Taiwan were established. Qingguang Market, the source of many of the commodities in the novel, is mentioned several times. Significantly, Zhen treats Allen as a commodity as well, referring to him as "a pretty American doll" she has purchased for a price and as "war spoils" she has obtained from her victory over Hong (143).

After Allen, Zhen's next sexual relationship stands as an explicit allegory of Taiwan's economic miracle, which further delineates the political dependency and material contexts of US-Taiwan relations. After running away from Allen, Zhen "grows up overnight" ("yi ye jian zhang da," 169) and becomes a resourceful, independent young woman. The language of "overnight growth," reminiscent of the discourse of miracle, explains Zhen's development in economic and emotional terms as a spectacular ascendancy without history. Through a combination of natural savvy, feminine beauty, initiative, and street-smart creativity, Zhen helps Lin, her new lover, transform a small local business into a large corporation. The narrative of land acquisition and inflated property value gives Xiao another opportunity to emphasize the determinations of commodities in the formation of peripheral social subjects. Indeed, her device of "narrative indirection" seems to substitute commodities for characters as the real protagonists. Although the characters live lives punctuated by this material history, they are largely unaware of the structural positions they have come to occupy and the economic terms in which they are related. The design of Xiao's queer materialist critique results in moments of narrative reticence, where the author simply "shows rather than tells," withholding authorial commentary in favor of a direct juxtaposition of material objects. In a scene where Xiao seeks to portray a shift in Allen and Zhen's personal dynamics, for example, she tells a story of the conflicting values and valuations of commodities instead:

> Sitting in Allen's old car, Zhen took out a small powder mirror and started retouching her makeup with difficulty, proposing, "Why don't we go out to eat?" Zhen was hoping she could take advantage of the high class, romantic ambience of the restaurant to talk Allen into having a baby with her. She wanted to bear a child with that magnificent American last name of his: Redford.
>
> "Nah—don't we still have leftovers in the refrigerator?"
>
> "We haven't had steaks in a while."
>
> "Let's not waste money. We'll eat at home."
>
> Now that they were living together, Allen became rather cheap. He bought Zhen a secondhand mini-refrigerator and rarely took her out to eat anymore. Not only so, he was having Zhen do his laundry now instead of sending it out to the cleaner's like he used to. However, for the sake of their future, Zhen did not argue with him. She waited until midnight, when he was finished with his beer and the radio show of the American military channel. She prepared hot water in the bathtub and a clean change of clothes for him.
>
> "Hot! Taiwan is so hot."
>
> Allen walked out half naked, sweating and moving himself closer to the fan.
>
> "Why don't we buy an air conditioner? Or move to Yangming mountain district?" (148)

In this passage, which significantly begins with another mirror and looks more like a carefully crafted floral arrangement of objects—an air conditioner, a beer, noises on the radio, a mini-refrigerator, a makeup kit, a buzzing fan—than like a dialogue or event, there is virtually no commentary on the characters' inner psychological turmoil, yet the seemingly ordinary conversation marks one of the climactic points in the story. These objects convey a wealth of condensed information: Zhen blindly worships Americanism (she wishes to have a biracial child with a Caucasian man and take on his "magnificent" American name); she plots a betrayal (to trap Allen in a marriage through conception, as she has done the first time with Huang); and Allen's sham begins to crumble (he turns out to be an ordinary, lower-middle class American soldier pretending to be a person of means to impress local girls in Taiwan), all amid mutual verbal manipulation (Zhen's sarcasm—"Yangming mountain" is the most expensive district in Taipei at the time, with a high concentration of political and cultural elites—comparable to Beverly Hills in the US context). While the objects in the text speak louder than the characters, the construction of the subjects by material possessions (and dispossession) captures a relation between the illusory appearance of personhood and substance in the matrix of the social field. Xiao's gendered realism provides a potent model for representing the atomizing and fragmenting effects of capitalism. The novel emphasizes the incomplete character of Zhen's development in cultural and psychological terms, allowing for a more nuanced reflection of capitalism's dehumanizing effects.

The Problem of the Bourgeoisie

After Lin, Zhen takes over the housing development company and becomes the mistress of Liu, an elderly man of considerable political clout and prestige in Taiwan. With Liu, she becomes a connoisseur of art, drinks Chinese tea, rebuilds a wardrobe of simple, elegant, and tasteful attire, acquires her own collection of Chinese calligraphy, and begins to reevaluate her expensively decorated but (in Liu's opinion) gaudy apartment. After Liu passes away, Zhen becomes romantically and sexually entangled with Luo, a young struggling artist she meets through Liu's daughter. While in previous relationships Zhen is accustomed to using her beauty as a bargaining chip for economic gains and unprincipled social climbing, her final relationship with this handsome young man turns into a role reversal, where she offers material benefits in exchange for "the touch of a muscular man in her life" (303). To further fill the void created by her material success, Zhen decides to be a mother again, reacquiring custody of her abandoned daughter with money. Zhen's experience with her daughter, however, only heightens her social alienation and the limits of capitalism. In the young woman, Zhen sees the spitting image of her youth, and comes face-to-face with the recalcitrant young girl she once was when she ran away from home. In another sense, Zhen also witnesses an aspect of herself frozen in an ever-renewing youthfulness that has become alienated from her body. If Zhen ever believed that she has managed to undo all the mistakes of her youth with the accumulation of financial and symbolic capital, that belief is brutally shattered when she discovers, at the end of the novel, that her fourteen-year-old daughter is a pregnant drug addict.

It is in the "economic miracle" phase that Zhen's "maternal instincts" awake. The economic transformations of Zhen, in other words, produce multiple lacks and fissures in her life and alienate her from herself. While Zhen's former self is unified by an unshakable desire for upward economic mobility, the organicity of her being is destroyed once that goal is achieved. As a result of this fragmentation, the self is severed, but this development also makes possible an ethical reflection on the self, where Zhen is able to reexamine her own life as an object. "Looking at herself in the front mirror of her car, Zhen suddenly fails to recognize the woman in the image behind her heavy makeup. Every person changes with time, including herself, her daughter, Huang . . . what will happen in the future? She wants to know, but is afraid to know" (157). This textual moment accentuates the symbolism of the mirror that launches the novel, but it also transforms the various mirrors and mirror images in the novel into a larger social critique of the alienation of the self under economic modernization in a queer Marxist fashion.

Xiao's genealogy of the self, in the final analysis, characterizes the self as a process of alienation and externalization, analogous to Marx's dissection of the alienation of labor from the body under capitalism. In the last line of the novel, Xiao finally explains the novel's title through an interior monologue. Pacing next to her daughter's pale body in the operation room after the teenage girl's abortion, Zhen "suddenly realized that it was herself lying on the bed . . . She clasped Guofen's cold hands in her own, wishing everything was nothing but a song of dreams" (342, the ending of the text). The representation of time shifts from a progression to a cyclicality. Zhen realizes that her life has been a *Rumengling*—a song of dreams. Like the work of the eleventh-century Chinese female poet, Zhen's own genealogy reflects nothing but the vicissitudes and changing fortunes of life. The book's title is not only another kind of mirror object, against which life becomes nothing but a dream, an alienated effect flashed in front of our eyes, but also a meta-commentary on the relation between the two Chinas. Invoking the Chinese female poet as the novel's antecedent, Xiao imagines a historical continuity of queer poetics in the Chinas. The invocation of ancient Chinese poetry in the last line returns the novel to its title, creating a temporal trajectory that recoils and redoubles unto its referent.

The Taiwanese literary critic Ni Luo suggests that this novel is "about everyone and no one," and that Zhen's story is "a sketch of a social type rather than a portrait":

> Song of Dreams is a snapshot of our social psyche during an epochal change . . . Reading Song of Dreams, we suddenly realize that the society we used to know has become so foreign to us. It has evolved so fast that our beliefs and worldviews simply cannot catch up. . . . Yu Zhen is a social type, a product of circumstances . . . Xiao Sa presents a slice of contemporary society and its materialism with stunning precision and realism.[27]

As Ni explains, Xiao's intent is to capture the inherent movements and dynamics of history, as they produce ideologically polarized outcomes, characters, and interpretations. On the structural level, the book is organized around a series of "illegitimate" relationships between Zhen and various romantic and sexual partners. On the thematic level, what drives the narrative plot forward is Zhen's constant search for upward social mobility through the acquisition of economic and, later, cultural capital. By integrating the narrative of sexual desire into the ebbs and flows of capital that structure the dispositions and worldviews of the characters, Xiao develops a queer Marxist narrative that casts a cold, sobering light on the genealogies of the self. The novel's thematic focus must thus be differentiated from its narrative dynamic. In thematic terms, the novel appears to be a story about love—or, more precisely, failed loves. As an embodiment of the directional dynamic of capitalism, however, Song of Dreams emphasizes the failures of heterosexual marriage and the failures of capitalism. Zhen's struggles as a "fallen" woman represent the constraining and sometimes destructive effects of gender as a regulatory cultural ideal. As the story progresses and Zhen accumulates more Western commodities, she brings herself closer to the center of the world economy, but her economic ascendancy is also mirrored by an unambiguously linear movement away from sexual normativity that ends in the complete privation of human connectedness. In this instance, Zhen's position as a progressively marginalized woman helps particularize what are otherwise abstract and illegible forces of international capitalism. The libidinal economy of the text does not celebrate love and marriage. Rather, it offers a constellation of failed relationships, scenes of social persecution, ethical dilemmas, and a gendered logic of development to deliver a queer Marxist critique of capitalism. For Xiao, the genealogies of the self are multiply constituted. By mapping the overdetermined relations between these seemingly discrete spheres of the self—the self-making of the middle class, nonprocreative desires, and a US-defined space of commodities—Xiao also makes a strong, and distinctively queer, case against the neoliberal imagination of Free China during the height of the Cold War.

CHAPTER 5

QUEER HUMAN RIGHTS

IN AND AGAINST THE TWO CHINAS

Like "women's human rights," the idea of queer human rights is a paradox. Queer human rights advocates ask us to imagine individuals as bearers of certain inalienable rights by virtue of a particularity (their queerness) and of a universality (their humanness) at the same time. Despite these logical contradictions, however, the concept of queer human rights has proven to be an extremely potent legal fiction. Organizations such as the International Gay and Lesbian Human Rights Commission (IGLHRC) have accomplished important work around the globe through a strategic invocation of the concept of gay and lesbian human rights. In 2004, I worked with IGLHRC and helped organize a workshop in Taipei to train local activists in documenting queer human rights violation cases. The workshop was immensely successful; the discussion of queer issues as human rights created a powerful political discourse, and the presence of an international nonprofit organization put some much needed pressure on the government that local activists could leverage. Being able to imagine oneself as part of a global community immediately changed the dialogue, even if that dialogue did not actually involve the entire human population in the world. From conversations with local activists in Asia, I learned a powerful lesson: that the contradiction between the universalizing conception of the human and the emphasis on the particularities of the queer does not render the concept useless in local political contexts. Queer activists in the two Chinas offer inspiring examples of how we can leverage the contradiction between the human and the queer to advance socially progressive agendas.

Although some critics understand the international or the "human" dimension of queer rights to be a politically suspect concept in the service of the colonial epistemology of the West, the concept of the human can also serve as a means of political organization and enfranchisement for local activists in the Chinas. IGLHRC, for one, has provided important resources for queer human rights activists in both the PRC and the ROC. It hands out an annual Felipa de Souza Award in recognition of international queer human rights activists and organizations. In 2002 Cui Zi'en from the PRC won the Felipa Award, and in 2004 the Gender/Sexuality Rights Association Taiwan (G/SRAT) won the same award.[1] In the case of Cui, not surprisingly, the invitation for a PRC national to receive a human rights award (queer or not) in the United States immediately became a source of political discomfort, but with a twist of irony. After Cui was announced as the recipient of the Felipa Award, his application for a visa to enter the United States was denied by the US embassy. The embassy asked him if he was "persecuted" by the Chinese government, to which he answered no. The US embassy decided that a recipient of a human rights award from mainland China who was not persecuted by communism must be a fraud with secret intents for immigration, and denied his visa application. International human rights organizations protested, and the US government eventually reversed its decision under media pressure. The events became an example of queer activism against the US government's discriminatory practice toward a Chinese national. However, the Beijing municipal government then began monitoring Cui after learning of his nomination for the Felipa Award. The public security bureau tapped his phone line and requested him to decline the awards from the United States. Cui did not comply with these requests, but did not suffer any consequences either.[2] In this case, neither the US government nor the PRC government is actually concerned about homosexuality, but the language of human rights, officially a "sensitive" (mingan) topic in the PRC, immediately places the controversy in the context of a long history of US interferences in Asian national affairs in the name of human rights, humanitarianism, and democracy. For this reason, queer human rights cannot be easily extricated from the dilemmas of sovereignty. There is always a gap between the universal rhetoric of queer human rights and its concrete practice, since any local discourse of the human is inevitably fraught with national interests that exceed the domain of sexuality.

Another example of the complex interactions between sexual rights and national boundaries occurred in 2006, when the East Bay Community Law Center in California took on an asylum case of an HIV-positive Taiwanese national. The attorney sought to build a case for political asylum by proving to the US court that Taiwan is an oppressive country where homosexuals and people living with AIDS are "subject to discriminatory laws, prejudice, physical violence, economic deprivation, and limited access to medical facilities."[3] The attorney contacted queer human rights activists in Taiwan and asked them to make a declaration under penalty of perjury attesting to "Taiwan's discrimination, abuses, and/or discrimination against its homosexuals and people living with HIV/AIDS."[4] The case was unsuccessful, but it would have been the first legal case for a Taiwanese national to obtain a green card by disclosing his HIV status. Like Cui's case, the story highlights the difficulty of abstracting queer human rights from concrete national interests and political stakes, since it is nation-states, not divine sources that create laws and rights; conversely, the invocation of queer human rights expresses first and foremost a desire for national, rather than cosmopolitan, memberships and entitlements.

Queer Tactics and Minority Agency

These contradictions, however, do not mean that queer human rights discourses must be politically self-defeating. There are positive examples of queer tactics that consciously exploit the contradictions between national, universal, and sexual claims for progressive ends. In 2006, I helped organize a political event in Taipei and San Francisco with such possibilities in mind. At the time, Taipei was about to hold its gay pride event (Taipei Lesbian and Gay Civil Rights Movement Festival) in September. The mayor of Taipei, Ma Ying-jeou (who is now the president of the Republic of China), like most politicians, did not wish to openly endorse the event. The coalition of queer activist organizations I was working with wanted Pride to become a consciousness-raising rally instead of a depoliticized, carnival-like gathering. Knowing that appealing to the mayor's office with "queer human rights" would not get very far, we came up with a different strategy. Since San Francisco, where I was

living at the time, was Taipei's sister city, I contacted Mayor Gavin Newsom to ask him if he could send a rainbow flag and a proclamation of
queer human rights to the City of Taipei, and the San Francisco mayor
happily complied. The proclamation reads:

> Whereas, all human beings are entitled to human rights, equality,
> and freedom; and
> Whereas, Taipei seeks to eliminate prejudice, intolerance, and
> discrimination against lesbians, gays, bisexuals and transsexuals;
> and
> Whereas, the City of Taipei is holding its seventh annual Taipei
> Lesbian and Gay Civil Rights Movement Festival on September 17th,
> 2006 to increase our knowledge of and respect for sexual minorities;
> Whereas, the City of San Francisco is the Sister City of Taipei
> THEREFORE BE IT RESOLVED, that I, Gavin Newsom, Mayor
> of the City and County of San Francisco, in recognition of the 2006
> Taipei Lesbian and Gay Civil Rights Movement Festival, do hereby
> extend best wishes to the City of Taipei for endeavors improving
> individual lives across boundaries of differences in gender and
> sexuality.

The strategy worked beautifully. Although Ma would not want to be
seen as a pro-gay politician, the geopolitics of US-China-Taiwan relations greatly outweighed any discomfort he might have with gay issues.
Under diplomatic pressures, Ma appeared in person to receive the rainbow flag from the City of San Francisco, which became the first instance
of an ROC government official's endorsement of an LGBT event, and a
milestone in the history of Taiwan's queer human rights movement
(see figure 5.1).

For reasons I will explain more fully in this chapter, our strategy's
success owed a great deal to the political tensions between the PRC, the
ROC, and the United States that I characterize as (queer) human rights
in and against the two Chinas. Queer activism brings the tensions between the two Chinas to a productive use. The international and the
national spheres of politics will always have incompatible interests,
and it may be a long time before either sphere develops any genuine
concern for LGBT issues, but queer subjects continue to find strategies of survival and self-articulation in the interstices of competing
political systems. It is always possible to mobilize the contradictions

5.1. Ma Ying-jeou, mayor of Taipei, politely accepts the rainbow flag, signed by Gavin Newsom, mayor of San Francisco, that author sent from San Francisco (September 17, 2006). (Source: G/SRAT Archive)

between national interests in the two Chinas for queer use with the help of human rights discourse.

Queer issues add a layer of complexity to the philosophical, ethical, and legal conundrums faced by human rights discourse in, about, and against the Chinas. Before turning to these discourses, I'd like to first briefly sketch the problems of the human in liberal and nonliberal philosophy. I will trace the figure of the human in dialogues between Marxist and non-Marxist thinkers, before showing how a state-based understanding of liberalism produces limited, and counterproductive, assumptions about free and non-free subjects in the PRC and the ROC. The case of queer human rights calls for a renewed understanding of the human, one that casts this figure as neither the agent of social transformation nor the subject of universal rights. Instead, queer human rights discourse and its attendant problems show that the human is best understood as an ethical perspective on the equality of human time, which we can recuperate from Marx's writings. Reanimating the category of the human in Marx has a number of theoretical consequences. First, this move disrupts the comfortable division between cultural and economic categories that post-Marxist authors have often deployed in an attempt to characterize Marxism as an essentialist dogmatism. The phenomenon of queer human rights discourse compels us to understand the interrelatedness of cultural and economic forces in the formation of the subject. In Marx, the labors of all human beings, measured by units of time, are presumed to be morally equivalent. Coupled with this insight, China is no longer simply a site of "different humans" that we can collect as an anthropological specimen in a liberal framework. Instead, the question posed by queer Chinas becomes an occasion for rethinking the power differentials that produce the human and the subhuman in the era of global financial capitalism.

Liberal Understandings of Human Rights

The literature on human rights is vast, but we can extrapolate several concerns from the current critiques of liberal approaches to human rights that are particularly relevant to queer issues. First, it is well recognized that human rights talk in the West is deeply rooted in the philosophy of natural rights.[5] The Christian theological idea that rights are willed to people by divine sources has proven difficult in translations of international law.[6] The European notion of natural rights is radically different from, for example, the Confucian understanding of rights, rites, ethics, and personhood. While human rights are sometimes translated as "quanli," the Confucian philosophical system does not have the concept of negative freedom and does not regard the possessive individuals as repositories of rights and duties; instead, the Confucian system emphasizes reciprocal responsibilities in the social order.[7] The British liberal tradition promotes a theory of possessive individualism that obscures the fact that an individual does not have rights; rights only exist in relation to others. Only when a person enters a set of social relations does it become possible to speak of rights. This problem also distinguishes Marxist understandings of social relations from liberal attempts to cast sexual differences as private matters. Recent scholarship on the ontology of the human further shows that the human is configured not just in relation to other humans, but also through a violent disavowal of its ontological affinities to nonhuman species, entanglements with inanimate objects, and dependency on technology that allow for its survival.[8] To "queer the nonhuman," as Noreen Giffney and Myra Hird suggest, is not just to refuse the lure of "anthronormativity" or to extend the critique of the nature/culture divide to human morphology, but to provide an occasion for rethinking bodily contours and desires we have taken for granted as incontrovertible material evidence of our individuality and autonomy.[9]

Second, cultural theorists and political philosophers have long recognized that the discourse of the human often represents the hegemonic values of dominant groups, rather than what is actually human or universal. We hear this debate when countries denounced by the United States for human rights abuses produce counter human rights reports to demonstrate that the US Department of State is more interested in its own ideology than in understanding actual human rights practices around the world. As Zhang Xudong points out, between the Tiananmen events in 1989 and China's entry into the World Trade Organization in 2001, China's socialist reforms have again come "under assault by a Western triumphalism" that combined "old–fashioned right-wing hostility toward communism and a liberal discourse of universal human rights that has become unabashedly jingoistic."[10] The publication of Michael Hardt and Antonio Negri's Empire trilogy (Empire, Multitude, and Commonwealth) provoked questions of whether the conception of the humanity living under "a single logic of rule" is actually a liberal apologia for globalization in a reformist guise, and whether the authors' descriptions of the centrality of biopolitics and immaterial labor today merely generalize conditions of the advanced capitalist metropole at the expense of the global South.[11] Peter Gowan, for example, maintains that this new liberal cosmopolitanism is merely a "radicalization of the Anglo-American tradition that has conceived itself as upholding a liberal internationalism, based on visions of a single human race peacefully united by free trade and common legal norms, led by states featuring civic liberties and representative institutions."[12]

The controversies surrounding the unilateralism of "humanitarian interventions" heighten this difficulty. The recent queer critique of "Christian-secularist-financial time" offers textured examples of the US empire's attempt to project its values onto the universal realm of the human.[13] In his reflections on a fellowship year spent on Carol Vance's Program on Gender, Sexuality, Health, and Human Rights at Columbia University, queer scholar John Erni laments that the conversations within the interdisciplinary group were "colonized" by rights discourse and international law, which made it difficult to raise issues in cultural studies without "sacrificing its antireductionist stance."[14] Erni proposes three strategies for reframing human rights: "a conceptual reorientation of human rights as a political representation of modernities-in-struggle, a perspective of human rights as a nodal point of transnational social movements, and a utilization of human rights as a global legal apparatus with notable impact on the discourse of public social justice."[15] Erni's analysis points out the dangers of reducing human rights to an empiricist legalism. A meaningful human rights discourse, by contrast, must be grounded in the concrete struggles in transnational locations and informed by their interpretive communities, a task that it cannot do without an antireductionist cultural studies—such as queer theory. The same is true within each national community. Lisa Rofel argues that queer activists cannot demand rights from the Chinese state because in China, rights are legally defined as relations involving property, consumption, and commerce, a development that marginalized other kinds of rights.[16] However, the "fact that rights are not currently viable means that lesbians and gay men have the opportunity not to capitulate to heteronormative life. That is, the ability to press for a non-assimilationist, nonnormative life is enabled by this context."[17]

Third, at best, human rights discourse operates as a strategic essentialism, and therefore succumbs to many of the pitfalls that queer theory has been devoted to debunking in the past two decades. Heather Love, Carla Frecerro, Jasbir Puar, Lisa Duggan, Michael Warner, Lauren Berlant, David Eng, Roderick Ferguson, and the queer Marxists described in this book, all strive to show that "the new homonormativity" has displaced what Leo Bersani calls the culture of "gay outlaws" with a "rage for respectability." This displacement stems from queer people who believe that the primary task of the queer movement is to "persuade straight society that they can be good parents, good soldiers, good priests."[18] As Steven Seidman argues, gay normalization has actually resulted in a "narrowing of the range of legitimate sexual variation . . . The social integration of gays creates an anxiety that other 'deviant' sexualities (sex workers, sadomasochists, pedophiles, polygamists) will make similar claims to normality and also demand respectability."[19] In other words, the phenomena of gay normalization, queer liberalism, homonationalism, and homonormativity, discussed at length in chapter 1, are also attempts to *rehumanize* the queer without questioning our normative definitions of the human. By assimilating queer subjects into prescribed notions of what constitutes a human person, these projects place the human at the center of a rights movement that further alienates and disempowers members of the population who are already marginalized by the assimilative politics of gay normalization.

Finally, globalization has fundamentally transformed the nature of nation-based imperialism and created novel networks and institutions of power. This does not mean, however, that the rise of transnational corporations and accelerated rates of migration have created a global village where a unified humanity resides. Rather, globalization has rigidified existing hierarchies between nations and the differential axes along which the human and the subhuman are discursively produced. Hence, the human is not a pregiven concept, but one that is formed by virtue of new social norms and technologies of power that vary from culture to culture. Observing this point, Pheng Cheah proposes that the proper starting point for human rights thinking is not the common essence and conditions of humanity, but the inhuman conditions that human beings have created around the world—slavery, social hierarchy, inhumane labor conditions, mass poverty, and illiteracy. These conditions have prevented the realization of a new cosmopolitanism as the "vehicle of freedom."[20] In a similar vein, Judith Butler reminds us that while certain "human" lives are grievable, others may be remembered only as statistics of war casualties, embodying the "precarity of life."[21] Butler's rethinking of the human offers another iteration of what Giorgio Agamben terms "bare life" and what Elizabeth Povinelli terms "disposability."[22] In the latest collection of her writings on gender, Butler offers a succinct formulation of the problem:

> The terms by which we are recognized as human are socially articulated and changeable. And sometimes the very terms that confer "humanness" on some individuals are those that deprive certain other individuals of the possibility of achieving that status . . . The human is understood differentially depending on its race, the legibility of that race, its morphology, the recognizability of that morphology, its sex, the perpetual verifiability of that sex, its ethnicity, the categorical understanding of that ethnicity. Certain humans are

recognized as less than human, and that form of qualified recognition does not lead to a viable life. Certain humans are not recognized as human at all, and that leads to yet another order of unlivable life.[23]

As Butler's descriptions of the "recognizable" and "grievable" forms of human life indicate, the human is always differentially and hierarchically produced against something that is not human and hence in need of an analysis of how such hierarchies are created in the first place. In what follows, I propose a critical return to the problem of the human in Marx to highlight a historical alternative to the philosophical conundrums in the current queer critique of humanism that I outlined in the previous section. Insofar as the current suspicions of human rights discourse within queer theory have primarily relied on a poststructuralist critique of Enlightenment humanism, exploring the alternative genealogy of Marxism may also provide a different assessment of the relevance of the human in queer discourse and activism.

Figurations of the Human

The philosophy of humanism may appear as an antiquarian doctrine of Enlightenment philosophy that poststructuralist theory has decisively and irreversibly supplanted. *Humanism* today is a term we are more likely to associate with the conservative and outmoded works of Matthew Arnold, F. R. Leavis, and Lionel Trilling than with "critical theory." For some, that which makes theory critical is first and foremost owing to the influence of poststructuralist French thought of the 1970s and 1980s, which constituted a linguistic turn in theory that called into question the assumption of "man" as the sovereign maker and author of subjectivity. Instead of seeing the "I" as a social agent who speaks, antihumanists see the "I" as an effect of language: language "speaks me" into being.[24] A related problem is whether human beings from different cultures share any essential features with one another. On this problem, Kate Soper's *Humanism and Antihumanism* is quite helpful. Soper identifies two key points of contention between these two traditions: the notion of a core humanity and the status of history. As Soper explains, humanism takes history to be the product of human thought and action. All human beings participate in this history and share common interests, features, and origins; the fact that they do not always appear to do so is the result of a historical loss that Marxist authors term *alienation*. By contrast, antihumanists consider the "essence of man" to be an ideological myth that must be replaced by the scientific analysis of impersonal structures and forces. The postulation of a "core humanity" is thus analytically tied to the problem of subjectivity—whether we can think of the human as an effect of language or as the subject of political action.[25]

Ian Chambers offers a similar description of the debates in *Culture after Humanism*, but with a twist. Contemplating the art of Dunhuang in western China, Chambers identifies an instance of "mongrel past and hybrid incubation [that] betrays an altogether wilder and uncertain version of 'China,' its people, language, and culture, than that promoted officially."[26] Seeing Dunhuang as a historical example of "traveling culture" produced by the intermingling of Buddhist, Sanskrit, Tibetan, and Chinese manuscripts, Chambers suggests that the human is made and remade by forces beyond the subject's recognition and sense of purity. Extrapolating from the example of China, Chambers usefully outlines three central propositions of humanism that poststructuralist theory has rejected: the assumptions that the human subject is sovereign, that language is the transparent medium of its agency, and that truth is the representation of its rationalism.[27] For Chambers, the cultural history of China, with its "millenarian practice of calligraphy" and "the intriguing osmosis between writing and painting," opens up the possibility of a critical practice that surpasses the signified and directs our understanding to the material, historical, and psychic life in which we reside and recognize ourselves.[28] Whether the signifier of China can fulfill this ambitious task of displacing our naive humanist understandings of the self as Chambers suggests is difficult to say. We can, however, note that the construction of a linear relation between a progressive poststructuralist decentering of the subject and an antiquarian or naive humanism relies on a specific construction of China as the exterior of theory.

Soper's and Chambers's intellectual histories suggest that in the 1970s, the French thought of Jacques Derrida, Michel Foucault, Roland Barthes, and Jean Baudrillard brought about a conclusive and irreversible rupture in theory, after which the figure of the human became a monolithic foundationalism. In these accounts, the decentering of the subject in poststructuralist thought appeared as nothing less than a Co-

pernican revolution in theory. While classic works in the poststructuralist canon, such as Barthes's "The Death of the Author," focus on the
critique of the belief in the transparency of language, the decentering of
the subject in the tradition of antihumanism is not limited to the issue of
language and representation.[29] It is also an explicit critique of the meta-
physical assumptions about the essence of man associated with Marxism, and in some ways it is an attack on Marxism itself. Derrida's "The
Ends of Man," for example, criticizes Martin Heidegger's conception of
man as the shepherd of Being, but its main enemy is a naive "anthro-
pologism" and "personalism" of man as "the irreducible horizon and origin" that Derrida describes as "the unnoticed and uncontested common
ground of Marxism."[30]

While Derrida maps the theoretical opposition between humanism
and antihumanism onto the difference between Marxism and post-
Marxism, these charges against Marxist humanism are not limited to
poststructuralist thinkers. Indeed, Marxist authors themselves have
created, and by and large, accepted the impression that the advent
of antihumanist thought marked a mental shift within Marx, one that
helped him shed the trappings of German idealism to write his mature
and scientific works.[31] In Marxist criticism the distinction between humanism and antihumanism conventionally corresponds to two different Marxes, the young Marx of the *Economic and Philosophical Manuscripts
of 1844* and the scientific Marx of *Das Kapital*. Louis Althusser describes
the writings of "the young Marx" as developing through two humanist periods.[32] In the phase between 1840 and 1842, Marx's thought was
dominated by a liberal-rationalism derived from Immanuel Kant's
and Johann Gottlieb Fichte's ideas of human freedom and universal
rights. In the second phase, between 1842 and 1845, Ludwig Feuerbach's communalist humanism provided a new way for Marx to think
through the contradiction between man's essence (reason) and its
existence (unreason), and Marx's identification of the human shifted
from freedom to community. According to Althusser, it was not until
1845 that the mature or scientific Marx finally emerged, breaking with
every theory based on the history and politics of an essence of man to
develop a historical materialism grounded in the scientific analysis of
modes of production. Therefore, the protagonists of the social drama
of *Das Kapital* are capital and labor-power, rather than the capitalist (a
figure Marx rarely names in the text) and the proletariat (who is not an

individual in any case).[33] Althusser, in other words, portrays Marx as a thinker who once flirted with socialist humanism and theories of alienation but eventually came to see the errors of his own ways and became a staunch antihumanist.[34] This reading has profound ramifications; it also implies an attitude toward Marxism itself. Critics influenced by this reading are likely to argue that if there is anything worth salvaging intellectually in Marxism, it must be the antitotalitarian impulse of Marxism itself rather than its communalism. The so-called humanist phase of Marx's thinking is seen as yet another instantiation of totalitarianism, dogmatism, and foundationalism, which deconstruction overcomes by revealing what was already in the mature phase of his writing.[35]

In this sense, what Marx calls commodity fetishism refers precisely to this reverse anthropomorphism, an ideological process whereby deeply unequal relations between human beings take on the appearance of an equitable exchange between things. Contemporary Marxist theory almost invariably follows the second Marx, anthropomorphizing capital and labor-power as abstract forces that violently confront each other.[36] An example is Giovanni Arrighi's schematic redefinition of capitalism as four dynamic, systemic "cycles" of accumulation rather than social formations. These cycles appear to be impersonal forces; they may be centered on locations (such as Genoa) but they are never isomorphic with nation-states, races, and other cultural groupings.[37] While the interpretation of Marx as the ultimate antihumanist is attributed to Althusser's structuralist revolution, the reading of Marx as a humanist is associated with Jean-Paul Sartre.[38] Of course, not all Marxist critics find these two readings of Marx to be irreconcilable.[39] My reading of the discourse of queer human rights in the two Chinas demonstrates that the traditional opposition between the humanist and antihumanist Marxes is not inevitable, and that the poststructuralist and decentering readings of the subject do not necessarily result in the death of the human. Rather, we can recuperate a different notion of the human in Marx, one grounded neither in the essence of man nor in the structural and metahistorical movements of capital. I argue that Marx's scientific contributions come from a standpoint based on the moral equality of human time. His insistence on the equality of human time in Das Kapital is neither the same as a naturalistic understanding of the essence of man, nor an argument for the priority of economic processes in our interpretation of social life. Rather, the concept of the human in Marx brings to light the historical processes whereby human inequalities are produced and reproduced without resorting to mystifying causes such as geography or cultural differences. The example of the two Chinas illustrates the dangers of attributing human rights development to the outcomes of socialism and liberalism. These complexities reveal the tension between Marx the humanist and Marx the antihumanist to be an unstable, if not altogether false, distinction.

Althusser's relation to antihumanism is critically informed by his relation to China.[40] Like many leftist French thinkers of his generation, Althusser took an interest in China primarily because of Mao's Cultural Revolution. As Camille Robcis's study of Althusser's turn to the Chinese declaration of the rights of man shows, "the 'China' that seduced so many Maoist French intellectuals during the 1960s and 1970s had less to do with the reality of the communist nation than with the French political, social, and cultural context of the time. 'China' operated as a projection screen for a French Revolutionary tradition."[41] Nonetheless, Mao's ideas of contradictions, antihumanism, and ideology have also made a real impact on French politics and theory through figures such as Althusser, who further developed Mao's ideas into answers to the political predicaments of the French Party. As Robcis explains, the Sino-Soviet split and the Twentieth Congress (in which Khrushchev attacked the cult of personality) planted the seeds for a humanist turn within French Marxism. In response, Althusser turned to Mao's writings on contradictions as well as the symptomatic lacunae of Marx's early humanist writings in order to develop an antihumanist Marxism.[42] Observing that "Althusser embraced the Cultural Revolution to eradicate humanist ideology and to conduct a truly antihumanist structuralist revolution," Robcis suggests that China has been "structuralized" within the electoral politics of the French left.[43]

The meaning of humanism in Althusser's polemical appropriations of Maoism and its meaning in Chinese political philosophy are thus quite different. Despite the important connections between these traditions, Chinese intellectuals in the 1980s were careful to distinguish their discussion of the "humanist spirit" (renwen jingshen) from the Western philosophy of humanism (renwenzhuyi).[44] While Chinese discourse of the human is always conceived in some relation to Confucian humanism (rendao zhuyi), Mao has also deployed humanism to develop epistemologies of popular sovereignty and democratic centralism against Confucianism.[45] In the post-Cultural Revolution period, humanism again became an important system of thought against Maoism. The Chinese cultural critic He Zhaotian points out that in the 1980s humanism became the basis of the twin pillars of a literary revolution against Maoism, which championed two concepts: "literature is a human science" and "literature is an art of language." This humanist revolution prepared cultural studies to protest against the distortions of human nature during the Cultural Revolution.[46] In this tradition, Maoism came to be seen as the ultimate antihumanism. In Chinese intellectual thought, therefore, both Maoism and humanism are flexibly interpreted: at times, Maoism is closer to Marxist humanism, indicating a belief in the common essence of man as the basis for action; at other times, Maoism is closer to Marxist structuralism and grounded in the belief that history is governed by demonstrable laws such as the contradiction between the forces and relations of production.

Thus, humanism and antihumanism have enjoyed different fortunes in the recent history of France and China, often in response to changing political climates rather than new intellectual findings. Why, then, is queer theory today unanimously supportive of poststructuralist antihumanism? The popularity of the poststructuralist critique of humanism reflects, in part, the urgency of undoing the Eurocentrism of contemporary critical theory. Since humanism implies that all of humanity shares certain common essential features, while queer theory contains an implicit critique of Eurocentrism in its effort to extend recognition to a diversity of sexual experiences across the globe, humanism seems complicit with the cultural imperialism of the West that queer theory challenges. In other words, because poststructuralist queer theory maintains that the terms by which we are constituted as human are contingent on discursive regimes that vary from culture to culture, the postulation of a common humanity, according to this logic, must be a product of a falsely universalizing Enlightenment ideal in European philosophy, a nefarious and provincial practice that we have learned to correct with attention to cultural differences, hybridity, heterogeneity, local specificity, and contradictions in the production of human identity. Seen in this light, the critique of Eurocentrism and the critique of humanism are conflated with each other, while a humanist critique of Eurocentrism seems both intellectually outmoded and politically impossible.[47] Since the human is not a universally identical condition but a privileged status hierarchically produced across temporal and spatial sites of power, it has become politically and ethically imperative for poststructuralists to pluralize the human. However, we might pause to ask, are the problem of universalism and the problem of humanism really the same? And moreover, what are the consequences and implications of the equation between the critique of Eurocentrism and the destruction of the concept of the human?

Human rights discourse is an area that has been visibly affected by this conflation of humanism and Eurocentrism in the poststructuralist decentering of the subject. As with other intellectual and political projects issuing from aspirations for a common humanity, human rights discourse undeniably postulates and relies on a universality that is, in reality, legally, politically, and economically nonexistent. Indeed, the singular category of the human seems to be increasingly less meaningful. Not only is the theoretical concept of the human itself intellectually defunct with the decline of structuralism and humanism, the socioeconomic conditions that "the human" describes are also rapidly transforming. Identities are now described as hybrid, layered, multiple, indeterminate, heterogeneous, and internally contradictory. Under globalization, world cultures feel both more diversified and more interconnected, a phenomenon for which no ethical perspective on the human proves satisfactory.[48] In this sense, both the "rise of China" and the emergence of queer cultures bring new political claims to unsettle the monolithic constitution of the human as the Euro-American heteronormative and cisnormative subject. In the following section, I propose a rethinking of the relation between the poststructuralist assimilation of the Chinese difference and the queering of the humanist subject. I argue that the theoretical construction of China as a form of alterity in poststructuralist thought is itself a problematic consequence of liberal pluralist culture, and that this construction misses the more valuable lessons offered by the geopolitics of the Chinas. Through a case study of the ROC's invocation of queer human rights as a strategy to define its own differences from the PRC, I develop an alternative to the poststructuralist approach to the Chinese difference. My hope is to show that the concept of queer human rights is never a simple reflection of preexisting human diversity we can assimilate into a liberal pluralist framework; rather, this concept is always mediated by complex geopolitical relations and interests. Hence, it is important to resist the tendency to read the emergence of queer cultures in non-Western contexts in developmentalist terms, using the manifest status of queer human rights as a metric to assess the extent to which postsocialist and postauthoritarian regimes have evolved into liberal states under the contemporary logics of neoliberal globalization. My analysis shows that these assumptions of free and unfree queer subjects in the two Chinas are entangled with the unequal distribution of power and resources across the straits, for which reason a Marxist perspective on the construction of the human is both necessary and timely.

The Chinese Difference

In the current theoretical milieu, the universalizing tendency of structuralism has given way to projects focused on the exploration of alternative cultural sites, modes of subjectivity, and historical experiences. Put simply, the solution to the problem of the human is simply to pluralize it. Crucially, this solution does not ask us to analyze how the hierarchical relations between humans are produced and reproduced over time—it merely asks us to recognize the irreducible pluralism of ways of being human. As an understudied topic in European philosophy, China is instrumentalized by poststructuralist thinkers who believe that the invocation of its alterity provides a much needed corrective to European humanism. In this context, China is rarely examined as an object of critical interest itself; rather, China provides an ethnic specimen for antihumanist thought, a logic of supplement against which the entirety of Western logos comes undone, its metaphysics deconstructed, its hegemony challenged, and its attendant universals successfully refused. The name China becomes synonymous with human difference, a difference that the theoretical tenets of poststructuralism compel us to affirm. The human and the Chinese appear to be mutually exclusive terms, as though we must first accept this mutual exclusivity in order to free ourselves from the totalizing clutches of European theory.

There are many examples of how China becomes a figure for antifoundationalism in poststructuralist theory, insofar as the invocation of Chinese concepts of the human is assumed to have the ability to disrupt the fantasy of the universal Eurocentric subject. Julia Kristeva's *About Chinese Women* is a particularly telling example of how an imagined identification with China played a key role in the early formation of French posthumanist theory.[49] Writing in the post–1968 leftist circles of Paris, where Barthes, Althusser, Jacques Lacan, and others enthusiastically embraced Mao's China as a utopian site of revolution, Kristeva explores the problematic of what defines a unified female subject in psychoanalysis. She criticizes Lacan's characterization of sexual difference as coextensive with language itself, as the binary symbolic positions of the masculine and the feminine through which the speaking subject emerges and acquires social intelligibility. Against Lacan's binary framework, she seeks to include racial and cultural differences in her theory of subject formation, suggesting that a Western woman's recognition of her self as a speaking subject is not a product of the binary symbolic positions in language, but what is accomplished through her cross-cultural identification with the Other.

Kristeva argues that the oppression of Western women is the result of the historical triumph of the patriarchal monotheism of Judaism over earlier matriarchal, fertility-based cultural systems. For Kristeva, the invariable law of the Symbolic, as Lacan describes, is specific to Western monotheistic culture. Kristeva uses Chinese myths, history, and cultural practices to construct a wild fantasy about an alternative matrilineal social space full of feminine *jouissance* that, she believes, subverts Lacan's phallocentric economy. In Kristeva's work, China represents an idyllic cultural space where the dynamics of maternal plentitude and presemiotic *chora* have not yet been suppressed by the development of monotheism and mercantile capitalism. Invoking an Orient grounded in a primitivistic, collective community organized under matriarchal authority, Kristeva believes that she has at last escaped the clutches of Western monotheism.[50]

Kristeva's work is a good example of a tendency in liberal discourses to invoke China in order to overcome an internal problem within Western theory. Here, a perceived *temporal* advance within European history—the passage from what seems to be a naive humanism to a sophisticated poststructuralism—becomes the *geopolitical* expansion from Europe to China with a reoriented intellectual gaze. If this geopolitical shift merely serves to solidify one's sense of moral supremacy and historical triumph over a conquered humanism or a phallogocentric system of signification, this narrative connects not China and the West but two points in European intellectual history—today's poststructuralist antihumanism and the structuralist humanism of Marx's and Lacan's generations. We should insist, however, that an important distinction exists between the analytical conundrum of (Marxist) humanism and the moral perils of Eurocentrism, and that the rejection of the latter need not result in the destruction of the former.

As I have argued in the first two chapters of *Queer Marxism in Two Chinas*, queer theory has always needed a theory of the incommensurability between East and West in order to demonstrate that notions like "symbolic," "women," "homosexuality," and "patriarchy" are culturally constructed and hence subject to resignification. This impulse has resulted in a contradiction between a queer critique of heteronormativity (the critique of the idea that heterosexuality is natural and universal) and the postcolonial critique of allochronism (the critique of the idea that the homo/heterosexual distinction, like modernity, was first invented in the West). The problem of allochronism is most clearly found in Foucault's work, whose emphasis on the discursive invention of the homosexual as a species leads him to characterize China (modern or classical), Japan, India, Rome, and the Arabo-Moslem societies as interchangeable examples of an *ars erotica* without history. Whether championed as an alternative system of pre-Oedipal signification (Kristeva) or condemned as a space of stagnation through the millennia (Foucault), China functions merely as a figure—and one whose empirical studies or archival evidence does not interest these French thinkers. Rather, China operates as a site of difference for antihumanist theory, producing a set of citable geopolitical specificities that hold for liberal Western thinkers the promise of undoing the universality of idealized Western norms and institutions. Foucault and Kristeva exemplify what I term theories of the radical generalizability of China, whereby vast differences between historical dynasties and ethno-linguistic regions are flattened out into a singular sign, such as women, *chora*, *ars erotica*, or the Cultural Revolution.

In what follows, I'd like to turn to a different kind of Chinese difference—not between China and the West, but between the perceived lack of liberalism in mainland China and the development of liberal queer culture in Taiwan. My aim is to historicize the category of liberalism through the case of queer human rights discourse against China. Instead of starting with political systems (between China, Taiwan, and the West) as the interpretive framework for reading queer culture, I suggest that liberalism, democracy, and queer rights are better understood as discursively produced identities. This analysis of queer human rights, I hope, will enable a new mode of cognitive mapping that presents an alternative to the traditional interpretation of the two Chinas as the embodiments of (post)socialism and liberal capitalism.

A Case Study: Queer Illiberalism in Taiwan

The discourse of queer human rights against China shows that neither liberalism nor socialism can be easily attributed to a mode of production. Rather, liberalism is a political narrative positioned in relation to the imagined sign of China, fueled by the ostensible tolerance, celebration, and recognition of queer subjects and other minorities in the ROC.[51] The category of the queer, in either China, does not describe the empirical existence of a social group. It is rather a sign of national difference, flashed for a global audience, between ROC's liberalism and PRC's lack of human rights. The queer refers to a discursively produced political subject, officially endorsed by the government of Taiwan as a minority group in need of state protection and entitled to human rights. The category of the queer plays a significant role in the global construction of the social and political meaning of the two Chinas today for both international China-watchers (including human rights watchers) and Chinese-speakers who identify or disidentify with Chineseness. China accrues its meaning in relation to the queer, whose social formation in turn defines China by restricting the definition of liberalism to the acquisition of rights.

Queer liberalism is a key tool with which Taiwan disciplines mainland China and produces its national sign of difference from its political enemy in the service of the Taiwanese independence project. Compared to mainland China or Singapore, Taiwan has indeed created greater civic space for queer subjects. The recent events of the Sunflower Student Movement (March to April 2014), during which protestors occupied the Legislative Chamber after a trade pact with the

PRC (the Cross-Strait Service Trade Agreement) was passed without clause-by-clause review, richly demonstrate the Taiwanese public's partisan passions, political liberty, and organized civic culture. It is also true that queer communities in Taiwan are both more organized and more visible than those in the PRC, Hong Kong, and Singapore. In addition to a large network of queer advocacy groups, Taiwan also has a robust culture of queer art, theater, literature, entertainment, and consumption. Despite these apparent advances in queer human rights, however, sexual minorities remain subject to a strong form of *queer illiberalism* in Taiwan. The space of the queer is accessible only to those who have met the state's definition of the human. Prostitutes, people living with AIDS, gay men and lesbians who use recreational drugs, and transgendered people all fall outside the normative definition of a "gay but healthy" image promoted by the state and remain excluded if not outright persecuted. In fact, the rhetoric of tolerance, liberalism, and progress is a political ruse designed to win over the sympathy of the American public, since Taiwan's continuous de facto and imagined future de jure status as a sovereign nation-state depends on American military protection and support.

At the present, the ROC parliament is reviewing a marriage equality bill that was submitted by NGOs in 2013. Since the bill was brought to the parliament, religious groups have organized massive rallies in protest of the bill. At the same time, many public figures, including pop singer A-Mei, have actively participated in its promotion. These events indicate that legal same-sex marriages have indeed entered a different phase of public consciousness in Taiwan. Long before the current marriage equality proposal, however, in 2001 Taiwan was already rumored to be on its way to becoming the first country in Asia to legalize same-sex marriage. The unsubstantiated news story was broadcast on all major media, including BBC News World and fridae.com (a Singapore-based English-language social networking website for gay men and women in Asia). The rumor quickly gained wide international attention, particularly from human rights watchers and gay activists. Even academics have misquoted the event. In a scholarly article by Jens Damm, "Same-Sex Desire and Society in Taiwan, 1970–1987," the author begins by commenting on the "stark contrast" between the dark years of the 1970s (symbolized by Pai's novel) "the recent announcement by Taiwan's president, Chen Shui-bian, that 'gay marriage' (*tong-*

zhi hunyin) is going to be legalized; the discourse of same-sex desire in Taiwan has clearly undergone dramatic changes in recent decades."[52]

The international media quickly described the news as a groundbreaking event in the global spread of human rights and applauded Taiwan as a model for the People's Republic of China. In reality, all that the Taiwanese congress had received at the time was a draft of a bill that both the public and the administration knew would never pass. In 2001, the Executive Yuan of Taiwan announced that a "protection of basic human rights" bill (*renquan baozhang jiben fa*) was in the planning stage as part of the new government's effort to create a "nation based on human rights" (*renquan liguo*), the campaign slogan of the DPP (Democratic Progressive Party) administration, the first "native" political party elected to power after forty years of the China-centered KMT (Kuomintang) autocracy. The announcement stated that homosexuals would be granted the right to organize families and adopt children—the word "marriage" was never mentioned. In July 2003, the government announced again that the "protection of basic human rights" bill was already fully drafted in accordance with international standards. The new bill, it was declared, would include protection against discrimination on the basis of gender and sexual orientation, and afford homosexuals the rights of marriage, adoption, and equality in the workplace. On October 27, 2003, the Executive Yuan announced to the global media that "Taiwan already has same-sex marriage," to the consternation of the citizenry.[53]

Unlike the current marriage equality bill, the 2003 rumor was merely a political ruse on the part of the newly elected DPP administration to promote its self-image as a liberal regime in distinction to mainland China.[54] To solidify its pro-independence, anti-PRC stance and to rally American support, the DPP regime fabricated a pro-same-sex marriage initiative, while carefully keeping it from realization to avoid alienating the conservative and religious electoral bases. These subtleties show that the concept of queer human rights is rarely a simple self-articulation by persecuted minorities; rather, the legal and ethical discourses of queer human rights are constantly bound up with the material and geopolitical demands of nation-states.

The global perception that Taiwan has made more progress in queer human rights than mainland China issues from the more fundamental assumption that capitalism and socialism define the differences between

Taiwan and China. This assumption also holds that a mode of production such as capitalism, socialism, or postsocialism determines the cultural formations of each country and serves as a satisfactory explanatory paradigm for understanding the freedom and constraints facing queer lives. This idea stems from a common academic argument that the legitimatization of homosexuality constitutes the last step of a globalizing liberalism, after which human history will be fully, and finally, rational.[55] This argument presumes, on the one hand, that liberalism is the motor behind every form of social progress ever achieved by humankind, holding it responsible for human emancipation as such. It posits, on the other hand, a chronological and analogical relationship between struggles that are actually overlapping and mutually constitutive, which ignores the historical specificity of race, gender, class, and other social axes of power. As a result, women's suffrage, the civil rights movement, and the present discourse of queer human rights are seen as structurally equivalent and historically successive movements.

The actual history of liberalism, democracy, and human rights in Taiwan, however, defies this chronological narrative. The DPP electoral campaign of "a new nation founded on human rights" was, in reality, an expression of anti-Chinese sentiments in Taiwan. The moral opprobrium heaped on communism in the PRC and on KMT dictatorship in Taiwan became virtually indistinguishable at the time when the awakening of "nativist consciousness" in Taiwan resulted in DPP's electoral success in 2000. The language of human rights afforded a political idiom that promised to end two nightmarish regimes—communism and KMT dictatorship—that had become conflated in the Taiwanese social imaginary. Contemporary intellectuals and politicians in Taiwan habitually describe the mainland Chinese as the primitive and the sub-human, as those not quite human subjects lacking in education, cultural refinement, and civilized manners. Recent bestsellers in the genre of political commentary and historical memoir contain a host of examples, though I will limit my discussion to the recent works of two prominent feminists, Lung Ying-tai and Chi Pang-yuan. Lung Ying-tai is a prolific writer and cultural critic who was Taiwan's Minister of the Ministry of Culture from 2012 to 2014. Lung's controversial but widely read book, *Big River, Big Sea—Untold Stories of 1949*, continues an earlier argument introduced in her *Persuade Us with Civilization, Not Force,*

Please that the obstacle to a unitary China lies in the deleterious effects of communism, such as mass illiteracy and lack of culture. *Big River, Big Sea—Untold Stories of 1949* sold over 110,000 copies in its first month of publication and was banned in the People's Republic of China.[56] Lung's work shares a certain nostalgia for the loss of Chinese culture with another contemporary work of enormous influence, Chi's *The Great River.* Chi's bestseller aims to do three things: it is a personal family history that documents the tumultuous years of China before her family emigrated to Taiwan, a feminist story of a woman's struggle between the old and the new, and, finally, Taiwan's heroic entry to become part of the modern West. Like Lung, Chi presents the modern revolutions in China as the loss and distortion of human nature. By contrast, Taiwan, thanks to its numerous Western-educated intellectuals, successfully evolved past the shackles of tradition (one that Chi cites throughout the book is discrimination against women) and entered a common global family of modern nations. The implication is that one becomes human only by shedding one's traditional, backward Chinese essence.

The idea of queer human rights and legalized same-sex marriage was formulated in this political context. Former DPP Vice President of Taiwan, Annette Hsiu-lien Lu, is a prominent feminist activist and literary icon. In addition to *New Feminism* (1974), one of the earliest and most influential works of feminist criticism in Taiwan, Lu also wrote, during her imprisonment as a political dissident, *These Three Women* (1985), a novel that depicts the differences between traditional housewives and independent career women.[57] Under the years of KMT autocracy, Lu was a political dissident who survived sedition charges, imprisonment, and political persecution. Scholars credit Lu with the establishment of "a Taiwanese feminist convention to make possible the overturn of governmental gender policies."[58] During her term as vice president, Lu formed the Presidential Office's Human Rights Advisory Committee and served as its spokesperson and convener. While Lu made important feminist contributions, she is the same person who told the citizenry in 2003 that "Heaven sent AIDS as a punishment so that we can distinguish men from animals" (*aizi tianqian shuo*) and therefore people living with HIV/AIDS should be rounded up and quarantined in a state-established "AIDS village."[59] Is Taiwan a liberal state for queers? How do we explain these paradoxes?

It was during the time of Lu's notorious speech that the bill for legalized same-sex marriage was proposed. Lu's own practice, however, betrayed that both human rights and the status of the human were conditional and retractable political choices, conferred upon only those who have met the state's definition of the human. While the law recognizes certain political subjects as human and therefore entitled to state protection, the same law alienates certain sexual minorities from the domain of the human, further exacerbating the conditions of their existence.

While rhetorically endorsing human rights, the Taiwanese state regularly mobilizes the police to raid gay home parties and harass gay bars. In several well-publicized events, the illiberal character of the regime became transparent. Gender/Sexual Rights Association, Taiwan holds an annual press conference on the "ten worst human rights violation cases in Taiwan," and an impressive list has been archived. In the AG Incident in 1998, the police raided a gay sauna (AG) and forced its patrons to simulate sex in front of the media. In 2004, the Taiwanese police (with paparazzi reporters) broke into a private residence during a gay "home party" (hong pa) (see figure 2). The police arrested the attendants, detained them in jail, screened them for sexually transmitted diseases, and published the test results to the media.

In 2003, the Taiwanese government prosecuted Lai, the owner of a bookstore, Gin Gin, for the possession and sale of gay adult magazines, despite the fact that all the magazines were legally imported, and sealed in plastic wrappings with a warning label of "18 and older only" in accordance with Taiwanese regulations. Moreover, heterosexual adult magazines have been legal and readily available in Taiwan, not to mention on the internet. In 2004, Lai was charged under the Criminal Code for the dissemination and distribution of obscene materials, and found guilty in 2005. The Gin Gin case paved the way for the "Zoophilia webpage incident," the prosecution of Central University Professor Josephine Ho for a hyperlink on her research center's website, which I discuss in detail in chapter two.

What is lacking in the global perception of Taiwan as a liberal counterpart to authoritarian China is precisely an account of the social conditions under which a sexual subject qualifies as a human being and becomes a recipient of political rights and entitlements. The ostensible support for or acceptance of gay men and lesbians in Taiwan, in fact,

5.2. Taiwanese police arresting gay men at a private party (Source: *Apple Daily*, Jan. 21, 2004. http://www.appledaily.com.tw/appledaily/article/headline/20040121/660437/

is extended only to specific groups of sexual subjects and is contingent on their abilities to meet certain social expectations and prove their human-like qualities. People living with AIDS, transgendered individuals, non-monogamous gay people, drag queens, transsexuals, drug-users, prostitutes, and their clients are excluded from the definition of a human being. In fact, the apparent legitimacy and visibility of Taiwan's gay culture has only further alienated those who live on the margins of society and do not identify with what society conceives of as a healthy, normal human being who "happens" to desire other persons of the same sex. The *tongzhi* movement in Taiwan, which began in the 1990s as a collective attempt to re-humanize stigmatized sexual subjects by dissociating homosexuality from the stereotypes—anal sex, drug use, diseases, and gender confusion—has been largely successful; one of its consequences is that social respect and normalcy have become the preconditions for queer subjects who seek the status of the human and its associated legal protection or social benefits. As discussed in the beginning of this book, queerness is now indeed a widely accepted lifestyle in Taiwan and part of its mainstream culture, but the newly earned legitimacy of *tongzhi* has deradicalized the queer movement and transformed homosexuality into an object of consumption and a site of political manipulation.

The Human in Marxism

The Chinese difference is thus an ideological fantasy predicated on the hierarchical constructions of the queer, the subhuman, and the liberal according to developmentalist logics. To counter this ideological narrative, we need to recuperate the figure of the human in Marx, one that is grounded in a non-liberal approach to ethics and equality. How does Marxism help immunize us against queer liberalism? Alternately, what does the case of queer human rights in and against the two Chinas teach us to rethink in Marxism?

Above all else, Taiwan's self-construction as a liberal state through a selective endorsement of queer human rights shows that liberalism is more of a discursively constructed political image than a generative infrastructure in relation to queer lives. This political image is discursively and retroactively constructed by the acknowledgment of sexual minorities, rather than being a social formation capable of bringing such minorities into being. Put differently, the case demonstrates that liberal democracy and socialist authoritarianism in the Chinas are better understood as discursive constructions than as modes of production that have a meaningful correlation to queer lives. Although Marxism is too often understood as a theory of modes of production, Marx's writing offers significant grounds for rejecting the categorizations of the two Chinas as liberal and illiberal queer spheres and economic formations. However easy it is for mainstream critics to reduce Marxism to a defense of socialist planning or collectivized labor in the PRC, I contend that Marx's own discussion of the human actually exposes the limits of mode-of-production narratives. The human in Marx is not a self-same identity, but a social relation. As the subject of a labor theory of value that emphasizes *the relationality of the self* and hence the limits of identity claims, the figure of the human in Marx is, as it were, already queered. To look for the queer human in Marx is to retrieve the ways in which the illusion of an autonomous self in bourgeois society is sustained by forces and relations beyond one's recognition. Marx's understanding of the constitutive sociality of the self formulates a queer theory *avant la lettre* that recasts the figure of the human as an effect of unanticipated forms of intimacy, desire, and connectedness in the world.

Although it is common to assume that the foundational premise of Marxism is the priority of economics in the determinations of social life and that Marx's project is an advocacy of socialist redistribution through a moral critique of capitalist consumption, an analysis of the figure of the human in Marx demonstrates the centrality of the labor theory of value for Marxist philosophy. The theory posits that the labors of all human beings, measured by time units, are morally equivalent. Through commodity-exchanges, the products of human labor take on different appearances and their prices may rise or fall (depending on the laws of supply and demand) but their values remain constant (as determined by the amount of labor expended in their creation). Crucial for Marx is the distinction between wealth and value: whereas wealth may appear to be something a person rightfully earns through hard work, risk-taking, foresight, or sheer luck, from the perspective of value the only way to accumulate greater wealth than the value of one's productive contributions to society is through the expropriation of the fruits of other producers. The concept of value describes the truly transindividual nature of the invisible and unequal mechanisms for redistributing social resources, whereas the language of private property creates the illusion that wealth is the individual achievement of the homo economicus at no expense of the others. The observation that any given commodity contains a quantum of labor from an unknown producer, who is in turn sustained by the labors of other unknown producers, allows Marx to make the argument that human beings are reproduced by an infinite aggregate of labors beyond the immediate scenes of production and direct exchange. The recognition of the invariability and indestructibility of value binds all of us to other human beings we do not know.[60] The labor theory of value forms the kernel of Marx's concept of the human as well as the basis of his communalism; I suggest that the labor theory of value is also the basis of a proto-queer theory of the constitutive links between the formation of the self and unknowable Others that anticipates contemporary theoretical efforts to redefine gender and sexuality as "ek-stasis," as "modes of being dispossessed, ways of being for another or, indeed, by virtue of another."[61]

Marx discusses the human in the sections of *Das Kapital* on the "organic" composition of capital. For Marx, the human figure (variable capital) is the sole producer of value, while the material objects that may be useful for the production of goods—capital, the machinery, raw materials, buildings, electricity, and commodities—are merely congealed forms of past human labor. Therefore, industrialization does not produce more value in a given society; it merely alters the value relationship between living labor and constant capital in the production process. This point is worth belaboring in the present context because it shows how erroneous it is to interpret Marxism as a recipe of socialist modernization, as well as how counterproductive it is to characterize the two Chinas as discrete national organizations in different stages of cultural and economic development, instead of understanding them as locations with unequal access to material and symbolic goods in the global chain of value. More important, Marx's labor theory of value does not limit itself to the reconstitution of labor-power and raw materials in the production scheme, but contains an account of the cost of the objective conditions that must be socially produced to renew the production process and paid for by the surplus value of the human worker. Althusser later rephrases Marx's insight as "a representation of the imaginary relationship of individuals to their real conditions of existence" necessary for the "reproduction of the conditions of production."[62] Classical Marxist authors discuss Marx's description of the labor process as the unity of three departments: department one refers to the branches of society that produce the means of production (raw materials, energy, machinery, tools, and buildings); department two refers to the branches that produce consumer goods and hence (re-)produce the labor force; and department three refers to the branches that do not directly enter the reproduction scheme and renew neither constant nor variable capital, such as the producers of luxury goods, weapons, churches, prisons, the police, and other ideological apparatuses that allow a society based on the first two departments to cohere and continue to function as a productive organism. Both Althusser's "reproduction of the conditions of production" (including ideology) and the three-department scheme in classical Marxist theory emphasize that the human figure is reproduced by *cultural forces* that contain value, not by material means of subsistence alone. Therefore, Marx's labor theory of value is not a description of the reconstitution of human beings in a narrowly economic sense. These cultural conditions of re-production encompass relations of gender and sexuality as well.

By turning our attention to the social conditions that produce and reproduce the human, Marx demonstrates the dialectical process whereby a human subject is constituted by forces and vectors of power that are beyond the immediate sense experience of the subject. Seen in this light, the traditional opposition between humanist and antihumanist is no longer irresolvable. Marx's understanding of the social matrix in which the subject acquires the status of the human (or becomes the sub-human) in *Das Kapital* is a cognitive supplement, rather than a logical corrective, to his early writings on the alienation of human beings from their species-being. The actual compatibility between Marx's early writings and contemporary poststructuralist theory of the queered and decentered subject designates fertile grounds for a rethinking of the meaning of socialism and liberalism in cultural contexts such as the two Chinas.

This analysis shows that, while we are accustomed to viewing Marxism and liberalism in antithetical terms and attributing queerness to the achievements of the latter, Marx's labor theory of value contains an ethical perspective on the relationality of the self that is more compatible with queer (rather than gay and lesbian) theory and movements, in contrast to liberalism's emphasis on individual autonomy, identity, and identity-based rights. In turn, queer perspectives also help disabuse us of the conventional, knee-jerk associations of Marxism and liberalism with the PRC and the ROC respectively by demonstrating that the history of minority struggles in concrete contexts is too complex to be reduced to an epiphenomenon of liberal or nonliberal economics. If we cease to understand Marxism and liberalism as contrasting modes of production and civic cultures of freedom of speech, queerness also acquires a more expansive and capacious definition that can benefit from Marxist theories of human interdependency and relationality.

A reinvigorated reading of the current discourse about queer human rights in (and for) the Chinas generates a textured description of the queer figuration of the human in its complexity without reducing it to a site of cross-cultural difference. This reading provides a way to disentangle the intellectual project of antihumanism from the moral requirements of multiculturalism by shifting, above all, the focus of progressive writings on queer Chinas away from a mode-of-production narrative to a theory of sociality grounded in the notion of shared time. Rather than insisting on the determining functions of economic factors in cultural life, this queer Marxism demonstrates the mutual complicity of moral and historical elements in the formation of the human. The discourse of queer human rights shows that the figure of the human is a powerfully operable legal form full of complexities. Neither an uncritical return to the values of humanism nor a wholesale destruction of the human would succeed in unraveling the powers and effects of contemporary iterations of queer human rights. What we need, rather, is a theory of the human that bridges the gap between the infinitely varied genders and sexualities in human cultures and our shared rights, responsibilities, and futures. As a corollary, we will need a theory that is capable of understanding the human as the subject of political action as well as an effect of social structuration. If, to some extent, this theory is already available in Marx's humanist and antihumanist writings, the problem of the human provides compelling reasons why a queer Marxism is not only possible but desirable. These connections are lost if we continue to view Marxism as a theodicy of a utopian classless society in the future or as a humanist defense of the primacy of economics that queer theory comes to challenge and displace. In this sense, the poststructuralist decentering of Marxist humanism appears to be a mischaracterization, for the figure of the human in Marx's labor theory of value already contains a critique of the sovereign subject and identity-based claims in a fashion that anticipates queer theory. Combined with each other, Marxism and queer theory are no longer mere descriptions of the rights and injuries of a historical subject (the proletariat or the homosexual). Rather, queer Marxists analyze the field of gender norms and social power in which desire, pleasure, intimacy, and human connectedness become possible, asking how such social relations are reproduced along unequal axes of power for differently positioned human beings. The geopolitical lessons of the Chinas highlight the urgency as well as the possibilities of renewing these dialogues between queer and Marxist methodologies.

Although the concept of queer human rights is paradoxically derived from the rights-bearers' differences (queerness) and their commonality (humanness), the Marxist uses of this paradox reveal it to be a powerful kind of catachresis in local strategic contexts. Nonetheless, our ability to deploy this catachresis has been vitiated by an uncritical use of the political status of sexual minorities as a metric to assess the extent to which neoliberal globalization has transformed postsocialist and post-authoritarian regimes. This story of the geopolitical rivalry between the two Chinas as the underlying cause for Taiwan's construction of a liberal, queer-friendly political image demonstrates that the intelligibility of sex and sexuality is often governed by material forces beyond sexual minorities' own initiative. Marx's labor theory of value is useful here because it shows that the human figure is reproduced by both cultural and material elements. Insofar as the "human" is both a material and a cultural concept, the subject of queer human rights is an appropriate paradox that cannot be defined by economic status or sexual identity alone. But perhaps the difference between the queer and the human, and between queer theory and Marxism, has been misconstrued from the start. The language of queerness reminds us that that is an infinite range of human sexualities, subjectivities, and differences which we cannot ethically define in advance, while Marxism emphasizes that, despite our differences in sexual orientation or nationality, we are one humanity who cohabits the same planet with shared responsibilities and interlocking fates. This dichotomous characterization misses one point about the meaning of "difference" in Marxism: queerness or difference does not simply exist; we have to create it. I am convinced that one day, for queers, living with a difference and making a difference will finally be the same.

NOTES

Chapter 1. Marxism, Queer Liberalism, and the Quandary of Two Chinas

1. Duggan, *Twilight of Equality?*, 50.

2. Warner, *The Trouble with Normal*, 168.

3. Phelan points out that the logic of homonationalism produces a secondary marginalization within "sexual strangers," who are compelled by the requirements of assimilation and group presentation to make their bid for entry as "good homosexuals" by condemning the "bad queers." Phelan, *Sexual Strangers*, 115–16. For new critiques of the alignment between the rise of homonormative politics and neoliberal values, see the essays in the special issue edited by Murphy, Ruiz, and Serlin, "Queer Futures."

4. Ferry, "Rethinking the Mainstream Gay and Lesbian Movement Beyond the Classroom," 104, 112.

5. The problems with China's neoliberal turn are well attested by many translated works by prominent PRC intellectuals, such as Wang Hui, *China's New Order*, 78–137; Wang Hui, *The End of the Revolution*, 19–66; and Dai Jinhua's *Cinema and Desire*, 213–34. Zhang Xudong succinctly summarizes the problem with China's neoliberal turn as the dilemma of "how to secure the freedom of a few against the demands for equality by the many." Zhang, *Postsocialism and Cultural Politics*, 52.

6. Rofel, *Desiring China*, 85–110.

7. Rofel, "The Traffic in Money Boys," 426–31.

8. Rofel, *Desiring China*, 25.

9. Lim, *Celluloid Comrades*, 24.

10. For examples of this approach, see the collection of essays in Chiang and Heinrich's edited volume, *Queer Sinophone Cultures*.

11. See Tang, *Conditional Spaces* for a treatment of the spatial configurations of desire in neoliberal Hong Kong, and Leung, *Undercurrents*, for a lucid analysis

of the interplay between subterranean expressions and public image culture in Hong Kong's postcolonial, neoliberalized sphere of production.

12. Yue and Zubillago-Pow develop the notion of "illiberal pragmatism" in their coedited volume, *Queer Singapore*. L. Chua's recent book, *Mobilizing Gay Singapore*, speaks from the activist side of the story, showing that the gay movements in the country deploy "pragmatic resistance" and creative strategies to gain visibility without direct confrontations with the law. See also B. Chua, "High Wage Ministers and the Management of Gays and the Elderly," for a lucid analysis of Singapore's "symbolic politics" that somehow manages to create social stability through oppressive laws the state has no real interest in enforcing. For an analysis of how queer performances and spectacles transform Singapore's national and transnational symbolic politics, see Lim, *Brown Boys and Rice Queens*, 91–101. Treat points out that Singapore's brief support of pinkwashing and homonationalism (2001–2004) was an economically motivated affair inspired by theories of creative class capitalism. Treat, "Rise and Fall," 349–65.

13. See Cohen, *Boundaries of Blackness*; Ferguson, *Aberrations in Black*; Manalansan, *Global Divas*; Muñoz, *Disidentifications*; Hong and Ferguson, *Strange Affinities*; Lim, *Brown Boys and Rice Queens*; McCune, *Sexual Discretion: Black Masculinity and the Politics of Passing*; Johnson and Henderson, *Black Queer Studies*; Holland, *The Erotic Life of Racism*; Allen, "Black/Queer/Diaspora."

14. Guillory makes this point in the context of the canon debate during the culture wars. *Cultural Capital*, 4.

15. Butler's classic essay, "Merely Cultural," offers an elegant defense of queer theory against "Marxist objection[s]" that such theory is "factionalizing, identitarian, and particularistic" (265) in its failure to consider the totality of the social system and more imperative tasks such as redistributive justice. Butler's *Bodies That Matter* is also, in many ways, an oblique response to the Marxist insistence on "materialism" as the domain of human productive activities that sustains and defines the viability of different human beings. In the triangulated debates between Butler, Laclau, and Žižek published as *Contingency, Hegemony, and Universality*, Butler further critiques the notion of capitalism as an all-encompassing structure that is elevated to an ahistorical, prediscursive, and transcendental category called the "Real."

16. Conversely, we can speculate that scholars of neoliberalism are turning to queer issues because of the theoretical distinction between liberalism and neoliberalism. As Aihwa Ong argues, whereas liberalism is a doctrine of "free economic action" in a negative relation to the state, neoliberalism is a mode of political optimization that cannot be understood as a strictly juridico-legal relationship between government and citizenship. Instead, this relationship concerns two kinds of optimizing technologies: technologies of subjectivity and technologies of subjection (Ong, *Neoliberalism as Exception*, 2, 6). If this analysis is right, we can further contend that any discussion of neoliberalism would remain incomplete without a consideration of queer sexuality as technologies of subjectivity and subjection.

17. Edelman's controversial *No Future* outlines the conflict between civilization's investment in the figure of the child and the antisocial, antirelational orientation of queerness he calls "sinthomosexual jouissance" (36, 38, 39). Against Edelman, Muñoz's *Cruising Utopia* outlines a different temporality that casts queerness as a future-oriented political project that must refuse pragmatism and assimilation. Edelman offers a renewed defense and explanation of living with negativity in his new coauthored (with Berlant) work, *Sex, Or the Unbearable*.

18. Freeman's *Time Binds* articulates this sense of erotohistoriography, which may be usefully contrasted with Love's *Feeling Backwards*, which offers another powerful argument for a recuperative history that can counter the loss of queer political radicality to gay assimilation.

19. Halberstam, *In a Queer Time and Place*.

20. Coviello, *Tomorrow's Parties*, and Nealon, *Foundlings*.

21. Halley and Parker, *After Sex? On Writing Since Queer Theory*; O'Rourke, "The Afterlives of Queer Theory"; and Ruffolo, *Post-Queer Politics*.

22. A short list of representative works published in the last few years include, Ahmed, *The Promise of Happiness*; Berlant, *Cruel Optimism*; Crimp, *Melancholia and Moralism*; Gould, *Moving Politics: Emotion and ACT UP's Fight Against AIDS*; Nealon, *Foundlings: Gay and Lesbian Historical Emotion before Stonewall*; Ngai, *Ugly Feelings*; Snediker, *Queer Optimism*; Cvetkvovich, *Depression*; Eng, *The Feeling of Kinship*; Muñoz, "Feeling Brown, Feeling Down."

23. Williams, *Marxism and Literature*, 128–35; Marcuse, *Eros and Civilization*, 78–105.

24. The affective turn in queer theory left many imprints on Chinese studies. See Schroeder, "On Cowboys and Aliens," for an example of an illuminating analysis of the new affective history of queer visual culture in contemporary China.

25. On money boys, see Kong, "Outcast Bodies," "Men Who Sell Sex in China," and *Hidden Voice*; Rofel, "The Traffic in Money Boys"; Tong, *Commercial Sex in MSM Community in China*. For early twentieth-century contexts, see Wu and Stevenson, "Male Love Lost"; and Kang, *Obsession*.

26. Martin, *Backward Glances*, 147–79.

27. See Shernuk, "Queer Chinese Postsocialist Horizons," for a provocative phenomenological reading of two queer texts from 1990s' Beijing, "Sentiments Like Water" and *Beijing Story*. Sernuk argues that these texts signify new postsocialist bodily horizons and bourgeoning individualistic subjectivities.

28. Sun et al. ("Sexual Identity") conducted extensive interviews with men who have sex with men, tracing complex and evolving patterns of their self-identifications with models popularized through the media such as *tongzhi*, homosexual, MSM, and gay.

29. See Ho, *Gay and Lesbian Subculture in Urban China*.

30. Schroeder, "Beyond Resistance."

31. See An, *Black Souls under the Red Sun*; Li, *Subculture of Homosexuality*; Li and Wang, *Their World*; Kam, *Shanghai Lalas*.

32. On women's same-sex marriage rituals and ceremonies in China, see Kam, "Opening Up Marriage"; He, "My Unconventional Marriage or ménage à trois in Beijing"; Engebretsen, "Conjugal Ideals, Intimate Practices"; Engebretsen, *Queer Women in Urban China*, 80–123; Wong, "Hong Kong Lesbian Partners in the Making of Their Own Families"; and Ding and Liu, eds. *Querying the Marriage-Family Continuum*. For an early authoritative study on the commonplaceness of women's same-sex marriages in the West, see Sharon Marcus, *Between Women*.

33. See Kang, "Decriminalization and Depathologization." See also Rofel, *Desiring China*, 137.

34. The inaugural event in December 2001, organized by university students, was called the "China Homosexual Film Festival." Later iterations of the event took place under the names of "Beijing Gay & Lesbian Film Festival," "Beijing Queer Film Forum," and, finally, in 2009, the present title of "Beijing Queer Film Festival."

35. On transgender, see Ho, ed., *Trans-gender*; Chiang, ed., *Transgender China*; Cheung, "GID in Hong Kong," 75–86.

36. Rofel, "Grassroots Activism," 156, 160.

37. The original website, http://www.tongqijiayuan.com, has been shut down due to the organization's allegedly fraudulent activities.

38. http://v.ifeng.com/documentary/society/201202/82b5c8a0-1e7f-476c-92c7-2a0efd90 0d92.shtml.

39. Cited in Pink Space's newsblog, April 12, 2011. http://www.pinkspace.com .cn/News/Show.asp?id=114.

40. The case is analyzed in Rofel, *Desiring China*, 136.

41. Cui, "Filtered Voices."

42. See chapter 2 for a fuller analysis of Li and Wang's project and similar works.

43. Butler, *Bodies That Matter*, 223–42, and *Undoing Gender*, 204–31. See also Žižek, "Class Struggle or Postmodernism? Yes, Please!" 90–95. Žižek's point (and joke) is that the postmodern condition of subject formation and class struggle are not mutually exclusive ethical priorities.

44. An archive is available online: http://pittqueertheoryf11.wordpress.com /2011/12/07/queer-involvement-in-the-occupy-movement/.

45. See Puar, *Terrorist Assemblages*, for a provocative reading of the construction of queers and terrorists as intimately related figures of death.

46. Rosenberg and Villarejo, "Queer Studies and the Crises of Capitalism."

47. Chen, *Asia as Method*, 7–8, 58, 111.

48. As Giovanni Arrighi wryly puts it, the postwar "system" of East Asia defies world systems analysis because it is not a system at all, but a situation that "has left the United States in control of most of the guns, Japan and the Overseas Chinese in control of most of the money, and the PRC in control of most of the labor." Neither first, second, nor third world, this "messy" political economic formation

is nonetheless so "capitalistically highly successful" that East Asia has emerged as the epicenter of global industrial output and capital accumulation. "The Rise of East Asia," 33–34.

49. See Shih et. al, *Sinophone Studies*, for an excellent collection of manifestos and critical essays outlining these predicaments.

50. See chapter 5 for a more detailed analysis of the rumor to legalize same-sex marriage in Taiwan.

51. Chang, "Representing Taiwan," 18–19. Chang argues that the research value of Taiwan has rested on three different models: as the speculative result of a nonsocialist path China could have taken, as a "surrogate China" for anthropologists who could not visit mainland China but wish to generalize from the part to the whole, and as a "former Leninist state undergoing democratic transformation" in East Asia for economists and political scientists interested in its "miracle."

52. Marx, *The Marx-Engels Reader*, 46.

53. The quotation is taken from Perry Anderson's preface to the interview he conducted with four of the alliance's founders: filmmaker Hou Hsiao-Hsien, novelist Chu Tien-Hsin, critic Tang Nuo, and National Taiwan University Professor Hsia Chu-joe. "Tensions in Taiwan," 18.

54. Ho, "Is Global Governance Bad for East Asian Queers?"

55. See, for example, Martin's *Situating Sexualities*, for a particularly sophisticated and productive reading of Taiwan's distinctive tongxinglian (queer) praxis, theory, and culture. Crucially, Martin's work is not grounded in an essentialist understanding of Chinese and Taiwanese cultures. She argues that queerness—for example, the female homoerotic imaginary—produces "a cultural archipelago where media cross-flows—both within and beyond 'transnational' China—interact with local histories to create distinctive yet interlinked contemporary cultural scenes." Martin, *Backward Glances*, 21.

56. Altman, "Global Gays/Global Gaze."

57. See chapter 2 for a fuller analysis of these positions.

58. Partially derived from Derrida's essay "Signature, Event, Context," Butler's notion of "citationality" is a reformulation of the theory of "performativity" she introduces in *Gender Trouble*. By renaming performativity as citationality, Butler hopes to clarity a misunderstanding of her work as suggesting that gender is a singular act performed by a humanist subject. Rather, Butler, suggests, performativity or citationality is the "iterative power of discourse to produce the phenomena that it regulates and constrains." Butler, *Bodies That Matter*, 2.

59. For Butler's critique of the psychoanalytic reformulation as the symbolic in Lacan, see Butler, *Gender Trouble*, 49–52; *Bodies That Matter*, 198–207; and *Undoing Gender*, 121–26; and Butler, Laclau, and Žižek, *Contingency, Hegemony, and Universality*, 11–14.

60. Butler, *Undoing Gender*, 208.

61. Lévi-Strauss, *The Elementary Structures of Kinship*, xxviii.

62. Butler, *Undoing Gender*, 103.

63. See Kristeva, *About Chinese Women*. For a collection of Žižek's perspectives on China and Chinese responses to his work, see the 2011 special issue of *positions*, "The Chinese Perspective on Žižek and Žižek's Perspective on China."

64. On the difference between her position and the Lacanian psychoanalysis of Žižek, Butler writes, "I agree with the notion that every subject emerges on the condition of foreclosure, but do not share the conviction that these foreclosures are prior to the social, or explicable through recourse to anachronistic structuralist accounts of kinship." *Contingency, Hegemony, Universality*, 140.

65. Many studies have criticized the construction of China (and Chinese gender and sexuality) as the outside of Western theory. See, for example, Wang's edited volume, *Other Genders, Other Sexualities? Chinese Differences* for a collection of essays on the topic.

66. Butler no longer holds these views. She discusses how her views on these points have changed in the 1999 new Preface to *Gender Trouble*, vi-xi, and in *Undoing Gender*, 207–19.

67. Butler, *Gender Trouble*, 3.

68. Sedgwick, *Epistemology of the Closet*, 1.

69. Segwick, *Between Men*, 21.

70. Sedgwick, *Tendencies*, 23–26.

71. Warner also makes this point in his *Fear of a Queer Planet*, x.

72. Sedgwick, *Epistemology of the Closet*, 13–14, emphasis added.

73. Significant efforts to elaborate or revise the argument include Katz, *The Invention of Heterosexuality*, Halperin, *One Hundred Years of Homosexuality*, Laqueur, *Making Sex*, D'Emilio, *Sexual Politics, Sexual Communities*, and Samshasha, *History of Homosexuality in China*. See chapter 2 for a fuller analysis of the "invention of homosexuality" thesis.

74. Foucault, *History of Sexuality*, 43.

75. Foucault, *History of Sexuality*, 57, 58.

76. Foucault, *History of Sexuality*, 67.

77. Stoler, *Race and the Education of Desire*, 95.

78. Foucault, *Society Must Be Defended*, 61–62.

79. Halperin, *How to Do the History of Sexuality*, 13.

80. Halperin, *How to Do the History of Sexuality*, 20.

81. Sedgwick, *Epistemology of the Closet*, 1–63.

Chapter 2. Chinese Queer Theory

1. Ironically, the invocation of "immutable characteristics" as a legal defense for gay people in Chinese discussion is a replay of an earlier moment in US queer theory and suggestive of that theory's influence. Janet Halley points out that these

equal protection claims require, first, "coherentist" assumptions about the shared interests of the group, as well as those about the advocates' ability to "speak for" the group. See Halley, "'Like-Race' Arguments," 41.

2. http://www.aibai.com/advice_pages.php?linkwords=Queer_theory. Accessed March 9, 2014.

3. For a further discussion of this problem, see Lim, "Queer Theory Goes to Taiwan," and Liu, "Why Does Queer Theory Need China?"

4. Liu, Petrus, interview with Cui Zi'en, New York City, November 5, 2012.

5. For a discussion of the state's and NGOs' efforts to collect and classify homosexuals and people living with AIDS in China, see He and Rofel, "I Am AIDS."

6. Some of the major non-public-health-focused organizations in China include Pink Space, Beijing Same-Path Work Group, and the Tongzhi Center. Lisa Rofel estimates that there are currently over three hundred active organizations throughout China ("Grassroots Activism," 156).

7. See Cui's documentary film, *Queer China, Comrade China* (2008), for an intellectual history of these works.

8. See Kang, "Decriminalization and Depathologization," 233–34. I expand on this point in a later section of this chapter.

9. Pletsch, "The Three Worlds."

10. Kam, *Shanghai Lalas*, 51–52.

11. Kam, *Shanghai Lalas*, 52.

12. McLennan, *Marxism, Pluralism, and Beyond*, 18.

13. See, among others, Chou, *Tongzhi*; Cristi, "The Rise of Comrades Literature"; and Lim, *Celluloid Comrades*, 11–12, for different explorations of the linguistic and social histories of *tongzhi*.

14. Cui's *Queer China, Comrade China* includes a documentary history of the dissemination of the term in mainland China.

15. As Tze-lan Sang explains, Qiu's Lazi became the "focus of a great deal of lesbian self-identification" due to the unprecedented literary talent and "extraordinary charisma" of the author, who, after giving such a beautiful and soulful expression to the community, completed the story with her own suicide in 1995. Sang, *The Emerging Lesbian*, 261.

16. Ning Yin-Bin observes that it was not a coincidence that the word "ku-er" first appeared in *Isle Margin*, a leftist journal where many Marxist works are published in Taiwan, which indicates that the emergence of queer discourse in Taiwan is historically linked to the a-statist intellectual tradition of the journal. "What is Queer Politics," 40. For an insightful comparison of the connotations and social cultures of "tongzhi" and "ku-er," see Lim, "How to be Queer in Taiwan," 235–50.

17. Chu, "Women, Queers (guai-tai), and Nation" and Chang, *Queer Family Romance*.

18. Guo, *Homosexuality in the Purview of Chinese Law*; Zhou, *Pleasure and Discipline*.

19. Kang, "Decrmininalization and Depathologization."

20. On the prosecution of homosexual behavior under "hooliganism," see also, Rofel, *Desiring China*, 137; Sang, *The Emerging Lesbian*, 167; and Sun et al., "Sexual Identity."

21. Kang, "Decrmininalization and Depathologization," 233, 238.

22. Sommer, *Sex, Law and Society in Late Imperial China*, 119–30, quoted in Kang, "Decriminalization and Depathologization," 234.

23. On the relation between the invention of new sexual terms and national survival, see Kang, *Obsession*, 1–29, 85–90. For a historical and literary analysis of the translations of homosexuality as a way of negotiating Western scientific knowledge, see Sang, *The Emerging Lesbian*, 99–126, and "Translating Homosexuality," 276–304.

24. Since Samshasha and Hinsch, more rigorous scholarship on primary sources has become available. A valuable contribution is Stevenson and Wu's edited volume, *Homoeroticism in Imperial China: A Sourcebook*.

25. *Postcolonial Tongzhi*, 319–20.

26. Chou's essentializing descriptions of Chinese culture have been criticized by numerous scholars, including Ding, Liu, and Parry, *Penumbrae Query Shadow*; Martin, *Situating Sexualities*; Sang, *The Emerging Lesbian*, 46, 99; Szeto, "Queer Politics"; Wong, "Rethinking the Coming Home," esp. 603–606; Kam, *Shanghai Lalas*, 90–93.

27. Geyer, "In Love and Gay," 262.

28. Vitiello, *The Libertine's Friend*, 58, 88, 100. See also Song, *The Fragile Scholar*; and McMahon, *Misers, Shrews, and Polygamists*.

29. Ding and Liu, "Reticent Poetics," 40.

30. Volpp, "Classifying Lust," 81. For an extended discussion of this debate, see Kang, *Obsession*, 2–4.

31. Hinsch, *Masculinities in Chinese History*, 124–27. See also Louie, *Theorising Chinese Masculinity*; and Huang, *Negotiating Masculinities in Late Imperial China*.

32. Mann, *Gender and Sexuality in Modern China*, 144.

33. Wu, *Homoerotic Sensibilities*, 27, 52.

34. Fabian, *Time and the Other*, 32.

35. Fabian, *Time and the Other*, 31.

36. In addition to Katz, *The Invention of Heterosexuality* and Halperin, *One Hundred Years of Homosexuality*, influential historicizations of "heterosexuality," "sex," or "homosexuality" include Laqueur, *Making Sex*; D'Emilio, *Sexual Politics, Sexual Communities*; and Samshasha, *History of Homosexuality in China*.

37. Other than the ones already cited in chapter one, see, Ho, *Gay and Lesbian Subculture in Urban China*; Huang, *Queer Politics and Sexual Modernity in Taiwan*; Leung, *Undercurrents: Queer Cultures and Postcolonial Hong Kong*; Tang, *Conditional Spaces: Hong Kong Lesbian Desires and Everyday Life*; and Yau, *As Normal as Possible: Negotiating Sexuality and Gender in Mainland China and Hong Kong*.

38. Pickowicz, "From Yao Wenyuan to Cui Zi'en," 42.

39. Pickowicz, "From Yao Wenyuan to Cui Zi'en," 47–48.

40. Indeed, it is difficult to separate Cui's formal experiments from his political and ethical concerns. Robinson makes this point when he observes that many of Cui Zi's dramaturgical and stylistic choices—such as the deliberate mixing of professional and nonprofessional actors—should "be understood not just as formally experimental, but also ethical." Robinson, *Independent Chinese Documentary*, 114.

41. Wang, "Embodied Visions," 666.

42. Rofel, "The Traffic in Money Boys," 446–47.

43. Paola Voci characterizes Cui zi's *Night Scene* as a "hybridized docudrama" that paradoxically shows abnormality "as an irrepressible desire, either the result of personal behavior or the defining trait of one's identity." Voci, *China on Video*, 208.

44. I published a translation of the story in *positions* (2004).

45. Chi Ta-wei argues that Cui's choice of science fiction as the generic preference for his queer creative works indicates a "heterotopic" impulse, a search for a utopia in difference, in alternatives to the present. *Ethics of Desire*, 204, 211, 213.

46. Wang, "Embodied Visions," 659–60.

47. Wang, "Embodied Visions," 660.

48. Leung, "Homosexuality and Queer Aesthetics," 530.

49. Xiao Bo is a character name we see in many of his films, and always played by Yu Bo.

50. Calling attention to the camera's use of impossible spaces for depicting the disconnected lovers, David Eng offers a powerful interpretation of the film as an evaluation of the ruptures among China's semicolonial past, revolutionary socialism, and incorporation into the global neoliberal order. "Queer Space of China," 464–72.

51. For an excellent analysis of this tragic-comic resolution in accordance with the requirements of a Chinese sentimental narrative tradition, see Hsu, "The Affective Politics of Home," 235–41.

52. Hall, "Queer China Onscreen," 19.

53. See, for example, Berry, "The Sacred, the Profane, and the Domestic," 196.

54. Cui, *Seven Stars*, 58, 150.

55. Interview by "Wenhua" on Phoenix Television, Feb. 9 2012. http://culture.ifeng.com/renwu/special/cuizien/?_from_ralated#005.

56. Zhang, *Invisible Images*, 106.

57. Cui, "Communist International," 420.

58. Yue, "Mobile Intimacies in the Queer Sinophone Films of Cui Zi'en," 97.

59. One of the most vivid accounts of this experience is Chen Yingzhen's autobiographical story, "Back Alleys," written under the pseudonym of Xu Nancun. Chen was sentenced to ten years of imprisonment in 1968 for participating in discussion groups on Marxist books.

60. The thirteen groups include the ROC Publication Appraisal Foundation, Christian Garden of Hope, Catholic Good Shepherd Sisters, and End Child Prostitution and Trafficking Taiwan.

61. Readers interested in the detailed stories about the administration's responses, the various judges' statements at the two trials, media opinions, and Ho's own legal preparation notes should consult a collection, Ho, *The Zoophilia Webpage Incident*, especially the first section, "The Birth of a Crime."

62. See chapter 5 for a fuller analysis of Lu's stance on queer human rights in Taiwan.

63. Lin, "Identity Politics in Taiwanese Feminism," 56–62.

64. For a detailed account, see Ning, "Women's Rights and Sexual Rights in Taiwan."

65. Butler, "Against Proper Objects," 4. The word *xing* (sex) in Chinese sees the same kind of semantic splitting in *nüxing* (female), *xingbie* (gender), and *xing xingwei* (sexuality or sexual activity). For an account of the evolution of *xing* from the original meanings of "human nature" and "personhood" to "gender" in Chinese feminism, see Liu, Karl, and Ko, *The Birth of Chinese Feminism*, 15.

66. For an assessment of the slogan's impact, see Chen, *The Many Dimensions of Chinese Feminism*, 97.

67. Several responses to "Josephine Ho and the myth of female orgasms" from medical professionals were published in Taiwan's leading newspapers and discussed in-depth in Ho, *The Gallant Woman*, 180–84, 125–36, and more extensively in the collection of critical responses to *The Gallant Woman*: Ho, ed., *Contestations over Female Sexuality*. On the historical connection between the institutionalization of medical, psychiatric, and journalistic knowledge and the creation of the "virtuous custom" in Taiwan, see Huang, *Queer Politics and Sexual Modernity*, 83–111.

68. On the perception of Ho as a threat to Taiwan's burgeoning feminism, see Farris, "Women's Liberation under 'East Asian Modernity' in China and Taiwan," 365. For a careful reconstruction of the academic debate between Ho and other feminists, see Huang, *Queer Politics and Sexual Modernity*, 134–39.

69. See Marx, "On the Jewish Question," 31.

70. Marx, "Contribution to the Critique of Hegel's *Philosophy of Right*: Introduction," 59–65.

71. Marx, "On the Jewish Question," 31. As Gondelier points out in an important study, Marx's interest lies less in a critique of religion per se than in the analogy between religion and commodity fetishism. Gondelier, *Perspectives in Marxist Anthropology*, 177.

72. Published in the early 1990s, Ho's work anticipates many of the current works on shame in queer theory, such as Munt, *Queer Attachments: The Cultural Politics of Shame*. Tarnopolsky's *Prudes, Perverts, and Tyrants: Plato's Gorgias and the Politics of Shame* reminds us of the differences between positive and negative forms of

shame, which are often conflated in queer theory. Many current studies owe a great deal to Sedgwick and Frank's work on Silvan Tomkins, *Shame and Its Sisters*.

73. Ho, *The Gallant Woman*, 46–56, 62, 161.

74. Rubin, "Thinking Sex," 20.

75. Ho, *The Gallant Woman*, 16.

76. Ho, *The Gallant Woman*, 16. '

77. Ho, "Asian Modernity and Its 'Gendered Vulnerabilities,'" 9–11.

78. Ho, "Sex Revolution and Sex Rights Movement in Taiwan," 123; Ho, "Sex Revolution—A Marxist Perspective on One-hundred Years of American History of Sexualities," 33.

79. Ho, *Gallant Woman*, 89, 113.

80. Ho, *Contestations over Female Sexuality*, 422.

81. Ho, "Sex Revolution—A Marxist Perspective on One-hundred Years of American History of Sexualities," 35.

82. Ho, "Sex Revolution—A Marxist Perspective on One-hundred Years of American History of Sexualities," 37–38.

83. Ho, "Sex Revolution—A Marxist Perspective on One-hundred Years of American History of Sexualities," 36–37.

84. Marx, *Capital*, Vol. I, 132

85. Marx, *Capital*, Vol. I, 274–75.

86. Freud's theory of *Trieb* is most systematically presented in "Instincts and Their Vicissitudes," in which Freud describes these mechanisms by first distinguishing between the pressure, source, object, and aim of each drive.

87. Marx, *Capital*, Vol. I, 169.

88. Ning, "A Sex Revolution Is Raging."

89. Ning, "What Is Queer Politics?" 44. On pluralism, see Ning, "Compound Society," 275–79.

90. Ning, "Is Sex Work Really 'Work'?—Marx's Theory of Commodity and the Social Constructionism of Sex Work," 87–139.

91. Ning, "Rudimentary Notes on the Intellectual History of Sexual Emancipation," 215.

92. Huang, "Utopian Socialism and Marxist Feminism," 60–66.

93. Fan, "Contemporary Socialist Feminist Theory," 181.

94. Ho, "Queer Existence under Global Governance," 548–51.

95. For a useful extension of Ho's work in the analysis of how religious and NGO organizations shape queer spaces in East Asia, see Tang, *Conditional Spaces*, 66.

96. "Betel nut beauties" (*binglang xishi*) in Taiwan are teenage girls who dress in scanty, sexy clothes and sell betel nuts and cigarettes to male working-class clients.

97. G/SRAT, "Women de lichang." http://gsrat.net/about/ourstand.php.

98. Wang, "A Brave New World of Gender-Crossings," 24–26.

99. The definitive Marxist treatise on this point is Engels's *The Origin of the Family, Private Property and the State*, 39. For modern discussions, see Bloch, *Marxism and Anthropology*, 53.

100. Wang, interview in "Marriage Equality or Revolution?"

101. For a collection of insightful critiques of the institution of marriage, see Ding and Liu, *Querying the Marriage-Family Continuum*.

102. For a representative essay, see Ding, "Stigma of Sex and Sex Work." In her analysis of the (in-)famous grape-arbor scene in the Ming novel *Jin Ping Mei*, Ding shows that certain "obscene objects" (red shoes, foot binding, and the swing) centrally organize the text's gender hierarchy and erotic imagination. *Obscene Things*, 165–279.

103. Ding, "Changji, jishengchong, yu guojia nüxing zhi jia," 376–78.

104. On "changying/cangying suixing," see Ning, "Recent Events in Taiwan's Gender/Sexual Politics," 64; and Ho, "Generational Shifts in Taiwan's Sexual Politics," 225. See also Ho, "Life of a Parasite."

105. Ding and Liu, "Penumbrae Ask Shadow," "Penumbrae Ask Shadow II," and "Reticent Poetics, Queer Politics"; Liu, "The Disposition of Hierarchy"; and Ding, "Penumbrae Query Shadow," These essays appeared in book form in 2007 as *Penumbrae Query Shadow: Queer Reading Tactics*.

106. The influence of this theory can be traced in many new works on queer Taiwan. Linus Lee ("Translating *Nie Zi*") offers a provocative reading of how the politics and poetics of reticence work in the service of a distinction of normative and aberrant homosexuality in the most canonical queer text in modern Chinese literature, Pai Hsien-yung's *Crystal Boys*. Lee argues that a reticent redeployment of "would-be" homosexual scenes is the underlying narrative logic of the recent TV adaptation by Public Television. For an intriguing interpretation of Lucifer Hung's fiction as a refusal of the binary frame of victim/hegemon instituted by reticent poetics, see Liu and Parry, "The Politics of Schadenfreude." Fran Martin develops an innovative theory of "masking" that is informed by Ding and Liu's notion of reticent poetics as a corrective to the Western notion of the closet of homosexual secrecy (*Situating Sexualities*, 189–205). Martin analyzes the language of Taiwan's *tongzhi* novels and of its social movements to show that "the mask" enacts a cultural logic of removable faces that is not organized by a true/false or secrecy/disclosure dichotomy. Hans Huang's brilliant analysis of Taiwan's virtuous custom, sexual shame, and state feminism in Taiwan has further developed the theory of reticent poetics. Huang, *Queer Politics and Sexual Modernity in Taiwan*.

107. For a detailed discussion of the parable, see also my translation of Liu Jen-peng's "The Disposition of Hierarchy and the Late Qing Discourse of Gender Equality," 69–70.

108. Lin, "Meili 'xing' shijie" [Brave 'sexual' world]. *China Times*, Oct. 13, 1994. See also Liu Yu-hsiu, "Zhengshi xing bantai lunshu de fuhua zuoyong" [Taking a

serious look at the corruptive effects of the discourse of sexual perversity], *China Times*, Jan. 11, 2002.

109. Lin, "Identity Politics in Taiwanese Feminism," 57.

110. Butler, "Against Proper Objects," 4. On several occasions, Butler has turned to psychoanalysis, in particular Freud's essay on "Mourning and Melancholia," to show why the analytical separation between sex and gender is difficult to maintain. *Gender Trouble*, 73–84; *The Psychic Life of Power*, 132–59; *Frames of War*, 174; and *Senses of the Subject*, 73–74. Butler argues that a distinction between a biological sex and a sociological gender is self-defeating if what is meant by sex is always going to turn out to be gender anyway, and this critique of the presumed dualism of gender underlies her disagreement with Gayle Rubin and Eve Sedgwick. On Butler's reading, feminism is informed by a theory of the fundamentality of "sexual difference" for language and culture, but it would be a mistake to reduce the constitutive ambiguity of "sexual difference" as both gender and sexuality to "male and female" and to evacuate feminism of all sexuality. Whereas Rubin understands "sexual difference" to mean the variety of human sexual preferences and acts, Butler understands "sexual difference" to mean "the structure of language, the emergence of the speaking subject through sexual differentiation, and how language subsequently creates intelligibility." Butler and Rubin, "Sexual Traffic," 75. For contemporary reflections on this problem, see Love, "Rethinking Sex"; and Rubin, "Blood under the Bridge" and her introduction to *Deviations*. For Butler's latest reflections on "sexual difference" as a question of ethics, see Butler, *Senses of the Subject*, 149–70.

111. Ho, *The Gallant Woman*, 166–70.

112. Ho, *The Gallant Woman*, 170. Here Ho's work offers a gendered response to Žižek's reformulation of Marx's ideology critique as a matter of doing rather than knowing ("false consciousness"). Žižek, *The Sublime Object of Ideology*, 28.

113. In *Assuming a Body*, Salamon observes that the critique of social constructionism often focuses on the issue of agency, which is derived from the view that "the materiality of the transgendered body renders transgendered people outside or beyond gender" (75), but this understanding of social constructionism misses the point that materiality is always circumscribed by intersubjectivity—what we cannot know or anticipate in advance. For this reason, "what constitutes something as real is not its materiality but a horizon of possibility" (91).

114. Marx, *Capital*, Vol. I, 655–67.

115. Marx insists that the worker's "means of subsistence must therefore be sufficient to maintain him in his normal state as a working individual," but "his natural needs, such as food, clothing, fuel and housing vary according to the climate and other physical peculiarities of his country. On the other hand, the number and extent of his so-called necessary requirements, and also the manner in which they are satisfied, are themselves products of history, and depend therefore to a great extent on the level of civilization attained by a country . . . In contrast,

therefore, with the case of other commodities, the determination of the value of labor-power contains a historical and moral element." *Capital I*, 275.

116. Althusser, "Ideology and Ideological State Apparatuses," 143.

117. Chen and Wang, "Obstacles to LGBT Human Rights," 406.

118. Brown, *States of Injury*, 55.

119. Warner, *The Trouble with Normal*, 45–61; Seidman, *Difference Trouble*, 139–61; Stychin, *A Nation by Rights*, 21–51.

Chapter 3. The Rise of the Queer Chinese Novel

1. Halperin, *How to Do the History of Homosexuality*, 17.

2. Foucault, *History of Sexuality*, 43.

3. Sedgwick, *Epistemology of the Closet*, 2.

4. See Sang, "Translating Homosexuality," 276–304. For an alternative history of the impact of Western sexology, see Kang, *Obsession*, 41–59. Unlike Sang, Kang emphasizes the continuities rather than rupture between premodern and modern discourses in China.

5. Chris Nealon describes several types of feelings "before Stonewall" characteristic of figures he calls "foundlings," and these include: "a secret, surpassing vitality that links American men in a Whitmanian brotherhood of hope for the future," "dreams of a diaspora of lonely, artisanal sensitives," the "fulfillment of Greek bodily and political ideals," and "erotic entanglements and struggles against prejudice [that] mark the beginnings of recognizably contemporary urban queer culture." *Foundlings*, 2.

6. Sedgwick's classic essay, "How to Bring Your Kids Up Gay," dissects the cultural impact of the lack of positive models—not just of same-sex desire, but also of effeminate boys and tomboy girls—on gay youths. For a historical treatment of the past fifty years before *Will and Grace*, *Ellen*, and *Queer Eye for the Straight Guy* became available for consumption and identification, see Chauncey, *Why Marriage*, 5–9. At the same time, as Muñoz argues in *Disidentifications* (1–36), such images, rather than serving as a socially progressive site of identification, also create an exclusionary framework that alienates queers of color and class differences. Against arguments in favor of community-building and identification, Denise Riley also reminds us of the importance of the "right to be lonely" in *Impersonal Passion*, 49–58.

7. I offer further elaboration of these points in a forthcoming article, "From Identity to Social Protest."

8. See Sieber, *Red Is Not the Only Color*, 19–28; Sang, *The Emerging Lesbian*, 163–74; Chu, "Queer Canon," 24–30.

9. As Scott E. Myers explains in his introduction to his English translation of *Beijing Comrades* (Myers, "Notes"), the novel was first published on a website called "Chinese Men's and Boy's Heaven" (Zhongguo nanren nanhai tiantang) in 1998 by

a young Chinese person living in New York City under the pseudonym Bei-Tong, whose real-world identity has never been determined.

10. The commercial success of *Lan Yu* is an important reason Helen Leung describes the 1990s and early 2000s as a period of "queer mainstreaming." "Homosexuality and Queer Aesthetics," 526. For David Eng, *Lan Yu* embodies the "expressive desire" of a melodrama of neoliberalism, opening up a new queer space for not just Hong Kong but postsocialist China. "The Queer Space of China," 481.

11. On the canonization of Pai's *Crystal Boys* as a site of queer identification in the 1980s, see Huang, *Queer Politics and Sexual Modernity in Taiwan*, 114–20; Martin, *Situating Sexualities*, 47–71; Zeng, *Orphans, Bad Sons and Taipei People*, 302–11; and Jui-yuan Wu, "As a 'Bad Son,'" 65–94.

12. The novel was published in Taipei by Zili in 1986, in Hong Kong by Sanlian in 1987, and in Beijing by Wenlian in 1987 (first edition) and by Huaxia in 1996 (second edition).

13. The story of a "paper marriage" between an American citizen and an immigrant woman from China was first invented by Chen. Lee and the screenwriters (Neil Peng and James Schamus) are clearly indebted to the original novel: in both versions, the woman is an artist from Shanghai who works odd jobs at restaurants and falls in love with the gay landlord she marries for a green card. For a persuasive reading of *The Wedding Banquet* as "a prescient harbinger for the evolution of queer liberalism in our global moment" that "configures the closet as the defining structure for gay oppression across the globe," see Eng, *The Feeling of Kinship*, 77–78. Song Hwee Lim argues that *The Wedding Banquet* bears a unique burden of representation as the first gay film in contemporary Chinese cinemas, which obscures its more radical and hybrid political energies and reduces the film to a gay liberationist discourse. Lim, *Celluloid Comrades*, 41–68.

14. Mao Feng, *The History of Homosexual Literature*, 129.

15. Chu, "Queer Canon," 9–35.

16. For a detailed study of these movements, see Chang, *Modernism and the Nativist Resistance*, 148–76. Per Chang's influential work, "xiangtu" is usually translated as "nativist" in English. However, while I was working on the translation of Chen Yingzhen's essay "What the 'Third World' Means to Me," Chen asked me to render the term as "rural" in our personal communication, May 2, 2005, suggesting that the xiangtu movement he espoused was concerned with the lower class rather than Taiwan's independence movement. For a reconsideration of the xiangtu debates from the perspective of Taiwan's passage from postcolonial nationhood to postmodern hybridity, see Yip, *Envisioning Taiwan*, 26–38.

17. For details, see my recent translation of Chen Yingzhen's autobiographical account of these events, which he originally published under the pseudonym of Xu Nancun. Chen, "Back Alleys," 342–48.

18. Significantly, Chen's literary strokes depict a broad range of sexual practices beyond homosexuality, including s/m and domestic sexual abuse (*Paper Marriage*,

53). Wang Ping argues that the stigma of s/m, paradoxically, provided the basis for the destigmatization of homosexuality in Pai's literary project. Wang, "Young Birds Flying Between Cha-Cha Dance Moves," 97–8.

19. Other than *Crystal Boys*, Pai has authored several stories depicting nonnormative sexual relations, communities, and longings, such as "Yue meng" (Moon dream), "Gu lian hua" (Love's lone flower), "Yuqing sao," (Sister Yuqing), "Hei Hong" (Black rainbow), and "Jin daban de zuihou yiye" (The last night of Madam Chin).

20. Liu, *Love and Beauty*, 206. See also Huang, *Queer Politics and Sexual Modernity*, 120, for a reading of Pai's humanist aesthetics.

21. Hsia, *A History of Modern Chinese Fiction*, 579–86.

22. For an excellent review of these allegorical readings of Pai's work, see Martin, *Situating Sexualities*, 57–71.

23. In an influential essay on Chen, Pai Hsien-yung characterizes Chen's creative career as a journey from the "quest for [socialist] utopia" to her disillusionment (Pai, "From Utopia," 143). Pai's interpretation set the tone for many years of Chen Ruoxi criticism, leading critic Ye Shitao, for example, to propose a tripartite distinction instead in a 1984 essay: "Idealism, Disillusionment, and Vacillation." Ye argues that Chen's hope for the freedom of the Chinese people has never changed even after she became disenchanted with the utopian vision of socialism. "From Idealism," 178.

24. The political reception of Chen has changed several times. While she was labeled as an anticommunist writer in the 1960s and 70s, Chen's support of the prodemocracy demonstrations after the 1979 Kaohsiung Incident in Taiwan also led some to call her a "stinky leftist." For a reading of Chen and her works as the expression of the dilemmas of the leftist intellectual, see Luo, "Unqualified Participants."

25. See Chen's autobiography, *No Regrets*, 155–58.

26. Chen, *No Regrets*, 172–75.

27. Wakeman, "The Real China," *New York Review of Books*. Wakeman predicts that Chen's stories will have a negative impact on China's tourism industry, which, he explains, has lured—with official propaganda and false advertisement—a throng of unsuspecting foreigners. Chen's writings will expose the truth of Communist China to "make that kind of blissful ignorance much harder to sustain in the future."

28. The Chinese version of this collection first appeared as *Yin xianzhang* in 1976.

29. Goldblatt, "Preface," in *The Execution of Mayor Yin*, ix.

30. Goldblatt, "Preface," in *The Execution of Mayor Yin*, ix.

31. Link, "Introduction," in *The Execution of Mayor Yin*, xi.

32. See also Chao, "1950s' Perverse Politics," for an insightful analysis of the conflation of anticommunism and sexual perversion in the 1950s' construction of

Taiwan as the basis of a "forever deferred" campaign to reclaim the "lost object" in both psychosexual and geopolitical terms.

33. Rubin, "Thinking Sex," 11.

34. Chu, "Queer Canon," 19.

35. Tsai Meng-Che offers an insightful analysis of the novel from the perspective of disability studies, showing that the romantic imagination of a "happy family" is inextricably linked to its abject conflation of AIDS and homosexuality as interchangeable disabilities. "Aizi, tongxinglian, yu hunjia xiangxiang," 53.

36. Sedgwick offers a trenchant critique of J. L. Austin's elevation of the heterosexual wedding ceremony into a source of fascination and the "pure, originary, and defining" example of performative utterances. Sedgwick reminds us that the effectivity of the performative that Austin takes to be natural and eternal depends on a cultural institution that not only varies from culture to culture, but remains open to contestations. "Queer Performativity," 1–16.

37. I am indebted to Brant Torres for this insight.

38. In "Transnational Queer Sinophone Cultures," Martin develops a useful distinction between roots-based, centripetal, and civilizational views of Chineseness and approaches that emphasize "the routes rather than the roots of Chineseness in a transnational frame" in queer thinking (39).

39. For a collection of recent critiques of the institution of monogamous heterosexual marriage in Chinese, see Ding and Liu, eds., *Querying the Marriage-Family Continuum*.

40. Chauncey reminds us that the current definition of marriage as a heterosexual monogamous union between a man and a woman is itself a construction, given that history shows "enormous variation over time and among cultures in how 'marriage' has organized sexual and emotional life, child-rearing, property, kinship, and political alliances." *Why Marriage*, 59. See also, Warner, *The Trouble with Normal*, 81–147; Boyd, "Sex and Tourism: The Economic Implications of the Gay Marriage Movement," 223–35; Halberstam, *Gaga Feminism*, 95–128; and Freeman, *The Wedding Complex*, 1–44.

41. In *Paper Marriage*, a minor character (Jiefu) refers to China as the Iron Curtain (148), which is a term usually used to describe the Eastern Bloc in Europe. The more common metaphor for socialist China is the "Bamboo Curtain."

42. As Carlos Rojas notes, the Great Wall is "a very queer thing" in global discourses about China and in China's own cultural history, a fungible concept that signifies both isolation and cosmopolitanism. *The Great Wall*, 148.

43. Fan, *A Historical Study of Contemporary Women's Fiction from Taiwan*, 236–44.

44. Yang, "On Chen Ruoxi's Fiction," *China Times*, March 4, 1976. Wei, "Xirou Zhengyan," *China Times*, March 17, 1976.

45. Yang, *A New History of Twentieth-Century Chinese Literature*, 331.

46. Wang, *After Heteroglossia*, 323, 322.

Chapter 4. Genealogies of the Self

1. For a helpful review of some of these historical debates, see White, *Developmental States in East Asia*.

2. My analysis of the miracle discourse resonates with Stephen Best and Saidiya Hartman's work on narratives of redress, in which they pose the important question of the "time of slavery": "Is it the time of the present . . . a death sentence reenacted and transmitted across generations?" "Fugitive Justice," 4.

3. Lye's *America's Asia* develops a detailed argument about the correlation between the model minority myth and the global signification of the East Asian economic miracle. "For reasons having to do with the necessarily international context of Asian American racialization . . . the domestic signification of Asian Americans has its counterpart in the global signification of Asia. While the new visibility of an Asian-American middle class was being used to support a neoconservative 'retreat from race' in domestic public policy, the expanding economies of the newly industrialized countries of East Asia—the 'Asian Tigers'—were being heralded by free market critics of import-substitution as evidence of the conceptual and political 'end of the Third World.'" *America's Asia*, 2–3.

4. My use of the term "genealogical critique" follows Foucault's influential interpretation of Nietzsche's imperative: "genealogy . . . must record the singularity of events outside of any monotonous finality; it must seek them in the most unpromising places, in what we tend to feel is without history." Foucault, "Nietzsche, Genealogy, History," 76.

5. Li Qingzhao (1081–1141) was China's most famous female poet who worked mostly in the *ci* form of poetry. *Ci* poems are written to be sung and their titles, such as "Rumengling," usually refer to the tunes of fixed rhythmic and tonal patterns rather than the contents of the individual poems. For this reason, the title is translated: "(To the tune of) Like a Dream."

6. On "reproductive futurism," see Edelman. For Edelman, the "conservatism of the ego compels the subject, whether liberal or conservative politically, to endorse as the meaning of politics itself the reproductive futurism that perpetuates as reality a fantasy frame intended to secure the survival of the social in the Imaginary form of the Child." *No Future*, 14.

7. You Suling, "Contemporary Taiwan Women Writers," www.pkucn.com/ view thread.php?tid=16422.

8. As Pei-Yin Lin's careful study shows, during the martial law era, women writers who depicted female desire and sexuality were routinely trivialized, censored, and penalized by the conservative establishment. The expulsion of Guo Lianghui from the Chinese Literary Association in the 1960s became a cautionary tale that further rigidified an already inclement social milieu. "Writing Beyond Boudoirs," 258. See also Lancashire, "The Lock of Heart Controversy in Taiwan, 1962–63," 462–88.

9. Ye, "Xiao Sa yu qi zuopin de shehui yishi." (lecture, Taipei, April 6, 2010).

10. For works in English that introduce Xiao in this context, see, for example, Carver and Chang, *Bamboo Shoots after the Rain*, and Hung, *City Women*.

11. Sheng, *Twentieth-Century Women's Literature*, 101.

12. Fan, *A Historical Study of Contemporary Women's Fiction from Taiwan*, 397–403.

13. Wu, "From a Dead End to a New Life," 427.

14. I am following the definition of peripheral realisms in Cleary, Esty, and Lye's recent effort to create an atlas of their analogous and interrelated developments in different social formations. Here realism, in both its classical and peripheral forms, does not refer to fiction's ability to create a photographic record of immediate reality, but to a text's aspiration to totality—its capacity to reflect on its systemic relation to what is not immediately present and visible. Cleary, Esty, and Lye, eds., "Peripheral Realisms."

15. The translation is available in Duke, *Worlds of Modern Chinese Fiction*, 227–45.

16. Markgraf, trans., "Die Verwandten in Hong Kong," in *Hefte für ostasiatische Literatur*, no. 52 (May 2012): 26–59.

17. Sima, "My Expectations," 206.

18. *Lianhebao*, 24.

19. Carver and Young, *Bamboo Shoots after the Rain*, 171–72.

20. Hung, "Introduction" to *City Women*, 13.

21. Nealon, *Foundlings*, 8.

22. Freeman, *Time Binds*, 105, 132–35.

23. Marx, *Capital*, Vol. I, 176.

24. Xiao, postscript, 343.

25. A "new residential quarter," or military dependents' village (juan cun), is a community of cheaply and hastily built houses for the large influx of ROC soldiers and their dependents when the KMT government retreated in the 1940s from the mainland to Taiwan, which the officials considered to be only a temporary base of operation. As these communities became permanent settlements, they suffered severe urban problems but also developed distinct cultures that are famously depicted by realist writers such as Xiao and Chu Tien-hsin.

26. Marx, "The Eighteenth Brumaire of Louis Bonaparte," 595.

27. Ni Luo, preface to *Song of Dreams*, 2.

Chapter 5. Queer Human Rights in and against the Two Chinas

1. See chapter 2 for an extensive analysis of Cui and G/SRAT's work on queer human rights.

2. Personal communication with Cui, March 15, 2013.

3. Email communication from East Bay Community Law Center to the Center for the Study of Sexualities, Taiwan, October 14, 2006. I am grateful to Josephine Ho and Wang Ping for their assistance with my research on the case.

4. Email communication from East Bay Community Law Center to the Center for the Study of Sexualities, Taiwan, October 14, 2006.

5. See Balibar et al., "Shadows of Universalism."

6. See Liu, "Legislating the Universal," 127–64.

7. For an excellent compilation of original Chinese documents from classical to contemporary sources that indicates a wide and disparate range of understandings of "human" and "rights" in China, see Angle and Svensson, *The Chinese Human Rights Reader*.

8. See Haraway, "The Promise of Monsters," 295–337, for a classic account of the imbrication of the human in the nonhuman. See also Chen, *Animacies*, 89–126, for an interdisciplinary understanding of queerness, affect, and critical animal studies.

9. Giffney and Hird, "Queering the Non/Human," 3, 5; see also Tang, *Conditional Spaces*, for a brilliant analysis of the queer formation of human subjects in relation to the nonhuman constraints of urban environments, spatial imaginaries, and spaces of everyday life.

10. Zhang, *Postsocialism and Cultural Politics*, 53.

11. For a representative collection of early criticisms, see Balakrishnan, ed. *Debating Empire*.

12. Gowan, "The New Liberal Cosmopolitanism," 51.

13. Patel, "Ghostly Appearances," 47–66.

14. Erni, "Who Needs Human Rights." Kindle edition, chapter 10.

15. Erni, "Who Needs Human Rights." Kindle edition, chapter 10.

16. Rofel, "Queer Positions, Queering Asian Studies," 183–93.

17. Rofel, "Queer Positions, Queering Asian Studies," 190.

18. Bersani, *Homos*, 103.

19. Seidman, *Beyond the Closet*, 155.

20. Cheah, *Inhuman Conditions*, 102.

21. Butler, *Precarious Life*, 20.

22. Agamben, *Homo Sacer*, 136–43; Povinelli, *Economies of Abandonment*, 4; see also Mbembe, "Necropolitics," 11–15.

23. Butler, *Undoing Gender*, 2.

24. This poststructuralist view has profoundly influenced a whole generation of queer thinkers. In her latest work, for example, Ahmed develops an account of the paradoxical relationship between will and willfulness by showing that the "'I' that is speaking is an 'I' that is spoken." *Willful Subjects*, 27.

25. Soper, *Humanism and Antihumanism*, 11–21.

26. Chambers, *Culture after Humanism*, 1.

27. Chambers, *Culture after Humanism*, 1–6.

28. Chambers, *Culture after Humanism*, 5.

29. Barthes, *Image–Music–Text*, 142–48.

30. Derrida, "The Ends of Man," 36.

31. For a rigorous reassessment of the work of the Frankfurt school as a critique of Marxist humanism, see Jay, *Permanent Exiles*, 14–27. Jay argues that although many commentators see the Frankfurt school as a regression into pre-Marxist Young Hegelians who reduced social criticism to philosophy, members of the *Institut für Sozialforschung* actually inhabited a wide ideological spectrum that should, in the final analysis, be summarized as antihumanist.

32. Althusser, *For Marx*, 223–25.

33. Althusser, *For Marx*, 221–45. Althusser also argues that history must be viewed as a process without a telos or a subject. See *Reading Capital*, 132–59.

34. Althusser, *For Marx*, 51–53. Contemporary critics are divided on the issue. Andrew Levine, for example, argues that Marxism is distinct from other forms of socialism precisely because of its scientific (rather than utopian) character, which was made possible by the analytical Marxism founded by Althusser (Levine, *A Future for Marxism?*, 122). By contrast, Fredric Jameson chastises Althusser (and analytical Marxism in general) for abandoning the dialect "for a return to the old Aristotelian or common-sense logic of the principle of non-contradiction," which, in Jameson's view, misses both the point of Marx's argument and the dialectical motions of capitalism itself. Jameson, *Representing Capital*, 128.

35. Gutting points out that "since humanist Marxists were strong critics of Stalinist repression, Althusser's antihumanism tended to be seen as a defense of Stalinism," but Althusser actually "saw his view as providing a Marxist response" to Stalinist totalitarianism. Gutting, *French Philosophy in the Twentieth Century*, 237–38.

36. For some influential examples, see Sayer, *The Violence of Abstraction*, 15–49; and Postone, *Time, Labor, and Social Domination*, 186–225.

37. Arrighi, *The Long Twentieth Century*, 96–239.

38. See also Soper, *Humanism and Antihumanism*, 96–119.

39. Spivak's deconstructive reading of Marx aims to show that the presumed mutual exclusivity between the materialist and idealist predications in Marx is an unstable one at best ("value is always in excess of exchange value"), since the subject of consciousness (the idealist predication) is always and already formed by objectified labor-power (the materialist predication), and the task of criticism is precisely to decouple or "blast open" the chain of continuity in the scheme of representation: "Marx is writing, then, of a differential representing itself or being represented by an agency ('we') no more fixable than the empty and ad hoc place of the investigator or community of investigators." Spivak, "Scattered Speculations," 154–75.

40. In "Is the Post- in Postsocialism the Post- in Posthumanism?" Shih proposes a "trialectical approach" that demonstrates the historical triangulation of developments in China, France, and the United States in the global reception and resignification of Althusser's antihumanism.

41. Robcis, "China in Our Heads," 51.

42. Althusser develops the technique of "symptomatic reading" in *Reading Capital*, 28–29, 95–97.

43. Robcis, "China in Our Heads," 59.

44. McGrath, *Postsocialist Modernity*, 31.

45. Howland, "Popular Sovereignty," 1–25.

46. He, "Postsocialist History," 128.

47. The relation between antihumanism and ethnocentrism is, of course, not always the same throughout history, and my comments are limited to contemporary discourses. In *On Human Diversity*, Todorov outlines a changing trajectory of different uses of universalism in French thought: while the discourse of human nature in early Enlightenment signified an extension of critical interests into the non-European world and hence was a progressive reaction against the provincialism of European intellectual thought, later use of the same beliefs in the universals of human nature has also resulted in genocide and persecution.

48. Spivak proposes a useful concept of "planetarity" against "globalization" that captures this dilemma: whereas globalization is "the imposition of the same system of exchange everywhere," planetarity recognizes the asymmetrical and irreducibly plural relations between cultures while insisting on the need to dialogue with and learn from others who inhabit the planet. *Death of a Discipline*, 72.

49. Kristeva, *About Chinese Women*. For an influential critique of Kristeva's Orientalism, see Spivak, *In Other Worlds*, 134–53; Chow, *Woman and Chinese Modernity*, 3–33; and Lowe, *Critical Terrains*, 136–89.

50. Kristeva, *About Chinese Women*, 47–62. See the essays in Wang's *Other Genders, Other Sexualities? Chinese Differences* for new critiques of this binary construction.

51. The construction of homosexuals as an official minority in Taiwan is entangled with the rise of Taiwanese independence nationalism and ethnic politics. See Chen Li-fen, "Queering Taiwan," 384–421, for an assessment of the potentiality of these ironies and problems.

52. Damm, "Same-Sex Desire," 67.

53. I am grateful to the Gender/Sexuality Rights Association (G/SRAT) for providing me with the archival information presented here.

54. Stychin makes a similar observation about Quebec: "Rather, the government saw itself engaged in the task of creating a culture of human rights for a new society. . . . From these passages can be discerned an example of how the amendment of human rights law to include sexual orientation became one of many sites for a new nationalist founding myth—one based on inclusion, openness, and a modernist discourse of progress." *A Nation by Rights*, 91.

55. John Erni emphasizes political liberalism's dependency on economic liberalism: queer human rights discourse in Asia cannot be understood as the simple manifestation of a global will; rather, it is the product of a complex process mediated by the rise of a new form of "networked sovereignty" and decentered constitutional cosmopolitanism, which generate occasions of self-reflection and

normative expectations for judges, courts, and voting members of society without embedding them in the judicial artifice of the state. "The Taiwan model" of queer cultural visibility requires and indicates a degree of market liberalization, a queer "middle class consumerism," a "logic of decadence that renders state biopower inconclusive," and an "accumulative sense of transnational 'successes' in queer cultural representations." Erni, "Run Queer Asia Run," 381–84.

56. "Lung Ying-tai becomes an Internet Pariah in China." *China Free Press*, September 18, 2009.

57. See chapter 2 for a fuller discussion of Lu's relationship to Taiwan's feminist movement.

58. Chen, *Many Dimensions of Chinese Feminism*, 58.

59. Lu made the speech on Dec. 7, 2003 at an AIDS prevention event. The speech was broadcast on national media, and cited as one of the "ten worst violations of queer human rights in 2003" by activist groups. http://gsrat.net/events /events_post.php?pdata_id=32 (Accessed April 3, 2015). A news story in English can be found at: http://www.taipeitimes.com/News/taiwan/archives/2003/12/09 /2003078887 (Accessed April 3, 2015).

60. Marx, *Capital*, Vol. I, 137–40.

61. Butler, *Undoing Gender*, 150, 19.

62. Althusser, "Ideology and Ideological State Apparatuses," 162.

BIBLIOGRAPHY

Agamben, Giorgio. *Homo Sacer: Sovereign Power and Bare Life*. Palo Alto: Stanford University Press, 1998.

Ahmed, Sara. *The Promise of Happiness*. Durham, NC: Duke University Press, 2010.

———. *Willful Subjects*. Durham, NC: Duke University Press, 2014.

Allen, Jafari S., ed. "Black/Queer/Diaspora." Special issue, GLQ: *A Journal of Lesbian and Gay Studies* 18, nos. 2–3 (2012).

———. *Global Sex*. Chicago: University of Chicago Press, 2001.

Althusser, Louis. *For Marx*. London: Verso, 1969.

———. "Ideology and Ideological State Apparatuses (Notes towards an Investigation)." In *Lenin and Philosophy and Other Essays*, 127–86. New York: Monthly Review Press, 1971.

———. *Reading Capital*. London: Verso, 2009.

Altman, Dennis. "Global Gays/Global Gaze." GLQ: *A Journal of Lesbian and Gay Studies* 3, no. 4 (1997): 417–37.

An, Keqiang. *Hong taiyang xia de hei linghun* [Black souls under the red sun]. Taipei: Re'ai chubanshe, 1995.

Angle, Stephen C., and Marina Svensson. *The Chinese Human Rights Reader: Documents and Commentary, 1900–2000*. Armonk, NY: M.E. Sharpe, 2001.

Arrighi, Giovanni. *The Long Twentieth Century: Money, Power, and the Origins of Our Times*. London: Verso, 1994.

———. "The Rise of East Asia and the Withering Away of the Interstate System." In *Marxism, Modernity, and Postcolonial Studies*, edited by Crystal Bartolovich and Neil Lazarus, 21–42. Cambridge: Cambridge University Press, 2001.

Balakrishnan, Gopal, ed. *Debating Empire*. London: Verso, 2003.

Balibar, Etienne, Souleymane Bachir Diagne, Lydia H. Liu, and Samuel Moyn. "Shadows of Universalism: A Conversation on 'Human Rights' in Comparative Perspective." Accessed March 22, 2014. http://ircpl.org/shadows-of

-universalism-a-conversation-on-human-rights-in-comparative-perspec
tive-2/.

Barlow, Tani E., ed. *Gender Politics in Modern China: Writing and Feminism.* Durham, NC: Duke University Press, 1993.

———. *The Question of Women in Chinese Feminism.* Durham, NC: Duke University Press, 2004.

Barthes, Roland. *Image–Music–Text.* New York: Hill, 1977.

Bei-Tong. *Beijing guishi.* [Beijing comrades]. First published online 1998. Accessed August 9, 2014. http://www.dzxsw.net/novel/38318/chapter.htm.

———. *Beijing Comrades.* Translated and edited by Scott E. Myers. New York: Feminist Press, forthcoming.

Benjamin, Walter. *The Arcades Project.* Cambridge, MA: Harvard University Press, 2002.

Berlant, Lauren. *Cruel Optimism.* Durham, NC: Duke University Press, 2011.

———. *The Female Complaint: The Unfinished Business of Sentimentality in American Culture.* Durham, NC: Duke University Press, 2008.

———. *The Queen of America Goes to Washington City: Essays on Sex and Citizenship.* Durham, NC: Duke University Press, 1997.

Berlant, Lauren, and Lee Edelman. *Sex, or the Unbearable.* Durham, NC: Duke University Press, 2013.

Berry, Chris. *Postsocialist Cinema in Post-Mao China: The Cultural Revolution after the Cultural Revolution.* New York: Routledge, 2004.

———. "The Sacred, the Profane, and the Domestic in Cui Zi'en's Cinema." *positions: east asia cultures critique* 12, no. 1 (2004): 195–201.

Berry, Chris, Fran Martin, and Audrey Yue, eds. *Mobile Cultures: New Media in Queer Asia.* Durham, NC: Duke University Press, 2003.

Berry, Michael. "China: 21st-Century Tiger." *Sight and Sound* 16, no. 9 (September 2006): 24–28.

Bersani, Leo. *Homos.* Cambridge, MA: Harvard University Press, 1995.

Best, Stephen, and Saidiya Hartman. "Fugitive Justice." *Representations* 92, no. 1 (Fall 2005): 1–15.

Bloch, Maurice. *Marxism and Anthropology: The History of a Relationship.* New York: Oxford University Press, 1983.

Boellstorff, Tom. *The Gay Archipelago: Sexuality and Nation in Indonesia.* Princeton, NJ: Princeton University Press, 2005.

Boyd, Nan Alamilla. "Sex and Tourism: The Economic Implications of the Gay Marriage Movement." *Radical History Review*, no. 100 (Winter 2008): 223–35.

Brown, Wendy. *States of Injury.* Princeton, NJ: Princeton University Press, 1995.

Butler, Judith. "Against Proper Objects." In *Feminism Meets Queer Theory*, edited by Elizabeth Weed and Naomi Schor, 1–30. Bloomington: Indiana University Press, 1997.

————. *Antigone's Claim: Kinship between Life and Death*. New York: Columbia University Press, 2002.

————. *Bodies That Matter*. New York: Routledge, 1993.

————. *Frames of War: When Is Life Grievable?* London: Verso, 2009.

————. *Gender Trouble*. New York: Routledge, 1990. Reprint 1999.

————. "Merely Cultural." *Social Text* 52/53 (Autumn/Winter 1997): 265–77.

————. *Precarious Life: The Power of Mourning and Violence*. London: Verso, 2004.

————. *The Psychic Life of Power: Theories in Subjection*. Stanford: Stanford University Press, 1997.

————. *Senses of the Subject*. New York: Fordham University Press, 2015.

————. *Undoing Gender*. New York: Routledge, 2004.

Butler, Judith, and Athena Athanasiou. *Dispossession: The Performative in the Political*. Malden, MA: Polity Press, 2013.

Butler, Judith, and Gayle Rubin. "Sexual Traffic." *differences* 6, nos. 2–3 (1994): 62–99.

Butler, Judith, Ernesto Laclau, and Slavoj Žižek. *Contingency, Hegemony, Universality: Contemporary Dialogues on the Left*. London: Verso, 2000.

Carver, Ann, and Sung-sheng Yvonne Chang, eds. *Bamboo Shoots after the Rain: Contemporary Stories by Women Writers of Taiwan*. New York: Feminist Press, 1990.

Chakrabarty, Dipesh. *Provincializing Europe*. Princeton, NJ: Princeton University Press, 2007.

Chambers, Ian. *Culture after Humanism: History, Culture, Subjectivity*. New York: Routledge, 2001.

Chang, Hsiao-hung. *Guaitai jiating luoman shi* [Queer family romance]. Taipei: Shibao, 2000.

Chang, Sung-sheng Yvonne. *Literary Culture in Taiwan: Martial Law to Market Law*. New York: Columbia University Press, 2004.

————. *Modernism and the Nativist Resistance*. Durham, NC: Duke University Press, 1993.

————. "Representing Taiwan: Shifting Geopolitical Frameworks." In *Writing Taiwan: A New Literary History*, edited by David Der-wei Wang and Carlos Rojas, 17–25. Durham, NC: Duke University Press, 2007.

Chao, Antonia Yen-ning. *Daizhe caomao daochu lüxing—xingbie quanli guojia* [Travelling everywhere with a sombrero: Gender, power, and nation]. Taipei: Juliu, 2001.

————. "Lao Ti banjia: quanqiuhua zhuangtai xia de ku'er wenhua shenfen chutan" [Moving house: The relational-materialistic aspect of queer cultural citizenship]. *Taiwan shehui yanjiu jikan* [Taiwan: A radical quarterly in social studies] 57 (2005): 41–85.

————. "Tongzhi hua: Wuling nian dai guo gong zhi jian de biantai zhengzhi/ xing xiangxiang." [1950's perverse politics/sexual imagination between nationalists and communists]. In Ho, ed., *Working Papers in Gender/Sexuality Studies* 3&4, 235–59.

Chauncey, George. *Why Marriage? The History Shaping Today's Debate over Gay Equality*. New York: Basic Books, 2009.

Cheah, Pheng. *Inhuman Conditions: On Cosmopolitanism and Human Rights*. Cambridge, MA: Harvard University Press, 2006.

Chen, Arvin, dir. *Will You Still Love Me Tomorrow?* Film. Taiwan: 1 Production Film Company, 2013.

Chen, Kuan-Hsing. *Asia as Method: Toward Deimperialization*. Durham, NC: Duke University Press, 2010.

Chen, Li-fen. "Queering Taiwan: In Search of Nationalism's Other." *Modern China* 37 (2011): 384–421.

Chen, Mel Y. *Animacies: Biopolitics, Racial Mattering, and Queer Affect*. Durham, NC: Duke University Press, 2012.

Chen, Ran. *Private Life* [Siren shenghuo]. Beijing: Zuojia chubanshe, 1996.

Chen, Ruoxi (Jo-Hsi). *The Execution of Mayor Yin and Other Stories from the Great Proletarian Cultural Revolution*. Translated by Nancy Ing and Howard Goldblatt. Bloomington: Indiana University Press, 1978.

———. *Jianchi, wuhui* [No regrets]. Taipei: Jiuge chubanshe, 2008.

———. *The Old Man and Other Stories*. Hong Kong: Renditions, 1986.

———. *Spirit Calling: Five Stories of Taiwan*. Taipei: Heritage Press, 1962.

———. *Yin Xianzhang* [Mayor yin]. Taipei: Yuanjing, 1976.

———. *Zhihun* [Paper marriage]. Taipei: Zili, 1986.

Chen, Xinyuan, ed. *Taiwan xian dang dai zuojia yanjiu ziliao huibian 45: Chen Ruoxi* [Research materials on modern and contemporary Taiwanese writers, vol. 45: Chen Ruoxi]. Taipei: Guoli Taiwan wenxue guan, 2013.

Chen, Ya-chen. *The Many Dimensions of Chinese Feminism*. New York: Palgrave Macmillan, 2011.

Chen, Yingzhen. "Back Alleys: The Creative Journey of Chen Yingzhen." Translated by Petrus Liu. *Inter-Asia Cultural Studies* 15, no. 3 (November 2014): 342–48.

———. "What the 'Third World' Means to Me." Translated by Petrus Liu. *Inter-Asia Cultural Studies* 6, no. 4 (December 2005): 535–40.

Chen, Yu-Rong and Wang Ping. "Taiwan xing/bie renquan xiehui jianjie." [G/SRAT: A brief introduction]. *Cultural Studies Monthly* 5 (2001). Accessed July 16, 2001. http://csat.org.tw/csa/journal/05/journal_forum_51.htm.

———. "Obstacles to LGBT Human Rights Development in Taiwan." Translated by Petrus Liu. *positions: east asia cultures critique* 18, no. 2 (Fall 2010): 399–408.

Cheng, Andrew Yusu, dir. *Welcome to Destination Shanghai*. Film. China: Ariztical Entertainment, 2013.

Cheung, Eleanor. "GID in Hong Kong: A Critical Overview of Medical Treatments for Transsexual Patients." In Yau, ed., *As Normal as Possible*, 75–86.

Chi, Pang-yuan. *Juliu he* [The great river]. Taipei: Tianxia, 2009.

Chi, Ta-wei. "Ethics of Desire: Sexual Alterity in Twentieth-Century Chinese-Language Fiction." PhD diss., UCLA, 2006.

———, ed. Ku'er kuang huan jie: Taiwan dangdai wenxue duben [Queer carnival: A reader of queer literature in Taiwan]. Taipei: Meta Media, 1997.

———, ed. Ku'er qishilu: Taiwan dangdai lunshu duben [Queer archipelago: A reader of queer discourse in Taiwan]. Taipei: Meta Media, 1997.

———. Wan an Babilun [Sexually dissident notes from Babylon]. Taipei: Tansuo wenhua, 1998.

Chi, Ta-wei, Dantangmo, and Lucifer Hung, eds. Daoyu bianyuan [Isle margin] 10 (July 1994).

Chiang, Howard, ed. Transgender China. New York: Palgrave Macmillan, 2012.

Chiang, Howard, and Ari Larissa Heinrich, eds. Queer Sinophone Cultures. London: Routledge, 2013.

China Free Press. "Lung Ying-tai becomes an Internet Pariah in China." September 18, 2009.

Chou, Wah-shan, ed. Beijing tongzhi gushi [Beijing tongzhi stories]. Hong Kong: Xianggang tongzhi yanjiushu, 1996.

———. Houzhimin tongzhi [Postcolonial tongzhi]. Hong Kong: Xianggang tongzhi yanjiushe, 1997.

———. Tongzhi: Politics of Same-Sex Eroticism in Chinese Societies. New York: Haworth Press, 2000.

Chow, Rey. Woman and Chinese Modernity: The Politics of Reading between West and East. Minneapolis: University of Minnesota Press, 1991.

Chu, T'ien-wen. Huangren shouji [Notes of a desolate Man]. Taipei: Shibao, 1994.

Chu, Wei-cheng. "Father China; Mother (Queer) Taiwan? Bai Xianyong Tongzhi Family Romance and National Imagination." Chung Wai Literary Monthly 30, no. 2 (July 2001):106–23.

———. "Linglei Jingdian" [Queer canon]. In Taiwan tongzhi xiaoshuo xuan [Queer stories from Taiwan], edited by Chu Wei-cheng, 9–35. Taipei: Eryu, 2005.

Chua, Beng Huat. "Singapore in 2007: High Wage Ministers and the Management of Gays and the Elderly." Asian Survey 48, no. 1 (2008): 55–61.

Chua, Lynette J. Mobilizing Gay Singapore: Rights and Resistance in an Authoritarian State. Philadelphia, PA: Temple University Press, 2014.

Cleary, Joe, Jed Esty, and Colleen Lye, eds. "Peripheral Realisms." Special issue, Modern Language Quarterly 73, no. 3 (2012).

Cohen, Cathy. The Boundaries of Blackness: AIDS and the Breakdown of Black Power. Chicago: Chicago University Press, 1999.

Coolloud. "Yao hunyin pingquan haishi geming? Dang tongxing hunyin zhengqu hefa" [Marriage equality or revolution? On the quest to legalize same-sex marriage]. Accessed April 15, 2014. http://www.coolloud.org.tw/node/71234.

Cornell, Drucilla. *Beyond Accommodation: Ethical Feminism, Deconstruction, and the Law*. New York: Routledge, 1991.

Coviello, Peter. *Tomorrow's Parties: Sex and the Untimely in Nineteenth-Century America*. New York: NYU Press, 2013.

Crimp, Douglas. *Melancholia and Moralism: Essays on AIDS and Queer Politics*. Cambridge, MA: The MIT Press, 2004.

Cristini, Remy. "The Rise of Comrade Literature: Significance and Development of a New Chinese Genre." Master's thesis, Leiden University, 2005.

Cruz-Malavé, Arnaldo, and Martin F. Manalansan, eds. *Queer Globalizations: Citizenship and the Afterlife of Colonialism*. New York: New York University Press, 2002.

Cui, Zi'en. Writer, director, producer. *Ai yaya qu buru* [Feeding boys ayaya]. Film. China: Cui Zi Studio, 2003.

———. *Beidou you qi xing* [Seven stars of the northern dipper]. Guangzhou: Huacheng chubanshe, 2012.

———. Writer, director. *Chou jiao deng chang* [Enter the clowns]. Film. China: Cui Zi Studio, 2002.

———. "The Communist International of Queer Film." Translated by Petrus Liu. *positions* (2010): 417–24.

———. "Endangered Species Rule!" Translated by Petrus Liu. *positions* (2004): 165–79.

———. "Filtered Voices: Representing Gay People in Today's China." Translated by Chi Ta-wei. *International Institute for Asian Studies Newsletter* 29 (November 2002): 13.

———. Writer, director. *Jiuyue* [Old testament]. Film. China: Cui Zi Studio, 2002.

———. Writer, director. *Nan nan nü nü* [Man man woman woman]. Film. China: Cui Zi Studio, 1999.

———. Director. *Wo ruhua shi yu de erzi* [My fair son]. Film. China: Cui Zi Studio, 2005.

———. Writer, director. *Xing xing xiang xi xi* [Star appeal]. Film. China: Cui Zi Studio, 2004.

———. Writer, director. *Yejing* [Night scene]. Film. China: Cui Zi Studio, 2003.

———. Writer, director. *Zhi Tongzhi* [Queer China, comrade China]. Film. China: Cui Zi Studio, 2008.

Culler, Jonathan. "The Performative." In *The Literary in Theory*, 137–65. Stanford: Stanford University Press, 2007.

Cvetkovich, Ann. *Depression: A Public Feeling*. Durham, NC: Duke University Press, 2012.

Dai, Jinhua. *Cinema and Desire: Feminist Marxism and Cultural Politics in the Work of Dai Jinhua*. Edited by Tani Barlow and Jing Wang. New York: Verso, 2002.

———. *Jing yu shisu shenhua* [The mirror and common myths]. Beijing: China Radio and Television Press, 1995.

Dai, Jinhua, and Meng Yue, eds. *Fuchu lishi dibiao: xiandai funü wenxue yanjiu* [Emerging from the horizon of history: Modern Chinese women's literature]. Beijing: Zhongguo renmin daxue chubanshe, 2004.

Damm, Jens. "Same-Sex Desire and Society in Taiwan, 1970–1987." *The China Quarterly* 181 (March 2005): 67–81.

———. "Contemporary Discourses on Homosexuality in Republican China: A Critical Analysis of Terminology and Current Research." In *Women in China: The Republican Period in Historical Perspective*, edited by Mechthild Leutner and Nicola Spakowski, 282–311. Münster, Germany: LIT Verlag, 2005.

D'Emilio, John. *Sexual Politics, Sexual Communities: The Making of a Homosexual Minority in the United States, 1940–1970*. Chicago: University of Chicago Press, 1983.

Derrida, Jacque. "The Ends of Man." *Philosophy and Phenomenological Research* 30, no. 1 (1969): 31–57.

———. "Signature, Event, Context." In *Limited, Inc*. Evanston: Northwestern University Press, 1988.

Ding, Naifei. "Changji, jishengchong, yu guojia nüxing zhi jia" [Parasites and prostitutes in the house of state feminism]. In Ho, ed., *Sex work studies*, 373–95.

———. "Feminist Knots: Shades of the Bondmaid-Concubine in Sex and Domestic Work." *Inter-Asia Cultural Studies* 3, no. 3 (December 2002): 449–67.

———. "Kanbujian dieying—jiawu yu xinggongzuo de biqie shenying" [Shades of the bondmaid-concubine in sex and domestic work]. *Taiwan shehui yan jiu jikan* [Taiwan: A radical quarterly in social studies] 48 (December 2002): 135–68.

———. *Obscene Things: Sexual Politics in Jin Ping Mei*. Durham, NC: Duke University Press, 2002.

———. "Parasites and Prostitutes in the House of State Feminism." *Inter-Asia Cultural Studies* 1, no. 2 (August 2000): 305–18.

———. "Penumbrae Query Shadow." In Ho, ed., *Introduction to the Politics of Sexuality*, 317–53.

———. "Stigma of Sex and Sex Work." *Inter-Asia Cultural Studies* 7, no. 2 (2006): 326–28.

———. "Weiyi yu liudong: jingying nüxing zhuyi jiaguo li de mao gou cang ying" [Transitions and movements: Pests and parasites in the classroom of elite state feminism]. In Ho, ed., *Sex work studies*, 397–420.

Ding, Naifei, and Liu Jen-peng. "Penumbrae Ask Shadow: Reticent Poetics, Queer Politics." In Ho, ed., *Working Papers in Gender/Sexuality Studies* 3&4, 109–55.

———. "Penumbrae Ask Shadow II: Crocodile Skin, Lesbian Stuffing, Half-man Half-horse Qiu Miaojin." Paper presented at the Third International Super-Slim Conference on Politics of Gender/Sexuality National Central University, Chungli, November 1999.

————. "Reticent Poetics, Queer Politics." *Inter-Asia Cultural Studies* 6, no. 1 (2005): 30–55.

————, eds. *Zhiyi hunyin jiating lianxu ti* [Querying the marriage-family continuum]. Taipei: Shenlou, 2011.

Ding, Naifei, Jen-peng Liu, and Amie Parry. *Wangliang wenjing: ku'er yuedu gonglue* [Penumbrae query shadow: Queer reading tactics]. Chungli: Center for the Study of Sexualities, National Central University, 2007.

Du, Bifen. "Cong chongjing, huanmie, dao zhuixun yu tuibian: Shixi Chen Ruoxi chang pian xiaoshuo Zhihun" [From utopia to *Paper Marriage*: Chen Ruoxi's fiction]. Master's thesis, Zhenli University, 2002.

Duggan, Lisa. *The Twilight of Equality? Neoliberalism, Cultural Politics, and the Attack on Democracy*. Boston: Beacon, 2003.

Duke, Michael S., ed. *Modern Chinese Women Writers: Critical Appraisals*. New York: Sharpe, 1989.

————, ed. *Worlds of Modern Chinese Fiction: Short Stories and Novellas from the People's Republic, Taiwan, and Hong Kong*. Armonk, NY: M.E. Sharpe, 1991.

East Bay Community Law Center, email communication to the Center for the Study of Sexualities, Taiwan, October 14, 2006.

Edelman, Lee. *No Future: Queer Theory and the Death Drive*. Durham, NC: Duke University Press, 2004.

Eng, David. *The Feeling of Kinship: Queer Liberalism and the Racialization of Intimacy*. Durham, NC: Duke University Press, 2010.

————. *Racial Castration: Managing Masculinity in Asian America*. Durham, NC: Duke University Press, 2001.

————. "The Queer Space of China: Expressive Desire in Stanley Kwan's *Lan Yu*." *positions: east asia cultures critique* 18, no. 2 (Fall 2010): 459–87.

Eng, David, Judith Halberstam, and José Muñoz, eds. "What's Queer about Queer Studies Now?" Special issue, *Social Text* 23, nos. 3–4 (2005).

Eng, David, Teemu Ruskola, and Shuang Shen. "China and the Human." Special double issue, *Social Text* 29, no. 4 (Winter 2011) and 30, no. 1 (Spring 2012).

Engebretsen, Elisabeth L. "Conjugal Ideals, Intimate Practices: Affective Ties and Relationship Strategies among Lala ('lesbian') Women in Contemporary Beijing." *Sexuality Research and Social Policy* 6, no. 3 (2009): 3–14.

————. *Queer Women in Urban China: An Ethnography*. New York: Routledge, 2014.

Engels, Friedrich. *The Origin of the Family, Private Property and the State*. New York: Penguin, 2010 [1884].

Erni, John N. "Run Queer Asia Run." *Journal of Homosexuality* 45 (2003): 381–84.

————. "Who Needs Human Rights? Cultural Studies and Public Institutions." In Morris and Hjort, eds., *Creativity and Academic Activism*, chapter 10. Kindle edition.

Evans, Harriet. *Women and Sexuality in China: Dominant Discourses of Female Sexuality and Gender Since 1949*. London: Blackwell, 1997.

Fabian, Johannes. *Time and the Other*. New York: Columbia University Press, 1983.

Fan, Luoping. *Dangdai Taiwan nüxing xiaoshuo shilun* [A historical study of contemporary women's fiction from Taiwan]. Taipei: Shangwu, 2006.

Fan, Qing. "Dangdai shehui zhuyi nüxing zhuyi" [Contemporary socialist feminist theory]. In Gu, ed., *Nüxing zhuyi yu liupai*, 181–214.

Fang, Fu Ruan, and Vern L. Bullough. "Lesbianism in China." *Archives of Sexual Behavior* 21, no. 3 (1992): 217–26.

———. "Same-sex Love in Contemporary China." In *The Third Pink Book: A Global View of Lesbian and Gay Liberation and Oppression*, edited by Aart Hendriks, Rob Tielman and Evert van der Veen, 46–53. Amherst: Prometheus Books, 1993.

Fang, Gang. *Tongxinglian zai Zhongguo* [Homosexuality in China]. Jilin: Jilin People's Press, 1995.

Farris, Catherine. "Women's Liberation under 'East Asian Modernity' in China and Taiwan: Historical, Cultural, and Comparative Perspectives." In *Women in the New Taiwan: Gender Roles and Gender Consciousness in a Changing Society*, edited by Catherine Farris, Anru Lee, and Murray Rubenstein, 325–76. New York: M.E. Sharpe, 2004.

Faurot, Jeannette L., ed. *Chinese Fiction from Taiwan: Critical Perspectives*. Bloomington: Indiana University Press, 1980.

Ferguson, Roderick. *Aberrations in Black: Toward a Queer of Color Critique*. Minneapolis: University of Minnesota Press, 2003.

Ferguson, Roderick, and Grace Kyungwon Hong, eds. *Strange Affinities: The Gender and Sexual Politics of Comparative Racialization*. Durham, NC: Duke University Press, 2011.

Ferry, Nicole. "Rethinking the Mainstream Gay and Lesbian Movement beyond the Classroom." *Journal of Curriculum Theorizing* 28, no. 2 (2012): 104–17.

Floyd, Kevin. *The Reification of Desire: Towards a Queer Marxism*. Minneapolis: University of Minnesota Press, 2009.

Foucault, Michel. *The History of Sexuality*, Volume 1. New York: Pantheon Books, 1978.

———. *Madness and Civilization: A History of Insanity in the Age of Reason*. New York: Vintage Books, 1988.

———. "Nietzsche, Genealogy, History." In *The Foucault Reader*, edited by Paul Rabinow, 76–100. New York: Pantheon Books, 1984.

———. *Society Must Be Defended: Lectures at the Collège de France, 1975–76*. New York: Picador, 2003.

Frecerro, Carla. *Queer/Early/Modern*. Durham, NC: Duke University Press, 2006.

Freeman, Elizabeth. *Time Binds: Queer Temporalities, Queer Histories*. Durham, NC: Duke University Press, 2010.

———. *The Wedding Complex: Forms of Belonging in Modern American Culture*. Durham, NC: Duke University Press, 2002.

Freud, Sigmund. "Instincts and Their Vicissitudes." In *General Psychological Theory*, 83–103. New York: Touchstone, 1997.

Fuss, Diana. *Essentially Speaking: Feminism, Nature, and Difference*. New York: Routledge, 1989.

Genet, Jean. *The Thief's Journal*. New York: Grove Press, 1994.

Geyer, Robert. "In Love and Gay." In *Popular China: Unofficial Culture in a Globalizing Society*, edited by Perry E. Link, Richard P. Madsen, and Paul G. Pickowicz, 251–74. Oxford: Rowman and Littlefield, 2002.

Giffney, Noreen, and Myra J. Hird. "Introduction: Queering the Non/Human." In *Queering the Non/Human*, edited by Giffney and Hird, 1–16. Burlington, VT: Ashgate, 2008.

Gilmartin, Christina, Gail Hershatter, Lisa Rofel, and Tyrene White, eds. *Engendering China: Women, Culture, and the State*. Cambridge, MA: Harvard University Press, 1994.

Goldblatt, Howard. Preface to *The Execution of Mayor Yin and Other Stories from the Great Proletarian Cultural Revolution* by Chen, Ruoxi (Jo-Hsi), ix. Translated by Nancy Ing and Howard Goldblatt. Revised ed. Bloomington: Indiana University Press, 2004.

Gondelier, Maurice. *Perspectives in Marxist Anthropology*. Cambridge: Cambridge University Press, 1977.

Gopinath, Gayatri. *Impossible Desires: Queer Diaspora and South Asian Public Cultures*. Durham, NC: Duke University Press, 2005.

Gould, Deborah. *Moving Politics: Emotion and ACT UP's Fight against AIDS*. Chicago: University of Chicago Press, 2009.

Gowan, Peter. "The New Liberal Cosmopolitanism." In *Debating Cosmopolitics*, edited by Daniele Archibugi, 51–66. London: Verso, 2003.

G/SRAT (2007). "Women de lichang" [Our positions.]. Accessed December 1, 2007. http://gsrat.net/about/ourstand.php.

Gu, Yanling, ed. *Nüxing zhuyi yu liupai* [Feminism: Theories and schools]. Taipei: Fembooks, 1996.

Guangtai [Song, Guangtai]. *Taobi hunyin de ren* [The man who does not want to be married]. Taipei: Haojiao, 1976.

Guillory, John. *Cultural Capital: The Problem of Literary Canon Formation*. Chicago: University of Chicago Press, 1993.

Guo Jingming. Writer and director. *Tiny Times 1.0*. Film. China: Le Vision Pictures, 2013.

———. *Xiao Shidai 1.0* [Tiny times 1.0]. Shanghai: Changjiang wenyi chubanshe, 2008.

———. *Xiao Shidai 2.0* [Tiny times 2.0]. Shanghai: Changjiang wenyi chubanshe, 2010.

———. *Xiao Shidai 3.0* [Tiny times 3.0]. Shanghai: Changjiang wenyi chubanshe, 2011.

Guo, Lianghui. *Di san xing* [The third sex]. Taipei: Hanlin, 1978.

Guo, Xiaofei. *Zhongguofa shiye xia de tongxinglian* [Homosexuality in the purview of Chinese law]. Beijing: Zhishi chanquan chubanshe, 2007.

Gutting, Gary. *French Philosophy in the Twentieth Century*. Cambridge: Cambridge University Press, 2001.

Halberstam, Judith/Jack. *In a Queer Time and Place: Transgender Bodies, Subcultural Lives*. New York: New York University Press, 2005.

———. *Gaga Feminism: Sex, Gender, and the End of the Normal*. Boston: Beacon Press, 2012.

Hall, Jonathan. "Queer China Onscreen." Promotional publication for the China Onscreen Biennial at Pomona College, October 15, 2012.

Halley, Janet. "'Like-Race' Arguments." In *What's Left of Theory: On the Politics of Literary Theory*, edited by Judith Butler, John Guillory, and Kendall Thomas, 40–74. New York: Routledge, 2000.

Halley, Janet, and Andrew Parker, eds., *After Sex? On Writing Since Queer Theory*. Durham, NC: Duke University Press, 2011.

Halperin, David. "Forgetting Foucault: Acts, Identities, and the History of Sexuality." *Representations* 63 (Summer 1998): 93–120.

———. *How to Be Gay*. Cambridge, MA: Harvard University Press, 2012.

———. *How to Do the History of Sexuality*. Chicago: University of Chicago Press, 2002.

———. *One Hundred Years of Homosexuality*. New York: Routledge, 1990.

Haraway, Donna. "The Promise of Monsters: A Regenerative Politics for Inappropriate/d Other." In *Cultural Studies*, edited by Lawrence Grossberg, Cary Nelson, and Paula Treichler, 295–337. New York: Routledge, 1992.

Hardt, Michael, and Antonio Negri. *Commonwealth*. Cambridge, MA: Harvard University Press, 2011.

———. *Empire*. Cambridge, MA: Harvard University Press, 2000.

———. *Multitude: War and Democracy in the Age of Empire*. New York: Penguin Books. 2004.

Harootunian, Harry. "Postcoloniality's Unconscious/Area Studies's Desire." In *Learning Places: The Afterlife of Area Studies*, edited by Masao Miyoshi, Harry Harootunian, and Rey Chow, 150–75. Durham, NC: Duke University Press, 2002.

He, Xiaopei. "My Unconventional Marriage or ménage à trois in Beijing." In Yau, ed., *As Normal as Possible*, 103–10.

He, Xiaopei, and Lisa Rofel. "I AM AIDS: Living with HIV/AIDS in China." *positions: east asia cultures critique* 18, no. 2 (2010): 511–36.

He, Zhaotian. "Postsocialist History and the Paradigmatic Shifts in Chinese Literary and Cultural Criticism." Translated by Petrus Liu. *Inter-Asia Cultural Studies* 6, no. 1 (2005): 126–35.

Heinrich, Larissa, and Fran Martin, eds. *Embodied Modernities: Corporeality, Representation, and Chinese Cultures*. Honolulu: University of Hawaii Press, 2006.

Hennessy, Rosemary. "Queer Visibility in Commodity Culture." *Cultural Critique* 29 (1994–95): 31–76.

Hershatter, Gail, Emily Honig, Jonathan Lipman, and Randall Stross, eds. *Remapping China: Fissures in Historical Terrain.* Stanford, CA: Stanford University Press, 1996.

Hillenbrand, Margaret. *Literature, Modernity, and the Practice of Resistance: Japanese and Taiwanese Fiction, 1960–1990.* Leiden, Holland: Brill, 2007.

Hinsch, Bret. *Masculinities in Chinese History.* Lanham: Rowman and Littlefield, 2013.

———. *Passions of the Cut Sleeve: The Male Homosexual Tradition in China.* Berkeley: University of California Press, 1990.

Hird, Derek. "The Paradox of Pluralization: Masculinities, Androgyny, and Male Anxiety in Contemporary China." In *Understanding Global Sexualities: New Frontiers,* edited by Peter Aggleton, Paul Boyce, Henrietta Moore, and Richard Parker, 49–65. New York: Routledge, 2012.

Ho, Aaron K. H. "The Lack of Chinese Lesbians: Double Crossing in *Blue Gate Crossing.*" *Genders* 49 (2009). Accessed April 2, 2013. http://www.iiav.nl/ezines /IAV_606661/IAV_606661_2010_52/g49_ho.html.

Ho, Josephine Chuen-juei. "Asian Modernity and Its 'Gendered Vulnerabilities.'" *Nordic Institute of Asian Studies Asian Insights* 1 (June 2008): 9–11.

———. *Butongguo nüren: xingbie, ziben, wenhua* [Gendered nation(s): Sexuality, capital, and culture]. Taipei: Zili, 1994.

———, ed. *Dongwulian wangye shijian bu* [The zoophilia webpage incident]. Chungli: Center for the Study of Sexualities, 2003.

———. "Is Global Governance Bad for East Asian Queers?" *GLQ: A Journal of Lesbian and Gay Studies* 14, no. 4 (Fall 2008): 457–79.

———. *Haoshuang nüren* [The gallant woman: Feminism and sex emancipation]. Taipei, Taiwan: Crown Publishers, 1994.

———, ed. *Huhuan Taiwan xin nüxing: haoshuang nüren shei bushuang?* [Contestations over female sexuality: Dissenting essays on the gallant woman]. Taipei: Yuanliu, 1997.

———. ed. *Kuaxingbie* [Trans-gender]. Chungli: National Central University, 2003.

———. ed. *Lianjie xing* [Connections: Trans-local exchanges on Chinese gender/ sexuality]. Chungli: Center for the Study of Sexualities, 2010.

———. "Life of a Parasite: One Survival Story in Cultural Stories." In Morris and Hjort, eds., *Creativity and Academic Activism,* chapter 3. Kindle edition.

———. "Queer Existence under Global Governance: A Taiwan Exemplar." *positions* 18, no. 2 (Summer 2010): 537–54.

———. "Sex Revolution and Sex Rights Movement in Taiwan." In *Taiwanese Identity from Domestic, Regional and Global Perspectives,* edited by Jens Damm and Gunter Schubert, 123–39. Münster, Germany: LIT Verlag, 2007.

————. "Taiwan xingbie zhengzhi de nianling zhuanxiang" (Generational shifts in Taiwan's sexual politics). In *Zhuanyan lishi*, edited by Josephine Ho, 221–63. Chungli: Center for the Study of Sexualities, 2012.

————, ed. *Xing/bie yanjiu* [Working papers in gender/sexuality studies] 1&2. Chungli: Center for the Study of Sexualities, 1998.

————, ed. *Xing/bie yanjiu* [Working papers in gender/sexuality studies] 3&4. Chungli: Center for the Study of Sexualities, 1998.

————, ed. *Xing/bie yanjiu* [Working papers in gender/sexuality studies] 5&6. Chungli: Center for the Study of Sexualities, 1999.

————, ed. *Xing/bie yanjiu de xin shiye* [Visionary essays in gender/sexuality studies] nos. 5&6. Taipei: Meta Media, 1997.

————, ed. *Xing gongzuo yanjiu* [Sex work studies]. Chungli: Center for the Study of Sexualities, 2003.

————. "Xing geming: yige Makesi zhuyi guandian de Meiguo bainian xingshi." [Sex revolution—a Marxist perspective on one-hundred years of American history of sexualities]. In Ho, ed., *Visionary Essays in Sexuality/Gender Studies*, 33–99.

————, ed. *Xing zhengzhi rumen* [Introduction to the politics of sexuality]. Chungli: Center for the Study of Sexualities, 2005.

————, ed. *Zhuanyan lishi: Lian an san di xingyun huigu*. [The personal is historical: Gender/sexuality studies/movements in greater China]. Chungli: Center for the Study of Sexualities, 2012.

Ho, Josephine, and Ning, Yin-Bin (Ka Wei bo). *Weishenme tamen bu gaosuni* [Why they didn't want to tell you—introduction to sexual politics]. Taipei: Fang Zhi, 1990.

Ho, Loretta Wing Wah. *Gay and Lesbian Subculture in Urban China*. New York: Routledge, 2009.

Holland, Sharon. *The Erotic Life of Racism*. Durham, NC: Duke University Press, 2012.

Hong, Guo-Juin. "Limits of Visibility: Taiwan's Tongzhi Movement in Mickey Chen's Documentaries." *positions: east asia cultures critique* 21, no. 3 (Summer 2013): 683–701.

Hou, Hsiao-Hsien, Chu Tien-hsin, Tang Nuo and Hsia Chu-joe. Interview with Perry Anderson. "Tensions in Taiwan," *New Left Review* 28 (2004): 18–42.

Howland, Douglas. "Popular Sovereignty and Democratic Centralism in People's Republic of China." In Eng et al., eds., "China and the Human, Part II": 1–25.

Hsia, C. T. [Chih-tsing]. *A History of Modern Chinese Fiction*. Bloomington: Indiana University Press, 1999.

Hsu, Walter Jen-Hao. "The Affective Politics of Home: Queer Familial Imaginations in Twentieth- and Twenty-First-Century Chinese Theatre and Film." PhD diss., Cornell University, 2013.

Hsu, Yousheng. *Nanhun nanjia* [Marriage between men]. Taipei: Kaixin yangguang chubanshe, 1996..

Huang, Hans Tao-Ming. *Queer Politics and Sexual Modernity in Taiwan*. Hong Kong: Hong Kong University Press, 2011.

Huang, Martin. *Negotiating Masculinities in Late Imperial China*. Honolulu: University of Hawai'i Press, 2006.

Huang, Shuling. "Wutuobang shehui zhuyi/Makesi nüxing zhuyi" [Utopian socialism and Marxist feminism]. In Gu, ed., *Nüxing zhuyi yu liupai*, 27–70.

Hung, Eva. *City Women*. Hong Kong: Renditions, 2000.

———, ed. *Contemporary Women Writers: Hong Kong and Taiwan; An Authorized Collection*. Hong Kong: Chinese University of Hong Kong, 1992.

Jameson, Fredric. *Representing Capital: A Reading of Volume One*. London: Verso, 2011.

Jay, Martin. *Permanent Exiles: Essays on the Intellectual Migration from Germany to America*. New York: Columbia University Press, 1985.

Jeffreys, Elaine, and Haiqing Yu. *Sex in China*. Cambridge, UK: Polity Press, 2015.

Ji, Ji. "Zhanzai lengjing de gaochu yu Xiao Sa tan shen huo yu xie zuo." [With Xiao Sa on life and writing]. *China Times*, August 14, 1987.

Johnson, E. Patrick, and Mae G. Henderson, eds. *Black Queer Studies: A Critical Anthology*. Durham, NC: Duke University Press, 2005.

Jolly, Susie, Andrea Cornwall, and Kate Hawkins, eds. *Women, Sexuality and the Political Power of Pleasure*. London: Zed Books, 2013.

Kam, Yip Lo Lucetta. "Opening Up Marriage: Married Lalas in Shanghai." In Yau, ed., *As Normal as Possible*, 87–102.

———. *Shanghai Lalas: Female Tongzhi Communities and Politics in Urban China*. Hong Kong: Hong Kong University Press, 2013.

Kang, Wenqing. "The Decriminalization and Depathologization of Homosexuality in China." In *China in and beyond the Headlines*, edited by Timothy B. Weston and Lionel M. Jensen, 231–48. Plymouth, UK: Rowan and Littlefield, 2012.

———. *Obsession: Male Same-Sex Relations in China, 1900–1950*. Hong Kong: Hong Kong University Press, 2009.

Katz, Jonathan. *The Invention of Heterosexuality*. New York: Dutton, 1995.

Khor, Diana, and Saori Kamano, eds. *Lesbians in East Asia: Diversity, Identities, and Resistance*. New York: Routledge, 2011.

Kong, Travis S. K. *Chinese Male Homosexualities: Memba, Tongzhi, and Golden Boy*. New York: Routledge, 2011.

———. "Fading Queer Heterotopia: Hong Kong Older Gay Men's Queer Use of Spaces." *Sexualities* 15, no. 8 (2012): 896–916.

———. *The Hidden Voice: The Sexual Politics of Chinese Male Sex Workers*. Hong Kong: Hong Polytechnic University, 2005.

----. "Men Who Sell Sex in China." In *Male Sex Work and Society*, edited by Victor Minichiello and John Scott, 314–41. New York: Harrington Press, 2014.

----. "Outcast Bodies: Money, Sex and Desire of Money Boys in Mainland China." In Yau, ed., *As Normal as Possible*, 15–36.

Kristeva, Julia. *About Chinese Women*. New York: Urizen Books, 1977.

Kwan, Stanley, dir. *Lan Yu*. Film. Hong Kong: Kwan's Creation Workshop, 2001.

Laclau, Ernesto, and Chantal Mouffe. *Hegemony and Socialist Strategy: Towards a Radical Democratic Politics*. London: Verso, 1985.

Lanchashire, Edel. "The Lock of the Heart Controversy in Taiwan, 1962–63: A Question of Artistic Freedom and a Writer's Social Responsibility." *The China Quarterly* 103 (1985): 462–88.

Laqueur, Thomas. *Making Sex: Body and Gender from the Greeks to Freud*. Cambridge, MA: Harvard University Press, 1990.

Lau, Joseph S. M. ed. *Chinese Stories from Taiwan: 1960–1970*. New York: Columbia University Press, 1976.

Lee, Ang, dir. *The Wedding Banquet*. Film. Taiwan: CMPC, 1993.

Lee, Linus. "Translating *Nie Zi* (1983) into *Crystal Boys* (2003)." Master's thesis, National Central University, 2004.

Leung, Helen Hok-Sze. "Homosexuality and Queer Aesthetics." In *A Companion to Chinese Cinema*, edited by Yingjin Zhang, 518–34. Malden: Blackwell Publishing, 2012.

----. "Notes on Sexual Dissidence in Hong Kong and Taiwan." *West Coast Line* 34, no. 3 (Winter 2001): 8–26.

----. "Thoughts on Lesbian Genders in Contemporary Chinese Cultures." *Journal of Lesbian Studies* 6, no. 2 (Summer 2002): 123–33.

----. *Undercurrents: Queer Culture and Postcolonial Hong Kong*. Vancouver: University of British Columbia Press, 2008.

Lévi-Strauss, Claude. *The Elementary Structures of Kinship*. Boston: Beacon Press, 1969.

Levine, Andrew. *A Future for Marxism? Althusser, the Analytical Turn and the Revival of Socialist Theory*. London: Pluto Press, 2003.

Li, Yinhe. *Ni ruci xuyao anwei* [You need to be comforted]. Beijing: Dangdai shijie chubanshe, 2005.

----. "Regulating Male Same-sex Relationships in the People's Republic of China." In *Sex and Sexuality in China*, edited by Elaine Jeffreys, 82–101. London: Routledge, 2006.

----. *Tongxinglian yawenhua* [The subculture of homosexuality]. Beijing: Zhongguo youyi chubanshi, 2002.

----. *Zhongguo nüxing de ganxing yu xing* [Love and sexuality of the Chinese women]. Beijing: Zhongguo youyi chubanshi, 2002.

Li, Yinhe, and Wang Xiaobo. *Tamen de shijie: Zhongguo nan tongxinglian qunluo toushi* [Their world: A penetrating look into China's male homosexual community]. Hong Kong: Cosmos Books, 1992.

Li Youxin (Alphonse Youth-Leigh). *Nan tongxinglian dianying* [History of films of, by, and for gay men]. Taipei: Zhiwen, 1993.

Li Ziyun, ed., *Anthology of Chinese Women's Fiction* [*Zhongguo nüxing xiaoshuo xuan*]. Hong Kong: Joint Publishing, 1991.

Lianhebao liuba niandu duanpian xiaoshuo jiang zuoping ji [Collection of the annual prize-winning stories and commentaries]. Taipei: Lianhebao, 1979.

Lim, Eng-Beng. *Brown Boys and Rice Queens: Spellbinding Performance in the Asias*. New York: NYU Press, 2014.

Lim, Song Hwee. *Celluloid Comrades: Representations of Male Homosexuality in Contemporary Chinese Cinemas*. Honolulu: University of Hawaii Press, 2006.

———. "How to Be Queer in Taiwan: Translation, Appropriation, and the Construction of a Queer Identity in Taiwan." In Martin et al., eds., *AsiaPacifiQueer*, 235–50.

———. "Queer Theory Goes to Taiwan." In *The Ashgate Research Companion to Queer Theory*, edited by Noreen Giffney and Michael O'Rourke, 257–75. Aldershot: Ashgate, 2009.

Lin, Bai. *One Person's War* [*Yigeren de zhanzheng*]. Nanjing: Jiangsu wenyi chubanshe, 1994.

Lin, Fang-mei. "Identity Politics in Taiwanese Feminism: On the Example of the Licensed-Prostitutes Debate." *Chung-Wai Literary Monthly* 27, no. 1 (1998): 56–87.

———. "Meili 'xing' shijie" [Brave 'sexual' world]. *China Times*, Oct. 13, 1994.

Lin, Pei-Yin. "Writing Beyond Boudoirs: Sinophone Literature by Female Writers in Contemporary Taiwan." In Shih, Tsai, and Bernards, eds., *Sinophone Studies*, 255–69.

Liu, Jen-peng. "The Disposition of Hierarchy and the Late Qing Discourse of Gender Equality." Translated by Petrus Liu. *Inter-Asia Cultural Studies* 2, no. 1 (2001): 69–79.

Liu, Jen-peng, and Amie Parry. "The Politics of Scahdenfreude: Violence and Queer Cultural Critique in Lucifer Hung's Science Fiction." *positions: east asia cultures critique* 18, no. 2 (Fall 2010): 351–72.

Liu, Jun. *Qing yu mei—Bai Xianyong zhuan* [Love and beauty: A biography of Pai Hsien-yung]. Taipei: Shibao, 2007.

Liu, Lydia H. "Legislating the Universal: The Circulation of International Law in the Nineteen Century." In *Tokens of Exchange: the Problem of Translation in Global Circulations*, edited by Lydia Liu, 127–64. Durham: NC: Duke University Press, 1999.

Liu, Lydia H., Rebecca E. Karl, and Dorothy Ko. *The Birth of Chinese Feminism: Essential Texts in Transnational Theory*. New York: Columbia University Press, 2013.

Liu, Petrus. "From Identity to Social Protest: The Cultural Politics of Beijing Comrades." In Bei-Tong, *Beijing Comrades*, translated and edited by Scott E. Myers. New York: Feminist Press, 2016.

————. Interviews with Cui Zi'en, Berkeley, April 24, 2005; Beijing, June 15, 2011; New York City, November 5, 2012; Beijing, September 21, 2014.

————. Personal communication with Cui Zi'en, March 15, 2013.

————. "Why Does Queer Theory Need China?" *positions: east asia cultures critique* 18, no. 2 (Fall 2010): 291–320.

Liu, Petrus, Lisa Rofel, and Shi Tou. "Interview with Shi Tou." *positions: east asia cultures critique* 18, no. 2 (Fall 2010): 409–16.

Liu, Petrus, and Lisa Rofel, eds. "Beyond the Strai(gh)ts: Transnationalism and Queer Chinese Politics." Special issue, *positions: east asia cultures critique* 18, no. 2 (Fall 2010).

Liu Yu-hsiu, "Zhengshi xing lunshu de fuhua zuoyong" [Taking a serious look at the corruptive effects of the discourse of sexual perversity], *China Times*, Jan. 11, 2002.

Louie, Kam. *Theorising Chinese Masculinity: Society and Gender in China.* Cambridge: Cambridge University Press, 2002.

Love, Heather. *Feeling Backwards: Loss and the Politics of Queer History.* Cambridge, MA: Harvard University Press, 2009.

————, ed. "Rethinking Sex." Special issue, *GLQ: A Journal of Lesbian and Gay Studies* 17, no. 1 (2011).

Lowe, Lisa. *Critical Terrains: French and British Orientalisms.* Ithaca, NY: Cornell University Press, 1991.

Lu, Annette Hsiu-lien. *Xin nüxing zhuyi* [New feminism]. Taipei: Youshi, 1974.

————. *Zhe sange nüren* [These three women]. Taipei: Zili wanbaoshe, 1985.

Lu, Tonglin, ed. *Gender and Sexuality in Twentieth-Century Chinese Literature and Society.* Albany, NY: State University of New York Press, 1993.

————, ed. "The Chinese Perspective on Žižek and Žižek's Perspective on China." Special issue, *positions: east asia cultures critique* 19, no. 3 (2011).

Lu, Zhenghui. *Xiaoshuo yu shehui* [The novel and society]. Taipei: Lianjing, 1992.

Lung, Ying-tai. *Dajiang dahai* [Big river, big sea—untold stories of 1949]. Taipei: Tianxia, 2009.

————. *Qingyong wenmin lai shuifu wo* [Persuade us with civilization, not force, please]. Taipei: Shibao, 2006.

Luo, Manli. "Bu hege de canyu zhe: lun Chen Ruoxi wenge shuxie zhong de zhishi fenzi xingxiang" [Unqualified participants—on the intellectual image in Chen Ruoxi's writings on the cultural revolution]. *Journal of Shantou University* (2012): 44–48.

Lye, Colleen. *America's Asia: Racial Form and American Literature, 1893–1945.* Princeton: Princeton University Press, 2005.

Mackie, Vera, and Mark McLelland, eds. *Routledge Handbook of Sexuality Studies in East Asia.* New York: Routledge, 2015.

Manalansan, Martin F. *Global Divas: Filipino Gay Men in the Diaspora.* Durham, NC: Duke University Press, 2003.

Mandel, Ernest, and George Novak. *The Marxist Theory of Alienation*. New York: Pathfinder Press, 1970.

Mann, Susan L. *Gender and Sexuality in Modern China*. Cambridge: Cambridge University Press, 2011.

Mao, Feng. *Tongxinglian wenxue shi* [The history of homosexual literature]. Taipei: Han Chung Book Co., 1996.

Marcus, Sharon. *Between Women: Friendship, Desire, and Marriage in Victorian England*. Princeton, NJ: Princeton University Press, 2007.

Marcuse, Herbert. *Eros and Civilization: A Philosophical Inquiry into Freud*. Boston: Beacon Press, 1974.

Martin, Fran. *Backward Glances: Contemporary Chinese Cultures and the Female Homoerotic Imaginary*. Durham, NC: Duke University Press, 2010.

———. Introduction to *Angelwings: Contemporary Queer Fiction from Taiwan*, edited and translated by Fran Martin, 1–28. Honolulu: University of Hawaii Press, 2003.

———. *Situating Sexualities: Queer Representation in Taiwanese Fiction, Film, and Public Culture*. Hong Kong: Hong Kong University Press, 2003.

———. "Surface Tensions: Reading Productions of Tongzhi in Contemporary Taiwan." *GLQ: A Journal of Lesbian and Gay Studies* 6, no. 1 (2000): 61–86.

———. "Transnational Queer Sinophone Cultures." In Mackie and McLelland, eds., *Routledge Handbook of Sexuality Studies in East Asia*, 35–48.

Martin, Fran, Peter A. Jackson, Mark McLelland, and Audrey Yue, eds. *AsiaPacifiQueer: Rethinking Genders and Sexualities*. Urbana: University of Illinois Press, 2008.

Marx, Karl. *Capital* [*Das Kapital*], Vol. I, Harmondsworth: Penguin Books, 1990.

———. "Contribution to the Critique of Hegel's *Philosophy of Right*: Introduction." In Tucker, ed., *The Marx-Engels Reader*, 53–65.

———. *Early Writings*. London: Penguin, 1975.

———. *Economic and Philosophical Manuscripts of 1844*. Moscow: Foreign Languages Publishing House, 1961.

———. "The Eighteenth Brumaire of Louis Bonaparte." In Tucker, ed., *The Marx-Engels Reader*, 594–617.

———. *Grundrisse: Foundations of the Critique of Political Economy*. London: Penguin, 1973.

———. *The Marx-Engels Reader*. Edited by Robert Tucker. New York: Norton, 1978.

———. "On the Jewish Question." In Tucker, ed., *The Marx-Engels Reader*, 26–52.

Massad, Joseph. *Desiring Arabs*. Chicago: University of Chicago Press, 2008.

Mbembe, Achille. "Necropolitics." *Public Culture* 15, no. 1 (Winter 2003): 11–40.

McCune, Jeffrey Q. *Sexual Discretion: Black Masculinity and the Politics of Passing*. Chicago: Chicago University Press, 2014.

McDermott, Joseph. "Friendship and Its Friends in the Late Ming." In *Family Process and Political Process in Modern Chinese History, Part I*, edited by Institute of Modern History, Academia Sinica, 67–96. Taipei: Institute of Modern History, Academia Sinica, 1992.

McGrath, Jason. *Postsocialist Modernity: Chinese Cinema, Literature, and Criticism in the Market Age*. Stanford: Stanford University Press, 2008.

McLennan, Gregor. *Marxism, Pluralism, and Beyond*. Cambridge, UK: Polity Press, 1989.

McMahon, Keith. *Misers, Shrews, and Polygamists: Sexuality and Male-Female Relations in Eighteen-Century Chinese Fiction*. Durham, NC: Duke University Press, 1995.

Moran, Thomas. "Same-Sex Love in Recent Chinese Literature." In *Columbia Companion to Modern East Asian Literatures*, edited by Joshua Mostow and Kirk A. Denton, China section, ed., 488–95. New York: Columbia University Press, 2003.

Morris, Meaghan, and Mette Hjort, eds. *Creativity and Academic Activism: Instituting Cultural Studies*. Hong Kong: Hong Kong University Press, 2012. Kindle edition.

Muñoz, José Esteban. *Cruising Utopia: The Then and There of Queer Futurity*. New York: NYU Press, 2009.

———. *Disidentifications: Queers of Color and the Performance of Politics*. Minneapolis: University of Minnesota Press, 1999.

———. "Feeling Brown, Feeling Down: Latina Affect, the Performativity of Race, and the Depressive Position." *Signs* 31, no. 3 (Spring 2006): 675–88.

Munt, Sally. *Queer Attachments: The Cultural Politics of Shame*. Burlington, VT: Ashgate Publishing, 2007.

Murphy, Kevin, Jason Ruiz, and David Serlin, eds. "Queer Futures." Special issue, *Radical History Review*, no. 100 (Winter 2008).

Myers, Scott E. "A Note from the Translator." In Bei-Tong, *Beijing Comrades*, translated and edited by Scott E. Myers. New York: Feminist Press, forthcoming.

Nealon, Christopher. *Foundlings: Lesbian and Gay Historical Emotion before Stonewall*. Durham, NC: Duke University Press, 2001.

Ng, Vivien W. "Homosexuality and the State in late Imperial China." In *Hidden from History: Reclaiming the Lesbian and Gay Past*, edited by Martin Duberman, Martha Vicinus, and George Chauncey, 76–89. New York: Meridian, 1989.

Ngai, Sianne. *Ugly Feelings*. Cambridge, MA: Harvard University Press, 2005.

Nguyen, Tan Hoang. *A View from the Bottom: Asian American Masculinity and Sexual Representation*. Durham, NC: Duke University Press, 2014.

Ni, Jiazhen. "The Subject of 1990's Homosexual Discourse and Movement in Taiwan." In Ho, ed., *Visionary Essays in Sexuality/Gender Studies*, 125–48.

Ni, Luo. Preface to *Rumengling* [Song of dreams], by Xiao Sa, 1–5. Taipei: Jiuge, 1981.

Ning, Yin-Bin (Ka Weibo). *Body Politics and Media Criticism*. Chungli: Center for the Study of Sexualities, 2004.

———, ed. *Changing Sexual Landscape: The China Turn*. Chungli: Center for the Study of Sexualities, 2011.

———. *An Ethical Inquiry into Prostitution*. Taipei: Taishe Academic Books, 2009.

———. "Fuhe shehui." [Compound society]. *Taiwan: A Radical Quarterly in Social Studies* 71 (2008): 275–79.

———. "Fuquan pai yu xingquan pai de liang tiao nüxing zhuyi zai Taiwan" [Women's rights and sexual rights in Taiwan]. Accessed June 2, 2005. http://intermargins.net/repression/theory/difference.htm.

———. *Introduction to Politics of Sexuality: Lectures on Sex Rights Movement in Taiwan*. Collaborative work with Josephine (Chuen-juei) Ho and Naifei Ding. Chungli: Center for the Study of Sexualities, 2005.

———. "Is Sex Work Really 'Work'?—Marx's Theory of Commodity and the Social Construction of Sex Work." *Taiwan shehui yanjiu jikan* [Taiwan: A radical quarterly in social studies] 46 (June 2002): 87–139.

———. "Jinnian Taiwan zhongdai xing/bie shijian" [Recent events in Taiwan's gender/sexual politics]. In Ho, ed., *Introduction to the Politics of Sexuality*, 41–98.

———. *Lectures on Sex/Gender Studies in Taiwan*, Vols. I and II. Beijing: Jiuzhou Press. 2007.

———. "Renshi Taiwan shehui mailuo: wenhua yu shehui yundong" [Understanding Taiwan's social context: Cultural and social movements]. In Ho, ed., *Introduction to the Politics of Sexuality*, 1–39.

———. "Shenme shi ku'er?" [What is queer politics?]. Edited by Josephine Chuen-juei Ho. *Working Papers in Gender/Sexuality Studies* 3/4 (1998): 32–46. Chungli: Center for the Study of Sexualities.

———, ed. *Xin daode zhuyi: Liang an sandi xingbie xunsi* [New moralism: Sexual reflections in greater China]. Chungli: Center for the Study of Sexualities, 2013.

———. *Xing gongzuo yu xiandai xing* [Sex work and modernity]. Chungli: Center for the Study of Sexualities, 2004.

———. "Xing jiefang sixiang shi chubu zha ji." [Rudimentary notes on the intellectual history of sexual emancipation]. In Ho, ed., *Working Papers in Gender/Sexuality Studies* 3&4: 179–234.

———. *Xing wuxu daode: Xing lunli yu xing pipan* [Sex is not a moral issue: Sexual ethics and sexual critique]. Chungli: Center for the Study of Sexualities, 2007.

———. "Yichang xing ge ming zheng zai fasheng." [A sex revolution is raging]. In Ho, ed., [Contestations over female sexuality], 348–67.

———. "Zhenji zhengzhi yu gongchang zhengzhi." [Ethnic politics and prostitute politics]. In Ho, ed., *Working Papers in Gender/Sexuality Studies* 5&6, 455–58.

Ong, Aihwa. *Neoliberalism as Exception*. Durham, NC: Duke University Press, 2006.

O'Rourke, Michael. "The Afterlives of Queer Theory." *Continent* 1, no. 2 (2011): 102–16.

Pai, Hsien-yung. *Crystal Boys* [Niezi]. Taipei: Yuanjing, 1983.

———. "Gu lian hua" [Love's lone flower]. In *Taibei ren* [Taipei people], 143–62. Taipei: Erya, 1983 [1971].

———. "Hei Hong" [Black rainbow]. In *Jimo de shiqi sui* [Lonely seventeen], 107–21. Taipei: Yuanjing 2012 [1976].

———. "Jin daban de zuihou yiye" [The last night of Madam Chin"]. In *Taibei ren* [Taipei people], 71–90. Taipei: Erya, 1983 [1971].

———. "Wutuobang de zhuiqiu yu huanmie" [From the quest of utopia to disillusionment]. In *Taiwan xian dang dai zuojia yanjiu ziliao huibian*, edited by Xinyuan Chen, 141–50. Taipei: Guoli Taiwan wenxue guan, 2013.

———. "Yue meng" [Moon dream]. In *Jimo de shiqi sui* [Lonely seventeen], 72–79. Taipei: Yuanjing, 2012 [1976].

———. "Yuqing sao" [Sister Yuqing]. In *Jimo de shiqi sui* [Lonely seventeen], 2–37. Taipei: Yuanjing 2012 [1976].

Pan, Suiming. *Zhongguo xing geming zonglun* [Sex revolution in China]. Kaohsiung: Wanyou chubanshe, 2006.

Pan, Suiming, and Yingying Huang. *Xing geming chenggong de shizheng* [Evidence of the success of sex revolution in China]. Taipei: Universal Press, 2008.

Parker, Andrew, Mary Russo, Doris Sommer, and Patricia Yaeger. *Nationalism and Sexuality*. New York: Routledge, 1992.

Patel, Geeta. "Ghostly Appearances: Time Tales Tallied Up." *Social Text* 18, no. 3 (Fall 2000): 47–66.

Peng, Li-hui. "Sexuality and Its Implications in Married Women's Extramarital Affairs." *Journal of Women's and Gender Studies* 18 (December 2004): 39–107.

Phelan, Shane. *Sexual Strangers: Gays, Lesbians, and the Dilemmas of Citizenship*. Philadelphia: Temple University Press, 2001.

Pickowicz, Paul, "From Yao Wenyuan to Cui Zi'en: Film, History, Memory." *Journal of Chinese Cinemas* 1, no. 1 (2007): 41–53.

Pickowicz, Paul and Yingjin Zhang, eds. *From Underground to Independent: Alternative Film Culture in Contemporary China*. Lanham, MD: Rowman and Littlefield, 2006.

Pletsch, Carl. "The Three Worlds; or the Division of Social Scientific Labor, circa 1950–1975." *Comparative Studies in Society and History* 23, no. 4 (October 1981): 565–90.

Postone, Moishe. *Time, Labor, and Social Domination: A Reinterpretation of Marx's Critical Theory*. Cambridge: Cambridge University Press, 1993.

Povinelli, Elizabeth A. *Economies of Abandonment: Social Belonging and Endurance of Late Liberalism*. Durham, NC: Duke University, 2011.

Povinelli, Elizabeth, and George Chauncey. "Thinking Sexuality Transnationally: An Introduction." Special issue, GLQ: A Journal of Lesbian and Gay Studies 5, no. 4 (1999): 439–50.

Puar, Jasbir. Terrorist Assemblages: Homonationalism in Queer Times. Durham, NC: Duke University, 2007.

Qiu, Miaojin. Eyu shouji [The crocodile's journal]. Taipei: Shibao, 1995.

Ricardo, David. The Principles of Political Economy and Taxation. London: Dover, 2004 [1817].

Rich, Ruby B. New Queer Cinema: The Director's Cut. Durham, NC: Duke University Press, 2013.

Riley, Denise. Impersonal Passion: Language as Affect. Durham, NC: Duke University Press, 2005.

———. The Words of Selves: Identification, Solidarity, Irony. Palo Alto: Stanford: 2000.

Robcis, Camille. "China in Our Heads: Althusser, Maoism, and Structuralism." In Eng, et al., eds., "China and the Human," 51–69.

Robinson, Luke. Independent Chinese Documentary: From the Studio to the Street. New York: Palgrave Macmillan, 2013.

Rofel, Lisa. Desiring China: Experiments in Neoliberalism, Sexuality and Public Culture. Durham, NC: Duke University Press, 2007.

———. "Grassroots Activism: Nonnormative Sexual Politics in Postsocialist China." In Unequal China: The Political Economy and Cultural Politics of Inequality, edited by Wanning Sun and Yingjie Guo, 154–67. London: Routledge, 2013.

———. Other Modernities: Gendered Yearnings in China after Socialism. Berkeley: UC Press, 1999.

———. "Queer Positions, Queering Asian Studies." positions: east asia cultures critique 20, no. 1 (2012): 183–93.

———. "The Traffic in Money Boys." positions: east asia cultures critique 18, no. 2 (Fall 2010): 425–58.

Rojas, Carlos. The Great Wall: A Cultural History. Cambridge, MA: Harvard University Press, 2010.

Rojas, Carlos, and David Der-wei Wang, eds. Writing Taiwan: A New Literary History. Durham, NC: Duke University Press, 2011.

Rosenberg, Jordana, and Amy Villarejo, eds. "Queer Studies and the Crises of Capitalism." Special issue, GLQ: A Journal of Lesbian and Gay Studies 18, no. 1 (2012).

Rubin, Gayle. "Blood under the Bridge: Reflections on 'Thinking Sex.'" In Deviations, Chapter 8.

———. Deviations: A Gayle Rubin Reader. Durham, NC: Duke University Press, 2011. Kindle edition.

————. "Thinking Sex: Notes for a Radical Theory of the Politics of Sexuality." In *The Lesbian and Gay Studies Reader*, edited by H. Abelove, M. A. Barale, D. M. Halperin, 3–44. New York: Routledge Press: 1993. First published 1984. Reprinted in *Deviations*, Chapter 5.

Ruffolo, David. *Post-Queer Politics*. Burlington, VT: Ashgate, 2009.

Sakai, Naoki. "The Dislocation of the West and the Status of the Humanities." In *Traces I: Specters of the West and the Politics of Translation*, edited by Naoki Sakai and Yukiko Hanawa, 71–91. Hong Kong: Hong Kong University Press, 2002.

Salamon, Gayle. *Assuming a Body: Transgender and Rhetorics of Materiality*. New York: Columbia University Press, 2010.

Sang, Tze-lan. "At the Juncture of Censure and Mass Voyeurism: Narratives of Female Homoerotic Desire in Post-Mao China." *GLQ: A Journal of Lesbian and Gay Studies* 8, no. 4 (2002): 523–52.

————. *The Emerging Lesbian: Female Same-Sex Desire in Modern China*. Chicago: University of Chicago Press, 2003.

————. "Lesbian Feminism in the Mass-Mediated Public Sphere of Taiwan." In *Spaces of Their Own: Women's Public Sphere in Transnational China*, edited by Mayfair Mei-hui Yang, 132–61. Minneapolis: University of Minnesota Press, 1999.

————. "Lesbianism in Literature." In *Encyclopedia of Contemporary Chinese Culture*, edited by Edward Davis, 448–49. New York: Routledge, 2005.

————. "Restless Longing: Homoerotic Fiction in China." *International Institute for Asian Studies Newsletter* 29 (Autumn 2002). Accessed March 18, 2007. http://www.iias.nl/iiasn/29/IIASNL29_6_Restless.pdf.

————. "Translating Homosexuality: The Discourse of Tongxing'ai in Republican China (1912–1949)." In *Tokens of Exchange: The Problem of Translation in Global Circulations*, edited by Lydia Liu, 276–304. Durham, NC: Duke University Press, 1999.

Sayer, Derek. *The Violence of Abstraction: The Analytical Foundations of Historical Materialism*. Oxford: Basil Blackwell Inc., 1987.

Schroeder, William F. "Beyond Resistance: Gay and Lala Recreation in Beijing." In *Understanding Global Sexualities: New Frontiers*, edited by Peter Aggleton, Paul Boyce, Henrietta Moore, and Richard Parker, 108–23. New York: Routledge, 2012.

————. "On Cowboys and Aliens: Affective History and Queer Becoming in Contemporary China." *GLQ: A Journal of Lesbian and Gay Studies* 18, no. 4 (2012): 425–52.

Sedgwick, Eve Kosofsky. *Epistemology of the Closet*. Berkeley: University of California Press, 1990.

————. *Between Men: English Literature and Male Homosocial Desire*. New York: Columbia University Press, 1985.

————. "How to Bring Your Kids up Gay." In *Tendencies*, 154–64.

————. "Queer Performativity: Henry James's The Art of the Novel." *GLQ: A Journal of Lesbian and Gay Studies* 1 (1993): 1–16.

————. *Tendencies*. Durham, NC: Duke University Press, 1993.

Sedgwick, Eve Kosofsky, and Adam Frank, eds. *Shame and Its Sisters: A Silvan Tompkins Reader.*

Seidman, Steven. *Beyond the Closet.* New York: Routledge, 2002.

————. *Difference Troubles: Queering Social Theory and Sexual Politics.* Cambridge: Cambridge University Press, 1997.

Sheng, Ying, ed. *Ershi shiji nüxing wenxue shi* [Twentieth-century women's literature]. Tianjing: Tianjing renmin chubanshe, 1995.

Shernuk, Kyle. "Queer Chinese Postsocialist Horizons: New Models of Same-Sex Desire in Contemporary Chinese Fiction, 'Sentiments Like Water,' and *Beijing Story.*" Master's thesis, University of Oregon, 2012.

Shih, Shu-mei. "Is the Post- in Postsocialism the Post- in Posthumanism?" In Eng et al., eds., "China and the Human," Part II, 27–50.

Shih, Shu-mei, Chien-hsin Tsai, and Brian Bernards, eds. *Sinophone Studies: A Critical Reader.* New York: Columbia University Press, 2013.

Sieber, Patricia, ed. *Red Is Not the Only Color: Contemporary Chinese Fiction on Love and Sex between Women, Collected Stories.* Lanham, MD: Rowan and Littlefield, 2001.

Sima, Zhongyuan. "Dui cainü Xiao Sa de qiwang." [My expectations for the talented Xiao Sa]. Postscript in *Wo,er Hansheng* [My son, Hansheng], by Xiao Sa, 206. Taipei: Jiuge, 1981.

Snediker, Michael. *Queer Optimism: Lyric Personhood and Other Felicitous Persuasions.* Minneapolis: University of Minnesota Press, 2008.

Sommer, Matthew. *Sex, Law and Society in Late Imperial China.* Palo Alto: Stanford University Press, 2000.

Song, Geng. *The Fragile Scholar: Power and Masculinity in Chinese Culture.* Hong Kong: Hong Kong University Press, 2002.

Soper, Kate. *Humanism and Antihumanism.* London: Hutchinson, 1986.

Spencer, Norman. "Ten Years of Queer Cinema in China." *positions: east asia cultures critique* 20, no. 1 (Winter 2012): 373–83.

Spivak, Gayatri. *Death of a Discipline.* New York: Columbia University Press, 2003.

————. *In Other Worlds.* New York: Routledge, 1998.

————. "Scattered Speculations on the Question of Value." In *In Other Worlds: Essays in Cultural Politics*, 154–75. New York, Routledge: 1987.

Stevenson, Mark, and Cuncun Wu, trans. and eds. *Homoeroticism in Imperial China: A Sourcebook.* New York: Routledge, 2013.

————. "Male Love Lost: The Fate of Male Same-Sex Prostitution in Beijing in the Late Nineteenth and Early Twentieth Centuries." In Heinrich and Martin, eds., *Embodied Modernities*, 42–59.

Stoler, Anne Laura. *Race and the Education of Desire: Foucault's History of Sexuality and the Colonial Order of Things*. Durham, NC: Duke University Press, 1995.

Stychin, Carl F. *A Nation by Rights: National Cultures, Sexual Identity Politics, and the Discourse of Rights*. Philadelphia: Temple University Press, 1998.

Sun Zhongxin, James Farrer, and Kyung-hee Choi. "Sexual Identity among Men Who Have Sex with Men in Shanghai." *China Perspectives* 64 (March-April 2006). Accessed March 15, 2009. www.chinaperspectives.revues.org/598.

Szeto, Mirana May. "Queer Politics and Its Discontents: The Case of the Postcolonial Tongzhi Community in Hong Kong." Paper presented at the eighth annual conference of the Cultural Studies Association, Taipei, Jan. 7, 2007.

Tang, Denise Tse-Shang. *Conditional Spaces: Hong Kong Lesbian Desires and Everyday Life*. Hong Kong: Hong Kong University Press, 2011.

Tarnopolsky, Christina. *Prudes, Perverts, and Tyrants: Plato's Gorgias and the Politics of Shame*. Princeton: Princeton University Press, 2010.

Todorov, Tzvetan. *On Human Diversity*. Cambridge, MA: Harvard University Press, 1993.

Tong, Ge. *MSM renqun yufang* AIDS *xingwei ganyu fangfa yanjiu* [AIDS prevention for the MSM (men-who-have-sex-with-men) community]. Beijing: Ji'ande jiankang jiaoyu yanjiusuo, 2004.

———. *Zhongguo nan nan xing jiaoyi zhuangtai diaocha* [An inquiry into commercial sex in the MSM (men-who-have-sex-with-men) community in China]. Beijing: Beijing Gender Health Education Institute, 2007.

Tongson, Karen. *Relocations: Queer Suburban Imaginaries*. New York: NYU Press, 2011.

Treat, John W. "The Rise and Fall of Homonationalism in Singapore." *positions: east asia cultures critique* 23, no. 2 (2015): 349–65.

Tsai, Meng-Che. "Aizi, tongxinglian, yu hunjia xiangxiang: Zhihun de can/ku zhengzhi" [AIDS, gay men, and aspirations to marriage: The politics of the disabled and the queer in Chen Ruoxi's *Paper Marriage*]. *Nüxue zashi* [Journal of women's and gender studies] 33 (December 2013): 47–78.

Tse, Audrey. "Queering Chinese Comrades! Through the Lens of Director Cui Zi'En." Honors Theses, Dietrich College of Humanities and Social Sciences, Carnegie Mellon University, May 2013.

Vitiello, Giovanni. "Exemplary Sodomites: Chivalry and Love in Late Ming Culture." *Nan Nü* 2, no. 2 (2000): 207–58.

———. *The Libertine's Friend: Homosexuality and Masculinity in Late Imperial China*. Chicago: Chicago University Press, 2011.

Voci, Paola. *China on Video: Smaller-Screen Realities*. New York: Routledge, 2010.

Volpp, Sophie. "Classifying Lust: The Seventeenth-Century Vogue for Male Love." *Harvard Journal of Asiatic Studies* 61, no. 1 (June 2001): 77–117.

———. *Worldly Stage: Theatricality in Seventeenth-Century China*. Cambridge, MA: Harvard University Asia Center, 2011.

Wakeman, Frederic. "The Real China." *New York Review of Books*, July 20, 1978.

Wang, David Der-wei. *Zhongshen xuanhua yihou: Dianping dangdai zhongwen xiaoshuo* [After heteroglossia: Critical reviews of contemporary Chinese fiction]. Taipei: Maitian, 2001.

Wang, David Der-wei, and Carlos Rojas. *Writing Taiwan: A New Literary History*. Durham, NC: Duke University Press, 2007.

Wang, Hui. *China's New Order: Society, Politics, and Economy in Transition*. Edited by Theodore Huters. Cambridge, MA: Harvard University Press, 2003.

———. *The End of the Revolution: China and the Limits of Modernity*. London: Verso, 2011.

Wang, Lingzhen, ed. *Other Genders, Other Sexualities? Chinese Differences*. Durham, NC: Duke University Press, 2013.

Wang, Ping. "The Moving Subject of the Anti-Sexual Harassment Movement." In Ho, ed., *Visionary Essays in Sexuality/Gender Studies*, 169–87.

———. Interview in "Marriage Equality or Revolution?" Accessed April 15, 2014. http://www.coolloud.org.tw/node/71234.

———. "Qia qia wu bu li qingniao gaofei" [Young birds flying between cha-cha dance moves]. *Zhanglaoshi yuekan* 304 (April 2003): 97–100.

———. "Xingbie yuejie de meili xin shijie" [A brave new world of gender-crossings]. *Re'ai zazhi* 25 (June 2000): 24–26.

Wang, Qi. "Embodied Visions: Chinese Queer Experimental Documentaries by Shi Tou and Cui Zi'en." *positions: east asia cultures critique* 21, no. 3 (2013): 659–81.

———. "Festivals: Closed and Open Screens: The 9th Beijing Independent Film Festival." *Film Criticism* 37, no. 1 (Fall 2012): 62–69.

———. "The Ruin Is Already a New Outcome: An Interview with Cui Zi'en." In *positions: east asia cultures critique* 12, no. 1 (2004): 181–94.

———. "Writing Against Oblivion: Personal Filmmaking from the Forsaken Generation in Post-socialist China." PhD diss., UCLA, 2008.

Warner, Michael, ed. *Fear of a Queer Planet: Queer Politics and Social Theory*. Minneapolis: University of Minnesota Press, 1993.

———. *The Trouble with Normal: Sex, Politics, and the Ethics of Queer Life*. Boston: Harvard University Press, 2002.

Wei, Ziyun. "Xiruo Zhengyan." *China Times*, March 17, 1976.

White, Gorden, ed. *Developmental States in East Asia*. New York: Palgrave Macmillan, 1998.

Whitehead, Jaye Cee. *The Nuptial Deal: Same-Sex Marriage and Neo-Liberal Governance*. Chicago: University of Chicago Press, 2011.

Williams, Raymond. *Marxism and Literature*. Oxford: Oxford University Press, 1977.

Wong, Day K. M. "Hong Kong Lesbian Partners in the Making of Their Own Families." In *International Handbook of Chinese Families*, edited by Kwok-bun Chan, 575–87. New York: Springer, 2013.

————. "Rethinking the Coming Home Alternative: Hybridization and Coming Out Politics in Hong Hong's Anti-Homophobia Parades." *Inter-Asia Cultural Studies* 8, no. 4 (2007): 600–16.

The World Bank. *The East Asian Miracle: Economic Growth and Public Policy.* New York: Oxford University Press, 1993.

Wu, Chunsheng, and Chou Wah-shan, eds. *Women huozhe* [We are alive]. Hong Kong: Xianggang tongzhi yanjiushe, 1996.

Wu, Cuncun. *Homoerotic Sensibilities in Late Imperial China.* New York: Routledge Curzon, 2004.

Wu, Fatima. "From a Dead End to a New Road of Life: Xiao Sa's Abandoned Women." *World Literature Today* 65, no. 3 (1991): 427–31.

Wu, Jui-yuan. "As a 'Bad Son': The Emergence of Modern Homosexuals in Taiwan." Master's thesis, National Central University, 1998.

Wu, Tingrong, *Xiao Sa jiqi xiaoshuo de san zhong zhuti* [Three motifs in Xiao Sa]. Tainan: Guoli Chenggong Daxue, 2002.

Xiao, Sa. "The Aftermath of the Death of a Junior High Co-ed." Translated by Chen I-djen. In *Bamboo Shoots after the Rain: Contemporary Stories by Women Writers of Taiwan,* edited by Ann C. Carver and Sung-sheng Yvonne Chang, 171–87. New York: Feminist Press, 1990.

————. *Chang di* [The long dike]. Taipei: Shangwu chubanshe, 1972.

————. "The Colors of Love." Translated by Eva Hung. *Renditions,* nos. 35–36 (1991):103–20.

————. "Floating Leaf." Translated by Howard Goldblatt. In *The Columbia Anthology of Modern Chinese Literature,* edited by Joseph S. M. Lau and Howard Goldblatt, 373–82. New York: Columbia University Press, 1995.

————. "Letter to My Ex-Husband." *China Times,* Oct. 18–19, 1986.

————. "My Relatives in Hong Kong." Translated by Loh I-cheng. *The Chinese Pen* (Autumn 1987): 1–46. Rpt. in *The Last of the Whampoa Breed,* edited by Pang-yuan Chi and David Der-wei Wang, 151–89. New York: Columbia University Press, 2003.

————. "My Son, Han-sheng." Translated by Eve Markowitz. In *Worlds of Modern Chinese Fiction: Short Stories and Novellas from the People's Republic, Taiwan, and Hong Kong,* edited by Michael S. Duke, 227–45. Armonk, NY: Sharpe, 1991.

————. "Old Mrs. Kuo's Distress." Translated by David Steelman. *The Chinese Pen* (Summer 1989): 1–11.

————. "Second Honeymoon." Translated by Patia Yasin. *The Chinese Pen* (Spring 1982): 82—96.

————. *Rumengling.* [Song of dreams]. Taipei: Jiuge, 1981.

————. "Die Verwandten in Hongkong." Translated by Katharina Markgraf. In *Hefte für ostasiatische Literatur* Nr. 52 (Mai 2012): 26–59.

————. Writer. *Wo de ai* [This love of mine]. Directed by Zhang Yi. Film. Taiwan: Taiwan Central Motion Picture Corporation, 1986.

———. Writer. *Wo zheyang guole yisheng* [Kuei-mei, a woman]. Directed by Zhang Yi. Film. Taiwan: Taiwan Central Motion Picture Corporation, 1985.

Xiaomingxiong [Samshasha]. *Zhonggguo tongxing'ai shilu* [A history of homosexuality in China]. Hong Kong: Fenhong sanjiao chubanshe, 1997.

Xuan Xiaofo. *Yuan zhi wai* [Outside the circle]. Taipei: Wansheng, 1976.

Yang, Changnian, et al., eds. *Ershi shiji zhongguo xin wenxue shi* [A new history of twentieth-century Chinese literature]. Banqiao: Luotuto, 1997.

Yang, Hanzhi. "Xierou ninglian de bishou—lun Chen Ruoxi de xiaoshou." [A dagger made of flesh and blood: On Chen Ruoxi's fiction]. *China Times*, March 4, 1976.

Yau, Ching, ed. *As Normal as Possible: Negotiating Sexuality and Gender in Mainland China and Hong Kong*. Hong Kong: Hong Kong University Press, 2010.

Ye, Shitao. "Cong chongjing, huanmie, dao panghuang" [From idealism to disillusionment to vacillation]. In *Taiwan xian dang dai zuojia yanjiu ziliao huibian*, edited by Xinyuan Chen, 173–84. Taipei: Guoli Taiwan wenxue guan, 2013.

Ye, Sifen. "Xiao Sa yu qi zuopin de shehui yishi" [The social consciousness of Xiao Sa and her works]. Lecture, Taipei, April 6, 2010.

Yip, June. *Envisioning Taiwan: Fiction, Cinema, and the Nation in the Cultural Imaginary*. Durham, NC: Duke University Press, 2004.

You, Suling, "Dangdai Taiwan nüxing zhuojia yu xifang nüxing zhuyi" [Contemporary Taiwan women writers and western feminism]. Accessed September 27, 2010. www.pkucn.com/viewthread.php?tid=16422.

Yue, Audrey. "Mobile Intimacies in the Queer Sinophone Films of Cui Zi'en." *Journal of Chinese Cinemas* 6, no. 1 (2012): 95–108.

Yue, Audrey, and Jun Zubillago-Pow, eds. *Queer Singapore: Illiberal Citizenship and Mediated Cultures*. Hong Kong: Hong Kong University Press, 2012.

Zeng, Xiuping, *Orphans, Bad Sons and Taipei People* [Guchen, niezi, taibeiren]. Taipei: Erya, 2003.

Zhang, Beichuan. *Tongxing'ai* [Homosexual love]. Jinan: Shandong kexue jishu chubanshe, 1994.

Zhang, Xianmin. *Kan bujian de yingxiang* [Invisible Images]. Shanghai: Sanlian, 2005.

Zhang, Xudong. *Postsocialism and Cultural Politics: China in the Last Decade of the Twentieth Century*. Durham, NC: Duke University Press, 2008.

Zhang, Yingjin. "Truth, Subjectivity, and Audience in Chinese Independent Film and Video." In Pickowicz and Zhang, eds., *From Underground to Independent*, 23–46.

Zhang, Yuan, dir. *East Palace, West Palace*. Written by Wang Xiaobo. Film. Hong Kong: Ocean/France: Quelq'un d'autre Productions, 1996.

Zhou, Dan. *Aiyue yu guixun: Zhongguo xiandaixing zhong tongxing yuwan de fali xiangxiang* [Pleasure and discipline: jurisprudential imagination of same-sex desire in Chinese modernity]. Guilin: Guangxi shifan daxue chuban-she, 2009.

Žižek, "Class Struggle or Postmodernism? Yes, Please!" In Butler, Laclau, and Žižek. *Contingency, Hegemony, Universality*: 90–135. London: Verso, 2000.

———. *The Sublime Object of Ideology*. London: Verso, 2008 [1989].

INDEX

About Chinese Women (Kristeva), 155, 209
Advocate, The, 100
aesthetic interest (*wenxue xing*), 110
"Against Proper Objects" (Butler), 61,
  180n65, 183n110, 196
Agamben, Giorgio, 146
Ai bao, 42
AIDS: epidemic, 14; people living with, 2,
  106, 140, 158, 163, 177n5; prevention organizations, 36; research funding, 36, 38
AIDS Prevention for the MSM Community
  (Tong), 37, 219
allegorical readings, 93
allegories: of continental philosophy,
  49; homosexualized, 101; of love, lust,
  and, transformation, 55; national, 93;
  political, 15, 93; postsocialist, 3; of queer
  community, 97; of sexual regulation, 52;
  of Taiwan's economic miracle, 132; of the
  tensions between PRC and ROC, 93
allochronism, 46–47, 156
alternative: Chinese sexuality, 46; to
  Euro-American queer theory, 44; form
  of "cultural communism," 96; genealogy
  of Marxism, 147; imagination of human
  creativity, fulfillment, and freedom, 33;
  interpretation of the two Chinas, 156; to
  liberal pluralist analysis, 30–33; to marriage and the social shame of divorce,
  118; matrilineal social space, 155; to the
  Oedipus complex, 22; to queer critique

of humanism, 147; to queer emancipation, 7; sexualities, 31, 36, 45, 92; sexual
  practices, 29; slogan of "pluralism of
  relationships," 73; social history of male
  same-sex relations, 45; system of pre-
  Oedipal signification, 156; to tolerance,
  respect, and diversity, 30
Althusser, Louis, 81–82, 149–51, 155, 166,
  195
Altman, Dennis, 21, 195
American Association of University Professors (AAUP), 59
anthronormativity, 144
Antigone's Claim (Butler), 22, 197
antihumanism: Althusser's, 151, 191n35,
  191n40; Derrida and, 149; "essence of
  man" is an ideological myth, 148; ethnocentrism, 192n47; Maoism, 152; Mao's,
  151; Marxist, 149, 151; multiculturalism
  and, 167; poststructuralist, 152, 156; of
  two different Marxes, 149–51. *See also*
  humanism
antihumanist: humanist *vs.,* 167; language,
  147; Marxism, 151; story, 131; structuralist revolution, 151; theory in China, 156;
  thought in China, 154; writings of Marx,
  168
antinuclear plant movement, 64
Arabo-Moslem societies, 28
Arcades Project (Benjamin), 125, 196
Arrighi, Giovanni, 150, 174–75n48, 195

Enlightenment humanism, 147

Enter the Clowns (Cui), 51, 200

Epistemology of the Closet (Sedgwick), 25, 30, 217

Erni, John, 144–45

erotic: *ars erotica* (sex as an art form), 27–28, 156; behavior, 79; desires, diversity of, 40, 55; encounter between a girl and a woman, 87; experiences outside the heterosexual family, 92; insurrectionary energies of the, 70; lack of *scientia sexualis*, 28; lacks of scientific and logical basis, 27; literature from Ming dynasty, 88; literature in premodern China, 85; ossified cultural essence, 28; pleasures, 67; relations, same-sex, 45; social agents, 69. *See also* homoeroticism

eroticism, same-sex, 98

erotohistoriography, 123

ethnic differences, 61

Euro-American: male, 26; modernity, 9; queer emancipation, 7; queer theory, 6, 22, 44; sexual knowledge, 21

Eurocentrism, 21, 29, 152–53, 156

European sexologists, 47

Evidence of the Success of Sex Revolution in China (Pan and Huang), 37, 215

exchange (*jiaohuan*), economic logic of, 66

Execution of Mayor Yin and Other Stories from the Great Proletarian Cultural Revolution, The (Chen), 95, 110, 198

exhibitionists, 65

existentialism, 128

extramarital affairs, 68, 118, 124

extraterrestrials, 49, 52

Fabian, Johannes, 46, 203

fallen women, 66

family from a queer perspective, 92

family values, 105–6

Fan, Luoping, 110, 118, 203

Fan, Qing, 71, 203

Fang, Gang: *Homosexuality in China*, 13, 37

Farewell My Concubine (film), 53

Feeding Boys, Ayaya (Cui), 51, 200

Feeling of Kinship: Queer Liberalism and the Racialization of Intimacy, The (Eng), 3–4, 202

Felipa de Souza Award, 139

female: binary definition of "female/male," 73; desire and sexuality, 188n8; eleventh-century, 116; factory workers, 72; gender as male/female, 73, 85; heterosexual, 116; homoerotic imaginary, 175n55; homosexual community, encounters with, 96; MTFS (male-to-female), 49; oppression, 67; orgasms, myth of, 180n67; politicians, 61, 63; prostitution, 46; subject in psychoanalysis, 155; T's and po's, 72

feminism: Gender/Sexuality Rights Association, 72; lesbian, 68; mainstream, 77, 79; Marxist, 71; premised on a common gender, 77; radical movements, 61; sex-positive, 62; sexuality and, 40; state, in Taiwan, 60–61, 75, 77, 83, 182n106; in Taiwan, 61, 79; universal basis for, 24

feminist(s): analysis, 62, 64; movement (1970s), new, 60; nonstatist, 61; sex-negative, 79; sex-positive, 60–62, 79; theory, French, 23

Ferguson, Roderick, 145, 203

Ferry, Nicole, 2, 203

fetishism, commodity, 150

Feuerbach, Ludwig, 149

Fichte, Johann Gottlieb, 149

"Floating Leaf" (Xiao), 120, 221

Floyd, Kevin: *The Reification of Desire: Towards a Queer Marxism*, 14

Foucauldian historians of sexuality, 99

Foucault, Michel: China's *ars erotica*, 27–28; homosexuality, invention of, 27; *Madness and Civilization*, 27, 203; poststructuralist thought, 148; *scientia sexualis*, 28

Frecerro, Carla, 145, 203

freedom, human, 73

Freeman, Elizabeth, 123, 173n18, 203

French feminist theory, 23

"From Yao Wenyuan to Cui Zi'en" (Pickowicz), 47–48, 215

Fuss, Diana, 35, 204

Gallant Woman, The (Ho), 64–68, 70, 77–78, 206

gay: bars, 11, 162; communities, desexualized nouveau riche in, 49; community, monogamists, 100; community, polyamorous, 100; consumers, middle-class, 11;

homosexuality: *ars erotica*, 27–28, 156; boundaries between homosociality and, 25, 45–46; China, as a venerable tradition in, 45; China, "vogue for male love" in seventeenth-century, 45; Chinese emperors and their male favorites, 44; Chinese Marxism and, 111–12; in Chinese screen cultures, 3; Chinese understandings of, 36; Chinese societies' tolerance of, 75; in classical Greece, 28–29; culturally undesirable practices and experiences, 2; decriminalized in China (1997), 43; gay researchers cannot come out of the closet, 37; gender and sexuality research and AIDS-prevention, 36–37; homosociality *vs.*, 25, 45–46; an immutable orientation, 35; invention from the West (1870), 27, 47, 85; invention of homosexuality in China, 85; *jijian* (illicit anal sex), 43; male, 89, 91, 98; male cohabitation, custom of, 45; male love, tolerance for, 46; modern invention, 27; nature/nurture debate, 35; object of consumption and political manipulation, 164; pathology of, 56; positive attitude toward, 46; public health and social order concern, 37; Qing period, 43; *scientia sexualis*, 27; self-identifying as gay undermines one's credibility, 36; sexuality studies experts present homosexuality as a mental health issue, 37; single origin in Greece or France (1870), 27, 30; threat to women's happiness, 12; in Western culture, 26; women married to homosexual men claiming to be victims of domestic abuse and psychological trauma, 12. *See also* hooliganism; same-sex; *tongxinglian*; *tongzhi* (same-sex love)

Homosexuality in China (Fang), 13, 37
Homosexual Love (Zhang), 37, 222
homosociality, 25, 45–46. *See also* same-sex
Hong Kong Sex Education Association, 59
Hong Kong's neoliberalism, 5
hooliganism (*liumang zui*), 11, 37, 43. *See also* homosexuality; *tongzhi*
How to Do the History of Sexuality (Halperin), 28, 205
Hsia, C. T., 93, 207

Huang, Chunming, 90
Huang Shuling, 71, 208
Huang, Yingying: *Evidence of the Success of Sex Revolution in China*, 37, 215
human, 146–47; connectedness, 31, 124, 136, 168; intimacy, heteronormataive model of, 124; morphology, 144; time, moral equality of, 150
humanism, Confucian (*rendao zhuyi*), 151
humanism (*renwenzhuyi*), 147–56, 167–68. *See also* antihumanism
Humanism and Antihumanism (Soper), 147, 218
humanist spirit (*renwen jingshen*), 151
humanist writings of Marx, 168
human rights: Christian theological idea of, 143; Confucian understanding of rights, 143; European notion of natural rights, 143; gay and lesbian, 138; human, ontology of the, 143; humanism and Eurocentrism, conflation of, 153; liberal understandings of, 143–47; ROC's queer, 153; in the two Chinas, queer, 150; watch groups, 20; women's, 138. *See also* queer human rights
Hung, Eva, 121, 208
Hung, Lucifer [Hong Ling], 42, 88, 182n106, 199

identity: disorder, gender, 79; homosexual, 3, 85–86, 98, 107; politics, 115; queer, 87–88; self-affirmative gay and lesbian, 98; sexual, 97
IGLHRC. *See* International Gay and Lesbian Human Rights Commission (IGLHRC)
Immigration and Naturalization Service (INS), 100
International Gay and Lesbian Human Rights Commission (IGLHRC), 138–39
intersexed individuals, 63
interventions, humanitarian, 144
Irigaray, Luce, 23
"Is Global Governance Bad for East Asian Queers?" (Ho), 71
Isle Margin (journal), 42, 177n16

Jameson, Fredric, 48
Jiang, Jiawen (G/SRAT), 72

Lung, Ying-tai (writer and politician), 118, 160, 193n56, 199; *Big River, Big Sea— Untold Stories of 1949*, 160–61, 211; *Persuade Us with Civilization, Not Force, Please*, 160–61, 211

Ma, Ying-jeou (mayor of Taipei), 42f5.1, 140–41
male: homosexuality, 89, 91, 98; nudity, 10; prostitution, 92. *See also* homosexual(s); homosexuality; same-sex
Male Queen (Nan wanghou) (Wang), 44
male-to-female (MTFs), 49
Man, Man, Woman Woman (Cui), 57
Mann, Susan: *Gender and Sexuality in Modern China*, 46, 178
Mann, Thomas, 90
Man Who Does Not Want to Be Married The (Guangtai), 89, 204
Mao, Feng: *The History of Homosexual Literature*, 90, 212
Marcuse, Herbert, 10, 212
marriage(s): cohabitation without, 124; dysfunctional, 124; failed, 108, 123; heteronormative assumptions about, 106–7; heterosexual, monogamous, 66, 78; heterosexual, queer-materialist critique of, 108; heterosexual, rebellion against, 116; unconventional, 108. *See also* same-sex marriage
Martin, Fran, 11, 212
Marx, Karl: *Das Kapital*, 80, 149–50, 166–67, 212; *Economic and Philosophical Manuscripts of 1844*, 149, 212; human interdependency and relationality, theories of, 167; humanist and antihumanist writings, 168; human subject is constituted by forces and vectors of power, 167; labor theory of value, 165–69; socialist redistribution, 165; society, utopian classless, 168
Marxism: academic subdiscipline in North America, 8; alternative genealogy of, 147; in anticommunist ROC, 4–5; antihumanist, 151; Chen Yingzhen, 91; China's postsocialist character, 4; China's socialist past and dialogues with, 4; Chinese queer Marxism, 7, 48,

91; Chinese queer writers' responses to, 87; classless society, theodicy of a utopian, 168; closed system incapable of dealing with the complexities of modern life, 9; Cold War bifurcations, 39; communalism *vs.*, antitotalitarian impulse of, 150; communism *vs.* capitalism, 112; communist bureaucracy and, 87, 94; contemporary queer thought and, 7; critique of capitalism, corporations, and consumption, 14; cultural materialism and society's economic base and ideological superstructure, 71; cultural narratives of two Chinas, 16; cultural struggles in anticommunist Taiwan, 91; culture associated with, materialist analysis of, 121; dialectical philosophy and historical materialism, 8; economic determination of social life, 83; economics and social life, 83, 165; the erotic, nonidentitarian approach to insurrectionary energies of, 70; formal *vs.* substantive equality (fetishism), 8; freedom, parliamentary, 63; freedom of religion *vs.* freedom from religion, 63; French, 151; gender and sexuality, inquiries into, 4; gender-blind historical materialism and subordination of women's needs for class struggle, 71; G/SRAT's work, 72; homosexuality and, 97, 111–12; homosexual male characters and Taiwan-based Chinese authors, 86; Ho's queer Marxism, 64, 66, 70–71; human, the moral and historical elements of, 168; human emancipation *vs.* liberal pluralism, 62; human in, 164–69; humanism *vs.* antihumanism, 149; humanist defense of the primacy of economics that queer theory comes to challenge and displace, 168; human sexuality, devoid of understanding of, 95; human sexuality, lacks understanding of, 95; intellectual resource *vs.* economic policy, 21; labor-power as reproduction of a social division, 82; labors of all human beings, 143; labor theory of value, 69, 80, 164–69; LGBTQ communities and Chinese queer, 7; liberalism *vs.*, 167; *Literature Quarterly*, 91; man, meta-

queer theory (continued)
  of radicality in queer movements,
  14; neoliberal homonormativity, 9;
  neoliberal social management and,
  7; political standoff between the two
  Chinas, 41; procreative heterosexuality
  vs. domestic partnership, 108; racism or
  Orientalism in, 30; rethinking of cultural
  comparison and comparability, 21; same-
  sex desire as a continuum of acts, 27;
  same-sex relations in China, 21; theoretical status of theory, 31; theory of cultural
  variability, 22; theory of geopolitics, 22;
  transnational and transcultural practice,
  15; United States, 2, 7, 26, 30; universal
  patriarchy, 22. See also Chinese queer
  theory
queer writers: Chinese, 87, 115; communism suppressed creativity of, 88;
  identity politics, 115; liberalism, 88, 115;
  Marxism, intellectual resource of, 87;
  Marxism and social thought, 8; Marxist
  critique of bourgeois individualism, 115;
  postmarket reform PRC, 88; postmartial
  law in Taiwan, 88; signifier of China fueled the imagination of, 93

Reich, Wilhelm, 68–69
Reification of Desire: Towards a Queer Marxism,
  The (Floyd), 14
Republic of China on Taiwan (ROC): American GI-club, 132; American military in,
  131–32; anti-Chinese sentiments, 160;
  Bai Xiaoyan, murder of, 65; bill to legalize same- sex marriage, 10; bookstore
  owner prosecuted for gay adult magazines, 162; China's "economic miracle,"
  6, 17, 19, 32; Cross-Strait Service Trade
  Agreement, 158; de-Sinicization, 19;
  division of China (1949), 4; doctrine of
  "two gender co-rule" (lianxing gongzhi),
  63; East Asian Economic Miracle, 19,
  114, 120, 122, 126, 188n3; economic
  and political liberalism, 17; economic
  liberalism (free trade), 17–18; economic
  miracle, China's, 114–15; execution of
  45,000–90,000 intellectuals (1950s), 20;
  feminism in, 61; feminism is premised

on a common gender, 77; feminist
  conventions, 161; free and nonfree
  subjects in, 142; Free China, historical
  claim as, 6; "Free China," 114; gay but
  healthy image, 158; gay culture, 163; gay
  marriage and Chen Shui-bian, 158–59;
  gay normalization, 61; Gay Pride parade
  (2003), 17; Gender Equality Employment Law (2001), 73; Gender Equity
  Education Act (2004), 73; geopolitical
  rivalry between PRC and ROC, 5; Gin Gin
  case, 162; global anticommunism, 19;
  homosexuality, legitimatization of, 160;
  homosexuality as an object of consumption, 164; homosexuals granted right to
  organize families and adopt children,
  159; housing subsidy program, 74;
  Kuomintang autocracy, 18; laissez-faire
  capitalism, 18; liberal democracy, 164;
  liberalism, 157; liberalized society, 19;
  male population oppresses women, 65;
  marriage equality bill, 158–59; martial
  law lifted (1987), 17–19, 58, 88, 118;
  Marxism in anticommunist, 91; massacre of Taiwanese protestors, 20; men
  and women are legally and formally
  equal, 62; modernism and cultural
  Marxism in, 90; multi-party system, 19;
  patriarchal domination, 63; personhood,
  liberal pluralist model of, 79; police
  raided a gay sauna, 162; police raided
  gay home parties and harassed gay bars,
  162, 163f5.2; political liberalism, 17;
  political liberalism (queer visibility), 17;
  political rivalry of parties, 19; postmarket reform, 88; postmartial law, 6, 10,
  88; postsocialism and postmartial law
  market economy, 6; Presidential Office's
  Human Rights Advisory Committee,
  161; protection against discrimination
  on the basis of gender and sexual orientation, 159; protection of basic human
  rights (renquan baozhang jiben fa) bill, 159;
  public bathrooms, design of, 66; queer
  advocacy groups, network of, 158; queer
  art, theater, literature, entertainment,
  and consumption, 158; queer communities in, 158; queer discourse and rigidity